THIRTY-THREE GOOD MEN

*This book is dedicated to my wife Anne Marie,
and my children Siobhán, Daragh, and Orlagh.*

John A. Weafer

Thirty-Three Good Men

CELIBACY, OBEDIENCE AND IDENTITY

A Sociological Study of the Lived Experience
of Irish Diocesan Priests in Modern Ireland,
1960–2010

the columba press

First published in 2014 by
the columba press
55A Spruce Avenue,
Stillorgan Industrial Park,
Blackrock, Co. Dublin

Cover design by David Mac Namara CSsR
Origination by The Columba Press
Printed by Bell & Bain Ltd

ISBN 978 1 78218 167 5

Acknowledgements

I wish to express my thanks to a number of people who helped me complete my study of Irish diocesan priesthood. First, I would like to thank Dr Máire Leane, and her colleagues in the Department of Applied Social Studies, UCC, for their encouragement in my undertaking and completing this study. It was not an easy task but the journey was greatly assisted by her interest and patient wisdom. I would like to thank Dr Eugene Duffy for his helpful comments on the original thesis, and Dr Lynn Levo, CSJ for her insights and friendship. I would also like to thank Eoin O'Mahony and the Bishops' Council for Research and Development for providing me with the statistical data on Church personnel appended to this publication. I would like to record my thanks to the publishers, Columba Press, for their professionalism and support. Finally, I would like to most sincerely thank the thirty-three priests and former priests who spoke so openly and honestly about their lives.

Table of Contents

SECTION I: THE IRISH DIOCESAN PRIEST AND THE IRISH
CATHOLIC CHURCH, 1960–2010

CHAPTER ONE: INTRODUCTION AND BACKGROUND

CHAPTER TWO: THE CHANGING SOCIO-RELIGIOUS
LANDSCAPE OF IRELAND, 1960–2010

CHAPTER THREE: THE CHANGING PROFILE
OF AN IRISH DIOCESAN PRIEST, 1960–2010

SECTION I

THE IRISH DIOCESAN PRIEST
AND THE IRISH CATHOLIC CHURCH, 1960–2010

Chapter One

Introduction and Background

The Dublin priest is first and foremost a man of God … Sometimes he gets support from the priests he works with, sometimes he doesn't. He is deeply hurt by the scandals that have tarnished the reputation of the priesthood and by the way these scandals have been treated in the media. He is not greatly impressed by authority. He is critical of those that hold power in the Church … He wants to see greater participation by the laity in the government of the Church … He feels that he is overworked … He has to be constantly available to his parishioners. He finds it impossible to live up to the expectations of others. He feels the sting of celibacy. He worries about the future. And yet, he is on the whole a fulfilled and happy man.

Forristal, 1997, pp. 27–8

1.1 AIM OF THE STUDY

This study is concerned with the lives of thirty-three Irish Catholic diocesan priests and former priests during a period of significant change in the Irish Church[1] and Irish society, 1960–2010. While a considerable amount of theological and historical material has been published on priesthood, relatively little social research has been published on the details of Irish diocesan priests' personal lives. Accordingly, in my research, I set out to explore the lived experience of Irish diocesan priests through their life stories, which I regard as 'interpretive devices through which people make sense of, understand and live their lives' (Lawler, 2008, p. 13). My study focuses on the way Irish diocesan priests understand and experience celibacy and obedience in modern Ireland, and how they understand their evolving identity as priests. Other related topics, such as the alleged crisis in priesthood, are also discussed.

During the course of the study I interviewed twenty-four Irish diocesan priests and nine former diocesan priests. Apart from their common gender, the research participants are quite different from each other, with diverse backgrounds, personalities, behaviours and attitudes. While most of them are active priests in good standing, others have left the priesthood; while some are young, most are middle-aged and elderly; while most are heterosexual, some are homosexual; while most live celibate lives, others are sexually active; while most hold orthodox Catholic beliefs, others are more liberal in some aspects of Church teaching; and while some are enthusiastic about their priesthood, others have become disillusioned. In short, the thirty-three participants reflect some of the many different strands of Irish diocesan priesthood. However, in spite of their many differences, my research will show that they are united by a common vocation to the diocesan priesthood, even if time and circumstances determined that some of these men would ultimately leave the priesthood.

A review of the literature, together with my knowledge of Irish diocesan priesthood, suggested three questions I considered worth investigating in furthering my understanding of Irish diocesan priests' lives in contemporary Ireland.

1. *How do Irish diocesan priests understand and experience celibacy in their day-to-day lives?* The literature suggests that priests experience celibacy along a continuum (Bordisso, 2011) and that many priests experience difficulties with the notion and practice of mandatory celibacy (Anderson, 2005; Hoenkamp-Bisschops; 1992, Sipe, 1995). My study supports the notion of a celibacy continuum amongst Irish diocesan priests, ranging from acceptance to rejection, with most priests somewhere in the middle of the spectrum. I will argue that Irish diocesan priests understand celibacy in diverse ways, with most priests against mandatory celibacy, including some priests who can see a value in celibacy for the priesthood. My study also suggests that younger post-Vatican II priests ordained in the 1990s and 2000s are most likely to embrace the ideal of celibacy, while their older counterparts ordained around the time of the Second Vatican Council experience most difficulties with the notion and also the lived experience of mandatory celibacy (Hoge and Wenger, 2003). The research participants' lived experience of celibacy is explored in chapter four.

2. *How do Irish diocesan priests negotiate their priesthood within a large and complex organisation?* Obedience is a key feature and indeed a virtue of Catholic spirituality and religious life. Yet, obedience, or rather disobedience, is not a major issue in the literature on Irish diocesan priests. Furthermore, there is little empirical evidence of diocesan priests speaking out against Church policy or practices, at least not in public. Anecdotal evidence suggests that diocesan priests are essentially loyal 'company men' who are firmly positioned within, and constrained by, a highly structured, centralised and strictly hierarchical Church. While my study corroborates this general view, it also suggests that Irish diocesan priests could more accurately be depicted as company men, 'with attitude'. Thus, while diocesan priests are typically loyal and obedient, they are not necessarily subservient or unthinking individuals. I will argue that diocesan priests typically learn to deal with senior authority figures in the Church by 'keeping their heads down' and 'doing their own thing' in the seminary, and by continuing this pragmatic, pastoral approach in their ministerial life following ordination. I will also argue that diocesan priests' relative freedom to act independently is only possible because of the symbiotic, if unequal, relationship priests have with Church leadership. This inter-personal dynamic allows priests a degree of flexibility in their actions, provided they are discreet and don't infringe the 'rules of the game' established by Church leadership. The research participants' lived experience of obedience is explored in chapter five.

3. *How do Irish diocesan priests understand their priesthood and how has this understanding changed over time, if at all?* The literature suggests that different generations of priests exist in the Catholic Church, each with its own distinctive understanding of priesthood and the Church. Research in the US by sociologists Hoge and Wenger, for example, concluded that the 'essence of priesthood has undergone two shifts' since the early 1960s, each with its own distinctive understanding of priesthood (Hoge and Wenger, 2003, p. 59). I will argue that generational differences also exist in the Irish diocesan priesthood but that they are largely confined to theological and liturgical issues, and that the cultural practice of Irish diocesan priesthood is more accurately depicted by similarity rather than difference.

The study will also provide some insights into the alleged crisis in diocesan priesthood and the Irish Catholic Church.[2] Various symptoms of a crisis in priesthood have been suggested by different commentators, including a crisis of ministry, morale, intimacy, and identity (Fitzgibbon, 2010). While each of these symptoms is serious, and there are clear signs that diocesan priesthood is in trouble, I will argue that Irish diocesan priesthood is not yet experiencing a crisis. For example, I will argue that the alleged crisis in priestly identity reflects the tension between two competing paradigms of priesthood rather than priesthood *per se*, where one model is on the ascent and another is struggling to maintain its position. The servant-leader model[3] prevailed for approximately twenty years following Vatican II[4] before being challenged by a neo-orthodox model of priesthood. The alleged crisis in priesthood is addressed in chapters three and seven.

1.2 Background to the Study

A Church in Crisis

There is considerable evidence and opinion to suggest that the Irish Church has 'been going through a period of intense crisis over the past decade or more' (Duffy, 2010b, p. 7). The Catholic Church is no longer the dominant force it once was in Ireland, and secularisation, 'formerly so slow to take hold in Ireland intensified in the 1990s and the early years of this century' (Fahey et al., 2005, p. 54). Nationwide social surveys have consistently indicated that substantially less Irish people are engaging with the Church or go to Mass nowadays. There are also fewer people who are willing to accept traditional Church teachings on morality (Association of Catholic Priests, 2012; *The Irish Times*, 2012; MacGréil and Rhatigan, 2009; *The Sunday Times*, 2013). Furthermore, many Irish people no longer trust the institutional Church (McGreevy, 2010), particularly following disclosures of child sexual abuse by priests and religious, and a perceived mismanagement of the process by Church leaders (Murphy et al., 2005).

Ireland is perceived by some commentators to be a missionary country in need of re-evangelisation and 'frontier work' (Dorr, 2003, p. 583). This view is endorsed by some Church leaders, such as Archbishop Diarmuid Martin, who believes that his diocese is facing the biggest crisis since emancipation in 1829 (McGarry, 2011), and that the Irish Church may be on the brink of collapse where it will 'inevitably become more a minority culture' (O'Doherty, 2011). The 'wonderful hope aroused by Vatican II' has, in the opinion of some 'all but vanished' (Hogan, 2013, p. 7). I will argue in chapter two that the Irish Catholic Church is in crisis.

A Decline in the Number of Priests in Modern Ireland

The primary concern of the present study is not, however, with the millions of lay Catholics that constitute the membership of the Irish Catholic Church. Rather, it is with the three thousand or so diocesan priests, most of whom work and live in Ireland's 1,365 parishes (O'Mahony, 2011). In 2006, there were 3,078 diocesan priests attached to Ireland's twenty-six dioceses, representing an average of 118 priests per diocese and a ratio of one priest per 1,416 Catholics (Table 1.1). The number of diocesan priests in Ireland has been declining steadily since the mid 1960s, and particularly since 1990 (Table A1, Appendix). A similar downward trend has also occurred in most of Western Europe, where the number of priests working in dioceses has declined quite rapidly in recent years (Kerkhofs, 1995). Conversely, hundreds of priests continue to be ordained in countries such as Poland, Italy, Spain, Brazil and Mexico (Vatican, 2009).

Table 1.1 General Statistics of the Irish Catholic Church 2006

Number of Dioceses in Ireland	26
Number of Diocesan Priests in Ireland	3,078
Percentage of Diocesan priests categorised as 'Active' in ministry (n=2,342)	76%
Number of Catholics in Ireland	4,359,908
Ratio of Diocesan priests to Catholics	1:1,416
Number of Parishes	1,365
Number of churches	2,645

Source: Council for Research and Development Fact Sheet Series '*Diocesan Priests in Ireland 2006*'.

A recent report from the Irish Catholic Bishops' Conference indicated that there are 2,067 priests currently assigned to parish ministry in Ireland and that the age profile of these priests is increasing (O'Mahony, 2013). The report found that three quarters of all priests in Ireland are aged between forty-five and seventy-four years of age, while the largest proportion of priests in Ireland is now in the sixty-five to seventy-four year age group and this proportion is increasing.

A Decline in Vocations

Irish people have traditionally perceived the priesthood very positively, with relatively high numbers of men seriously considering a vocation to the priesthood or religious life (Table A4, Appendix). In 1974 and 1984, approximately one sixth (15% and 18%, respectively) of Irish men said they had seriously considered a vocation to the priesthood or religious life (Breslin and Weafer, 1985). Twenty-three years later this figure had fallen to just less than one in ten Irish adult males (Weafer, 2007). The appeal of priesthood for many Irish people is also reflected in the proportions of people who would encourage their sons to be priests. In 1974, 91.5% of adults in the Republic of Ireland said they would encourage aspirants to the priesthood. Ten years later, in 1984, 70% of Irish adults said they would be willing to encourage a prospective priest (Breslin and Weafer, 1985). By 1998, a RTÉ/MRBI survey reported a further decline in support, although it was still relatively high at a time when considerable negative publicity surrounded the media coverage of clerical scandals: 63% would be either 'very happy' (35%) or 'fairly happy' (28%) if a member of their family entered the priesthood, with only 8% 'unhappy' with this prospect (RTÉ, 1998). A year later, only a third of respondents said they would be prepared to encourage someone to become a priest, brother or nun if they wanted to (Weafer, 2000).

Vocations to the priesthood have been declining since the late 1960s in Ireland and in many Western countries. Various studies have identified different factors that are linked to the decline, including mandatory celibacy, the counter-cultural nature of priesthood, and the ambiguous nature of a priest's vocation[5] (*Pro Mundi Vita*, 1987; Weafer, 1988; Newman, 1966; MacGréil, 1997). Celibacy is perhaps most often given as a reason for not pursuing a vocation (MacGréil, 1997; Newman et al., 1971; Breslin, 1981; Curcione, 1973; Dunn, 1994), and it has been identified in a number of studies as one of 'the high occupational demands for becoming a priest' (Brunette-Hill and Finke, 1999, p. 56). In brief, the argument is that men are reluctant to consider the priesthood because of the anticipated difficult nature of celibacy (Stark and Finke, 2000; Breslin, 1981; Breslin and Weafer, 1986).

A second factor associated with a decline in vocations is the counter-cultural nature of priesthood. A candidate for the diocesan priesthood is asked to live a celibate, holy, and obedient life. However, this can be difficult in a society where there is increasing sexual freedom, a focus on material gain, a rejection of traditional authority, and increasing secularisation (Curcione, 1973). A third factor linked to the decline in vocations is the ambiguous nature of priestly, religious and lay vocations that followed the Second Vatican Council. Prior to the council, a priest's vocation was widely regarded as a higher calling and theologically superior to other vocations. However, following the council, greater emphasis was given to the position of lay people in the Church, leading to 'a certain ambiguity' and a blurring of 'the distinction between the priesthood of the baptised and that of the ordained' (Bohr, 2009, p. 3). Increasingly, people began to question the distinction between different vocations in the Church, and, for a relatively short time the term vocation was used in a way that was not automatically synonymous with a religious vocation. However, it would appear that the Church is seeking to address this issue through its emphasis on the 'essential difference' between 'the ministerial priesthood and the priesthood of all believers' (Irish Bishops' Conference, 2006, p. 9). It is increasingly accepted that the life of a priest is 'different' to that of even the most 'involved lay person' because it is 'a celibate life' and one that will 'involve the burden of other people's troubles' (Murray, 1988, p. 23). The prayer for vocations at Mass is once again invariably for religious and priestly vocations. However, in spite of the difficulties highlighted above, men continue to present themselves for priesthood, albeit in much smaller numbers than in the past (see Table A4, Appendix).

1.3 THE NATURE OF DIOCESAN PRIESTHOOD

For the purposes of this study, a diocesan priest is defined as an ordained[6] man[7] who has a vocation or 'call' to the priesthood, who promises to live a celibate life,[8] and who ministers in a geographic area (diocese/parish), under the leadership and authority of the bishop of the diocese to which he belongs. Unlike his religious (regular) clergy counterpart, a diocesan priest does not belong to a religious order, live under a monastic rule, or take vows of poverty, chastity and obedience. He is however, bound by canon law,[9] the law of the Catholic Church, to live a celibate life and to be obedient and respectful to his bishop. Ordination to the priesthood is regarded as a solemn occasion in the life of the priest and the Church, as epitomised by the words of Cardinal Montini to newly ordained priests in 1965:

> You are now priests of Christ for eternity. The long and meticulous preparation that has led to this awesome and sublime moment; the solemnity of the rite that we have celebrated; the words of the Roman Pontifical, rich with wisdom and heavy with warnings; the sacrament you have received and the mysteries you have celebrated with me; all these are a sermon that speaks now and will forever speak to your consecrated souls.
>
> *Cardinal Montini, 1965, p. 11*

The Irish diocesan priest lives and works within a centralised and strictly hierarchical organisation, the main features of which include the pope as its supreme leader on earth (McGarry, 2012),[10] a bishop who is in charge of a diocese,[11] and a parish priest who is the pastor of a parish under the authority of his bishop.[12] *The Dogmatic Constitution of the Church* (*Lumen Gentium*) acknowledges the primacy of the pope as pastor of the entire Church and the supreme authority of the bishops (acting together with the pope). It is 'a Church of unequals' (Dulles, 1976, p. 35) where power passes down through the hierarchy from the pope and bishops to the clergy and laity. The laity have no formal role in the management of the Church.[13] In effect, bishops manage their dioceses without serious challenge from any quarter,[14] either internal or external, other than the pope in exceptional circumstances[15] (Fuller, 2002). The *Ferns Report* (Murphy et al., 2005), for example, highlighted the independence of each diocese as follows:

> The Bishop is free to organise the day-to-day running of his diocese as he sees fit, provided he operates within canon law … There is no central authority in Ireland to whom individual Bishops are accountable or to which they can turn for advice or support.
>
> *Murphy et al., 2005, p. 28*

The hierarchical nature of the Catholic Church is illustrated in the following chart (Figure 1.1).

Figure 1.1 The Hierarchical Structure of the Catholic Church 2014

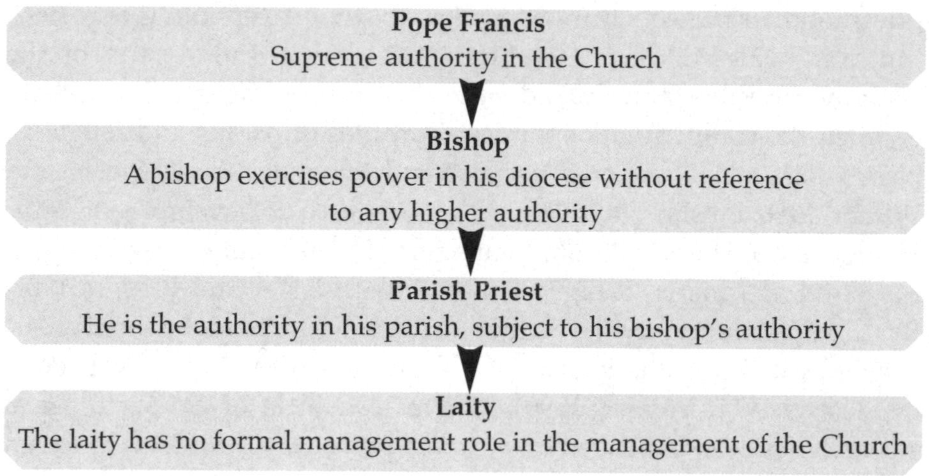

Pope Francis
Supreme authority in the Church

▼

Bishop
A bishop exercises power in his diocese without reference to any higher authority

▼

Parish Priest
He is the authority in his parish, subject to his bishop's authority

▼

Laity
The laity has no formal management role in the management of the Church

The priest is a familiar figure in Ireland and most Irish people are undoubtedly accustomed to the notion of priesthood or the person of a priest (Weafer, 2000),[16] whether it is through knowing their local priest as he carries out his public ministry and sometimes through home visitation (Irish Marketing Surveys, 1998).[17] Many people are also familiar with the portrayal of priests in the media, including the notorious activities of some 'paedophile' priests, the satirical portrayal of priests in the media, such as *Fr Ted*, or the contribution of some priests to Irish society (Bohan, 2013; Daly, 1998; Daly, 2000; Kerr, 1982; McVeigh, 2008; Moran, 1998). A priest's life is typically very public and, in spite of the increased irrelevance of religion to the everyday lives of Catholics in recent years (Andersen, 2010; *The Irish Times*, 2012), the priest's lifestyle can still attract national interest.[18] Yet, in spite of their public ministry, priests are undoubtedly a mystery to many lay people (Draper, 2001).[19] The literature supports the enigmatic image of priesthood when it suggests that a priest can be a 'lone ranger', a person who is set apart by virtue of his spiritual role, clerical garb, celibate lifestyle, position within the community, and his approach to work which is often one of 'rugged individualism' (Fitzgibbon, 2010, p. 175). My study seeks to address this gap in knowledge by exploring the stories of thirty-three diocesan priests and former priests.

1.4 MY RATIONALE FOR UNDERTAKING THE STUDY

I had various reasons for undertaking the research, both professional and personal. The main reason for undertaking this study is the dearth of qualitative sociological research on the lived experience of Irish diocesan priesthood. As previously mentioned, with some exceptions (Lane, 1997; Mulcahy, 1971; Mulcahy, 1974; Rice, 1990), most social research on the Catholic priesthood in Ireland since the Second Vatican Council has entailed the compilation of statistical profiles of priests and religious, paying particular attention to vocation and personnel trends (Breslin and Weafer, 1986; Breslin, 1981; Council for Research & Development, 2007; Hanley, 1995; Hanley, 2000b; Lennon et al., 1972; Lennon et al., 1971; MacGréil and Inglis, 1977; Newman, 1966; Weafer and Breslin, 1983; Ryan, 1972; Lennon, 1974).[20] Other research has explored related areas, such as preaching the homily and the views of priests to Vatican II (Mulcahy, 1974; Weafer, 1990). Conversely, little or no sociological research has been published on the more personal side of Irish diocesan priesthood.[21]

In recent years, some personal information on Irish diocesan priests has emerged in the form of autobiographies (Bohan, 2013; Daly, 1998; Daly, 2000; Daly, 2011; Gaughan, 2000; McVeigh, 2008; O'Callaghan, 2007; Tierney, 2010). Other priests have provided details of the lives of priests, and occasionally their own lives, in religious journals, such as *The Furrow*, or have had stories written about their lives (Murphy and de Rosa, 1993). Information on the Irish diocesan priest is also to be found in various surveys (*The Irish Catholic*, 2004; Lane, 1997), academic studies (Conway, 2013; Keenan, 2012), websites[22] and statutory tribunals of Inquiry (Murphy et al., 2005; Murphy et al., 2009). However, a gap in our knowledge and understanding of Irish diocesan priesthood remains, some of which will be addressed in this study. My research is also timely because of the access it has provided to elderly priests who experienced life before and following Vatican II.

I also had personal reasons for undertaking this study. At one time in my life I seriously considered the vocation of priesthood and I spent almost five years in the seminary discerning my vocation to the priesthood or rather, lack thereof. My initial choice of 'career' had a significant impact on my life and it took some years after leaving the seminary before I came to terms with my decision to leave. It was not an easy choice, even with the unspoken support of my family, bishop and most priests of the diocese. These thoughts were not, however, to the forefront of my mind when I decided to undertake the research. I did not consider my past to be significant in the research process, and I initially adopted the position of a relatively 'detached observer', which conformed to the parameters of traditional qualitative research (Denzin and Lincoln, 2000).[23] However, with hindsight I accept that my motivation for undertaking the research was possibly as much personal as professional, and that the project entailed a degree of reflexivity I had not anticipated (Etherington, 2004).[24] In some ways, the study has helped me to make sense of my own biography in the context of others with whom I had shared similar experiences. My research experience has confirmed for me that I do not have a vocation to the priesthood, although, like many others, there is a sense of unfinished business about what could have been if I, or the priesthood, were different.[25] I also believe that my background helped me to establish a rapport with the research participants and to bring an intuitive understanding to the planning of the study and analysis of the data.

1.5 METHODOLOGY

Conversations with a Purpose

I decided to adopt a qualitative research approach (personal interviews) for a variety of reasons, but mainly because I felt it would give the research participants a suitable environment in which to tell their stories. I also believed that the use of a qualitative research methodology would contribute to the discovery of a richer and more personal type of sociological knowledge that has not previously emerged from existing studies on diocesan priests, and which does not readily emerge when researchers are using quantitative approaches (Skinner et al., 2000; Inglis, 2007).[26] Exponents of qualitative research believe that this approach makes it possible to 'explore a wide array of dimensions of the social world, including the texture and weave of everyday life, the understandings, experiences and imaginings of our research participants, the ways that social processes, institutions, discourses or relationships work, and the significance of the meanings that they generate' (Mason, 2002, p. 1). I also envisaged that a qualitative methodology would address the perceived quantitative, positivist bias and limitations of Irish social research (Share et al., 2007).[27] Sociologist Perry Share (2007), for example, wrote that a 'major limitation of Irish sociological research into religion is that it has tended to be highly positivist' (Share et al., 2007, p. 398), while sociologist Tom Inglis argues that research into religion in Ireland 'concentrated on gathering facts and data, usually through social surveys, and has avoided dealing with the larger, more general questions about the position and influence of the Church' (Inglis, 1987, p. 2).

Personal interviews in sociology are sometimes referred to as 'conversations with a purpose' and in the present study, I conducted thirty-three such conversations with Irish diocesan priests and former priests. I decided to select a broad sample of priests from a variety of backgrounds. Of the thirty-three men interviewed, twenty-four priests are in active ministry (including four semi-retired priests), seven priests have left the priesthood, and two have changed their allegiance from a diocese to a religious order. Ten priests were ordained before the conclusion of the Second Vatican Council, fourteen were ordained in the 1970s and 1980s, and nine were ordained in the 1990s and 2000s. One priest and two former priests are gay; two priests had been falsely accused of sexually abusing young boys; and one former priest had become a minister in the Church of Ireland. In all, nine dioceses and the four Irish Provinces are represented in the study.

The interviews were usually held in the research participants' homes, resulting in more than forty hours of interviews and in excess of 3,500 miles travelled during the summer of 2010. The thirty-three priests and former diocesan priests were interviewed using a narrative-style introduction, followed by questions listed in a semi-structured topic guide (Mishler, 1999; Etherington, 2004).[28] The participants were initially asked to respond to the following narrative introduction:

> I am interested in hearing about your life and experiences as a diocesan priest; from the time you felt you had a vocation to the present day. Take your time and try to mention anything you feel is important because everything that is of interest to you is of interest to me. Where would you like to start?

The narrative introduction proved very effective in helping priests recollect their life stories in a relatively seamless and natural way, possibly stirring up memories they had forgotten, and allowing them to take control of the interview process by emphasising those aspects of their priesthood they deemed most important. While most priests spoke with the minimum of encouragement, others initially required prompting before they got into a rhythm and embarked on their stories. Most of the research participants began their stories chronologically, starting with accounts of their vocation and seminary life, before moving to other topics of interest to them. For example, once they had discussed their early years as students, older priests spoke a lot about the legalistic control in the pre-Vatican II Church and how their priesthood had changed following Vatican II. Conversely, priests ordained around the time of Vatican II were most concerned with the slow progress of Vatican II and the difficulties they had personally encountered with celibacy.

I chose not to ask the research participants direct questions about their sexuality or sexual experiences, partly because of the potential sensitivity of the topic and its potential adverse impact on the remainder of the interview. I was also wary of, and keen to avoid, sensationalising priests' stories. However, neither did I wish to arbitrarily exclude discussion on sexual behaviour. Accordingly, I created a space in the interview process, which invited the participants to discuss their experience of celibacy at whatever level of intimacy they felt comfortable. This was done by asking the research participants if they regarded their celibate lifestyle to have been a blessing or a hindrance to their life as a priest, together with some general questions on mandatory celibacy and clerical support networks. This process allowed some priests to give quite specific details of their sexual lives, while others chose not to make any personal disclosures.

The research was guided by the protocols of the SRA (Social Research Association, 2003) and the Ethical guidelines of the Sociological Association of Ireland (Sociological Association of Ireland, 2004). Each of the research participants was given a verbal account and a written explanation detailing the nature and purpose of the research. They were informed of the proposed research process, the expected duration of the interview, and given assurances of confidentiality and anonymity. They were also told that they could withdraw from the research, without repercussions at any time, and that if they withdrew their permission to use their data within two weeks of the interview, all their data would be deleted. Counselling was offered to all the research participants, although none availed of the service. Most of the participants opted to read a copy of their transcribed interview but, with the exception of some relatively minor details, they were all satisfied that their interviews reflected their views and experience of priesthood. Overall, I believe that the research process was successful and that my personal biography helped to create a rapport with the research participants that enabled them to speak openly about most areas of their lives. All of the research participants spoke very openly and honestly about their lives for more than one hour, and many of them voluntarily shared their 'more vulnerable side' (Fitzgibbon, 1996, p. 226). Indeed, some priests gave details of their lives that I regarded as too personal to warrant inclusion in this or any other publication.

1.6 STRUCTURE OF THE BOOK

The changing nature of Irish society vis-à-vis Catholicism since 1960 is explored in chapter two, in order to understand the changing context within which Irish diocesan priests live and work. I will argue that the modern Irish religious landscape is less supportive and more hostile towards the Church when compared with the 1960s. However, anecdotal evidence suggests that priests are still highly regarded in Irish society, particularly in rural areas and by older people in established parishes. Accordingly, chapter three will review the literature on Irish diocesan priests in contemporary Irish society and investigate what insights it can provide on the evolving position of diocesan priests in contemporary Irish society. Chapter three will also explore evidence, which suggests that different models of priesthood have emerged and prevailed in the Catholic Church at different times during the past fifty years. The empirical findings from the research are presented and analysed in chapters four to six, commencing with the topic of celibacy, and followed by obedience and identity, respectively. These empirical chapters will address the research questions outlined in chapter one. The final chapter draws together the main findings and insights from the research, and discusses the implications of the research findings for Irish diocesan priesthood. A range of statistical data relating to Irish diocesan priesthood is appended.

Chapter Two

The Changing Socio-Religious
Landscape of Ireland, 1960–2010[29]

The landscape of the Irish Church is being eaten away by sexual scandal, materialism, the dawning of new and welcome freedoms for women and minorities, the secularisation of minds.

O'Brien, 1995, p. 13

2.1 INTRODUCTION

Ireland's socio-religious landscape has changed dramatically during the past fifty years or so, with the result that Ireland has become a more modern, urban, cosmopolitan, educated, and secular society (Murphy, 2000b). During this period, the influence and dominance of the Catholic Church in Irish society has declined, while the position of the media and diverse interest groups has increased (Donnelly and Inglis, 2010).[30] Mass attendance, sacramental participation and religious vocations have fallen sharply, while referenda have been passed and legislation enacted, which permits the sale of contraceptives, divorce, homosexual behaviour between consenting adults, and abortion in certain circumstances. All of these are contrary to the teachings and ethos of the Catholic Church. Furthermore, large numbers of Irish Catholics have an unfavourable opinion of the Catholic Church (Iona Institute, 2011). They do not trust the Church and neither would they turn to it for guidance in moral issues (Association of Catholic Priests, 2012). No longer can it be said that Catholicism is the unquestioned orthodoxy of everyday Irish life (Inglis, 2005) or, to put it more simply in the words of writer and former priest, Michael Harding, for many people, maybe 'the religion we cling to doesn't work anymore' (Harding, 2013, p. 24).

Conversely, other indicators suggest Ireland is still a Catholic country, albeit a very different country to the theocratic society that existed in the 1950s and early 1960s.[31] For example, the vast majority of Irish people continue to identify themselves as Roman Catholic (Census 2011), and religious practice is significantly higher in Ireland than in most European countries (European Values Survey 2012).[32] A nation-wide survey conducted in 2007 found that the majority of adult Catholics (70%) felt valued by their Church (Weafer, 2007), with most of these people saying 'very much' or 'quite a lot'. The voice of the laity is also increasingly prominent in the Irish public arena, albeit more and more polarised between liberal and conservative interests. The Catholic Church retains a strong influence in education through its ownership and management of the vast majority of primary schools, and a Catholic ethos is present in many post-primary schools and hospitals (Maxwell, 2014). Furthermore, the ongoing significance of Catholicism for Ireland's national identity is evident from the regular coverage it receives in newspapers and other media.

The aim of this chapter is to review the changing socio-economic and religious landscape in Ireland since 1960, in order to understand the changing context within which Irish diocesan priests live and work. The chapter is divided into three parts, beginning with an overview of the 'swinging' 1960s,[33] followed by the 'disillusioned' 1970s and 1980s, and the turbulent years of 'Celtic Tiger' Ireland. I will argue that the Irish Catholic Church is in crisis, although not yet in terminal decline, and that the socio-religious landscape of contemporary Ireland is less welcoming and more hostile towards the Church. The implications of this altered environment for Irish diocesan priests will be explored in chapter three.

2.2 SOCIO-ECONOMIC AND RELIGIOUS CHANGE IN 1960S IRELAND

2.2.1 Socio-Economic Change

Something happened in the sixties that led to a fundamental change in attitude and lifestyle in Ireland and other Western countries (Fallon, 1998).[34] The 1960s were a 'time of rude energy' and 'a contempt for tradition', and 'like all such times', the 1960s 'threw up a generation that believed itself to have discovered the world anew and to have cracked codes that had eluded its elders' (Tobin, 1984, p. 1). It was a time when one generation 'superseded another' (Whyte, 1980, p. 361), when a 'new generation' came to the fore in 'politics, the media, health services, sport, music, cultural and legal life, and religion' (Ferriter, 2004, p. 536–7).

During this period, free post-primary education was introduced in Ireland (Coolahan, 1981), population decline reversed and for the first time, the majority of Irish people lived in urban areas (Fahey, 2007). Censorship was redefined and curtailed (Woodman, 1985), second-wave Irish feminism emerged (Connolly and O'Toole, 2005), and John F. Kennedy visited Ireland. A national television service was launched in 1961 and shows such as *The Late Late Show*, 'enabled widespread discussion to take place on topics [which would] otherwise have been swept under the carpet' (Coogan, 1987, p. 2), and 'sexual permissiveness was upon us' (Fallon, 1998, p. 257). The sexual revolution was just one of the revolutions that was 'unleashed' as many young people 'rejected the narrow, restrictive moral values of former generations, and opted for a freer, more spontaneous, ultimately unrestricted lifestyle' (Twomey, 2003, p. 136).

In contrast to the perceived 'archaic' country that prevailed during the 1950s, where 'all kinds of topics of everyday concern seemed to be under some kind of unspoken taboo' (Garvin, 2010, p. 2), the 1960s was a decade when Ireland engaged with advanced western societies. It was a decade of freedom, a time of openness and while 'the isolation and introspection' of previous generations did not disappear, 'the blinds were let up, the windows were thrown open, the doors were unlocked; and good, bad or indifferent, the modern world came in among us at last' (Tobin, 1984, p. 8). For young radicals in the western world, the 1960s represented an opportunity to fight imperialism, capitalism, and bureaucracy as 'part of an imagined community of global revolt' (Prince, 2006, p. 851). In the Republic of Ireland, radicalism took a 'gentler' form in Irish universities (Ferriter, 2004, p. 599), while, in Northern Ireland, a country dominated by the sectarian divide, the global revolt that was 1968 resulted in The Troubles[35] (Prince, 2006).

The success of the First Programme for Economic Expansion that followed the publication of T. K. Whittaker's celebrated report *Economic Development* in 1958, led to a dramatic increase in living standards during the sixties, giving the country the 'material and psychological basis for national recovery' (Tobin, 1984, p. 4). For the first time in many generations, the 1960s offered 'employment, security, and the prospect of reasonable material comfort' for all of Ireland's population (Tobin, 1984, p. 7). The 'associated expectations and excitement' that followed success in these state initiatives were captured in the catchphrase of the 1960s, 'the rising tide that would lift all boats' (Breen et al., 1990, p. 1). The widely acknowledged results from the change in direction in Ireland's economic policy also led to some benefits for social policy, in areas such as education, housing, healthcare, and the expansion of the social welfare system (Considine and Dukelow, 2009).

However, there was another side to the 1960s that was far from idyllic for people living on the margins of society. In 1960 'Ireland was a very poor country' (Garvin, 2005, p. 252) and for many, the 1960s was a decade of 'squalor and neglect in the midst of a new-found opulence' (Ferriter, 2004, p. 536). It was a decade when young pregnant women were sent to Magdalen laundries to hide their shame, and many young boys and girls were abandoned and abused in industrial schools (McAleese, 2013; Raftery and O'Sullivan, 1999; Murphy et al., 2005). Hidden behind the optimism of the 1960s lay 'much stagnation and class snobbery' (Ferriter, 2004, p. 537), where economic growth 'served to widen the gulf between rich and poor' (Ferriter, 2004, p. 537). Socio-logical studies highlighted the difficulties of living in isolated parts of rural Ireland and the widespread rejection of this life by many young people (Brody, 1973; Hannan, 1970; Healy, 1968). It was a time which Minister for Education, Ruairí Quinn recalls was 'a cultural prison, a censored ghetto. If you were not conforming, you either shut up or you left' (Hanafin, 2012, p. 21).

2.2.2 Irish Catholicism in 1960s Ireland

The early 1960s 'found the Irish Catholic Church much as it had been for the best part of a century' (Tobin, 1984, p. 38). The Church shared many of the features of the 1950s Catholic Church, which Church historian Louise Fuller believes represented the 'final phase of nineteenth century devotional revolution Catholicism' (Fuller, 2005, p. 42). The chief characteristics of 1960s Catholicism comprised a 'remarkably high level of religious practice, the legitimisation by the state of the Catholic ethos, the authoritarian approach of the bishops towards their followers, the high number of vocations to the religious life and the extent to which the thinking, rituals, language and symbols of Catholicism informed consciousness' (Fuller, 2005, p. 42). The vast majority of Irish people were dedicated Catholics who held the Church in very high standing (Biever, 1976). Most churches were full on Sundays (Ward, 1964) and there were long queues for confession on Saturday nights 'throughout the length and breadth of the country' (Fuller, 2005, p. 43). Vocations and ordinations to the diocesan priesthood were very high (Lennon et al., 1971), and thousands of Irish people worked in missionary countries as priests, religious and lay volunteers (Humphreys, 2010; Lennon et al., 1971; Hogan, 1990).

The list of devotional practices engaged in by most Catholics during the 1960s was lengthy, including Mass (said in Latin up to 1965), processions, pilgrimages, confraternities, sodalities, parish missions, benediction, novenas, the rosary, Marian devotions, First Fridays,[36] and indulgences.[37] Many people wore 'an array of accoutrements' (Kerrigan, 1998, p. 110), such as a miraculous medal, a pioneer pin or a scapular, and women were obliged to wear a scarf or mantilla on their heads when attending Mass. Thousands of people were members of Lay Catholic organisations, such as the Legion of Mary, the Children of Mary, and St Vincent de Paul (Inglis, 1998). Most Irish households displayed pictures of the Sacred Heart (with a red light), Pope John XXIII, and President John F. Kennedy.

The 'dominant form of religious behaviour' in Ireland during the 1960s was 'an adherence to the rules and regulations of the Catholic Church' (Inglis, 1998, p. 30). The fear of mortal sin appeared to be everywhere in the pre-Vatican II Church,[38] with no one totally sure what constituted a mortal or a venial sin.[39] The fear of committing a mortal or venial sin as set down in the *Penny Catechism*[40] underpinned the legalistic response of many people and priests to their faith. It was a time of fear and secrecy, and rules were broken at your peril, especially those concerned with sexuality and 'impure thoughts' (Banville, 2004).[41] In the 1960s, most people accepted the reality of eternal damnation, and the threat of mortal sin was used to control sexual urges (O'Morain, 2012). Social conformity was regulated by state censorship and the rules of the Catholic Church. Homosexuality was illegal, as was divorce, abortion, and the sale of contraceptives.

To complicate matters further, some dioceses had their own 'reserved sins', such as forbidding people to attend dances after midnight.[42]

Accordingly, most people depended on their local bishop and priests to keep them informed on such matters. Sociologist Máire Nic Ghiolla Phádraig observed that Irish Catholicism was a personalised faith that relied heavily on 'authority figures like the clergy to adjudicate on moral issues' (Nic Ghiolla Phádraig, 1986, p. 153). This was a time when the Catholic Church had 'almost total power' in Irish society, according to writer John McGahern, where it represented 'the dominating force' in his 'upbringing, education and early working life' (McGahern, 2009, p. 133). To be Irish was effectively to be Catholic and 'the discourse engaged in by Church personnel played a powerful role in the formation of consciousness and identity' (Fuller, 2002, p. 42). An orthodox Catholic world view was taken for granted by the majority of people (Andersen, 2010), and those who opposed the Church and its clerical culture, the intellectuals and educated, were typically forced to emigrate or to live silent and hidden lives (Garvin, 2005).

The Catholic Church had a 'special position' in the Constitution (Article 44) and the hierarchy was regarded as 'without peer in terms of power' (Humphreys, 1966, p. 53). Few politicians or civil leaders had the temerity to challenge the Church, although some individuals did try (Browne, 1986).[43] The dominant position of the Catholic Church in Ireland at this time is possibly best illustrated by the power exercised by individual Church leaders, such as Archbishop John Charles McQuaid (Cooney, 1999), and the influence of certain lay organisations, such as the Knights of Columbanus (Garvin, 2005).[44] Sociologist Tom Inglis believes that the 'symbolic domination' of the Catholic Church was 'manifested in the way Church teaching was enshrined in the Irish Constitution and social legislation, the censorship of publications and films, the control of the media, the public display of Catholic icons and symbols, clerical dress, and so forth' (Inglis, 2003, p. 44). However, this was to change following the Second Vatican Council (1962–5), when the certainties of the Church were questioned and a gradual change was evident in the nature of Irish Church–State relations (Whyte, 1980).

2.2.3 The Second Vatican Council (1962–5)
The holding of the Second Vatican Council 'represented an irrevocable turning-point' (Kung, 2001, p. 192) and the 'most significant influence on Catholic life and theology in general and moral theology in particular

in the last fifty years' (Curran, 2006, p. 410). Vatican II is generally regarded by Catholics as the 'most important religious event of the twentieth century' (O'Malley, 2008, p. 1), a time when the Catholic Church, like much of the Western world, was perceived to be on the brink of significant change and renewal. The Second Vatican Council marked the demise of the rigid institutional model of Church that prevailed up to the late 1960s (Hornsby-Smith, 1992).[45] The pre-Vatican II Church was a Church of certainties and unquestioning obedience, where people 'looked out from the Catholic ghetto on a life in which sacrifice, suffering, resignation, detachment and acceptance of things as "God's Will" were keys to salvation' (Nic Ghiolla Phádraig, 1982, p. 486).

The Second Vatican Council 'effected a transformation in the life and habits of the Church' (Tobin, 1984, p. 117). It initiated changes and pointed to the possibilities of enhanced participation in a hitherto remote and conservative Church (Flanagan, 1969). The new model of Church that emerged from Vatican II emphasised collegiality, ecumenism, community and the enhanced participation of the 'People of God'. It was a more open, optimistic and democratic vision of Church, albeit still hierarchical, where dialogue was encouraged. Archbishop Martin, who was a student at the time of the Second Vatican Council, recalls being 'inspired and energised' by the Council's Pastoral Constitution on the Church in the Modern World: *Gaudiem et Spes*.

> Coming out of a particular moment of a traditional and authoritarian Irish Church culture, the newness of this challenging and exciting notion of dialogue between the Church and the culture of the modern world … was almost thrilling to our young ears. Rather than telling the world what to do, the Church was to listen to what the modern world was saying to and telling the Church.
>
> *Martin, 2012*

In Ireland, the timing of the Second Vatican Council was somewhat fortuitous in that it coincided with 'a decisive shift in cultural experience', which had been taking place for the previous fifteen years or so (Connolly, 1979, p. 755). There was a 'desire for change' in Ireland and 'when change came that desire spiralled' (Martin, 2012). For most Irish Catholics, the various liturgical changes in the Mass,[46] such as the use of the vernacular in the Mass and the priest/altar facing the people

(Flannery, 1962; McCormack, 1962; McConville and McConville, 1962),[47] were 'the most visible and most dramatic signs of change in Catholic culture' (Fuller, 2002, p. 109). Change 'came much [more] slowly and hesitantly in other spheres', such as lay participation and ecumenical activity (Donnelly, 2000, p. 13).

The impact of the Second Vatican Council was, however, more than a set of liturgical changes. It 'ushered in a new mood – a more optimistic Catholic culture' (Fuller, 2005, p. 48), where the 'new brand of Catholicism underwritten by the Second Vatican Council' (Fuller, 2005, p. 48) was perceived by many to be more democratic than the traditional authoritarian Church. Although it is perceived to have lacked practical details on implementation, the documents of the Second Vatican Council 'contained enormous developments in the theology of the laity and their mission in the church' (Dolan, 2007, p. 52). The 'universal call to holiness' and the recognition of 'the dignity of lay men and women' energised and empowered lay people 'to fulfil their vocation in the church' (O'Malley, 2008, p. 5). Various Episcopal commissions were established in Ireland to coincide with the publication of Council documents, and lay organisations that were committed to working among the poor, such as the Young Christian Workers, were formed.

The Council also affirmed the primacy of moral conscience, thereby removing some of the traditional threat of mortal sin. Vatican II effectively gave 'permission' to question the way things were done in the Church, and 'possibly, the most important outcome for Catholic culture was that the era of certainties was undermined forever' (Fuller, 2005, p. 49). Irish theologian Fr Vincent Twomey wrote that the theological and liturgical renewal inaugurated by the Second Vatican Council 'shattered old certainties' and suddenly 'everything was, in principle, considered capable of being changed, including the teaching of the Church' (Twomey, 2003, p. 136). Historian James Donnelly contends that the Catholic Church in Ireland 'lost much of its once great moral authority by its persistent mishandling of issues connected to sexual behaviour and morality' (Donnelly, 2000, p. 14). Irish theologian, Fr Dermot Lane argues that 'the real significance' of *Humanae Vitae* was that it 'initiated an open discussion in the Irish Church, not only about the morality of family planning, but also about the authority of the bishops to teach on this subject – something unknown and unparalleled in the past' (Lane, 2004, p. 72). Irish theologian, Linda Hogan, makes a similar point concerning the 'radical transformation' that occurred in the field of ethics.

> Prior to the council, theological ethics was primarily a legalistic and casuistic enterprise, which aimed at giving universally applicable answers to a set of predetermined questions. This approach to morals was underwritten by a starkly hierarchical model of church, with its exaggerated account of the distinctive and unequal roles of laity, clergy, bishops and pope … The critical turning point was Vatican II, which utterly transformed the internal landscape of Catholicism and allowed questions concerning conscience, moral authority and the church's moral tradition to emerge in a different register.
>
> *Hogan, 2012, p. 16*

However, it became evident by the end of the 1960s that the promise and liberal spirit of the Second Vatican Council would face opposition from within the Church. The Irish Church was very conservative and the 'primary concern' of the Irish bishops in implementing Vatican II was 'to bring about the changes of the council without, however, disturbing the faith of the people' (Lane, 2004, p. 70). Some of the opposition to Vatican II came from people, priests and bishops who did not wish to change the way they did things (Flanagan, 1969; Houtart, 1968).[48] More significantly, perhaps, influential forces within the Vatican disapproved of the perceived liberal agenda. Consequently, the initial hopes and enthusiasm surrounding the Vatican Council were diminished by the end of the 1960s, with the issuing of an encyclical on Human Life (*Humanae Vitae*) in 1968,[49] together with other 'strains and tensions springing from contrasting ecclesiologies that underlay the conciliar discussion of various topics' (O'Riordan, 1990, p. 77). The landmark decision in *Humanae Vitae* to ban the use of contraceptives in 1968 was interpreted by some as a clear sign that the Church was not going to change, at least for the foreseeable future (Hoge and Wenger, 2003). This represented a significant response from the conservative forces to the perceived liberal agenda of Vatican II, and, what many would see as the beginning of a return to a more orthodox and conservative Church. It became increasingly evident to some observers that some anticipated features of Vatican II would not materialise, such as the expected change in the discipline of celibacy (O'Malley, 2008).[50]

The impact of Vatican II is a subject that would play out in subsequent decades. Almost three decades later, one Irish priest expressed his disappointment with the Church, which he felt was no longer the Church for which he was ordained in the 'heady-post Vatican II days of 1971':

> It is increasingly difficult to remain a priest in a Church, which has sidelined Leonardo Boff, Hans Küng, Charles Curran, Ernesto Cardenal, not to mention people nearer home. A Church which has lost more than a hundred thousand priests mainly due to its insistence on compulsory clerical celibacy, a Church which makes celibacy more important than Eucharistic ministry, a Church which preaches justice for all, yet refuses to contemplate equality for women in its ministry.
>
> *Standún, 1993, p. 85*

His view of Vatican II is shared by many others in the Irish and universal Church (Hogan, 2012; Hogan, 2013). Conversely, others, such as Bishop Michael Smith of the Meath diocese, have a more positive recollection of the council and its impact on the Church's life and mission (Smith, 2012).

By the end of the 1960s, traditional Catholicism was no longer taken for granted, as Ireland's emerging educated class began to increasingly challenge the Church. Various commentators have observed, often in hindsight, some cracks that appeared in the all-encompassing Catholic Church during this time. Sociologist Fr Conor Ward of UCD, for example, thought it likely that the prevailing stereotype of the Irish Catholic would 'not survive empirical investigation' (Ward, 1964).[51] Similarly, political scientist Tom Garvin, believes that Biever's 1962 study of political and religious attitudes in Dublin, and an earlier study by Jesuit sociologist, Fr Alexander Humphreys, in his sociological study of Dubliners (Humphreys, 1966), indicated the presence of 'an incipient anti-clericalism' amongst the educated Catholic upper middle class (Garvin, 2005, p. 261). Sociologist Tony Fahey also detected signs of change in the sixties, and argues that 'the high-point of religious commitment in Ireland had already passed by the late 1960s and signs of decline had appeared, as illustrated, for example, by the diminishing authority of the churches in the political sphere and the drying up of vocations to the religious life' (Fahey et al., 2005, p. 30). By the end of the 1960s, the traditional, devout Catholic Ireland was facing the prospect of change as it sought to coexist[52] with new, more radical, less deferential attitudes towards the Church. However, change was slow in the Irish Church and much remained the same as the Church entered the 1970s.

2.3 THE DISILLUSIONED DECADES, 1970–89

2.3.1 Socio-Economic Changes, 1970–89

The early 1970s continued more or less where the 1960s left off, 'upward, outward and onward seemed to be the direction in which the wagon was rolling' (Coogan, 1987, p. 2). Ireland joined the EEC in 1973 and expectations were high that Ireland would benefit from its membership. However, economic performance was 'mediocre' for the first two decades after Ireland joined the EEC (Haughton, 2000, p. 38). The international economy weakened following an oil crisis in 1973–4 and again in 1979–80, when the price of crude oil more than doubled, leading to very high inflation, high unemployment rates, and, ultimately, falling living standards and 'a resumption of heavy emigration' (Kennedy et al., 1988, p. 266). Ireland entered into a recession and did not begin to emerge from it until towards the end of the 1980s (Hagan, 1984). It was also a time when the Northern Troubles reignited, with Bloody Sunday and the fall of Stormont in 1972 being recognised as two significant events. In the opinion of some commentators, Ireland was a country in crisis (Crotty, 1986).

The 1970s was 'a decade of radicalism and protest for some organised groups, including community and women's groups and the trade union movement' (Considine and Dukelow, 2009, p. 51). This period was also marked by poverty and growing inequalities in Irish society (Collins and Kavanagh, 1998, p. 185). The establishment of the Combat Poverty Agency in 1986 served to highlight diverse aspects of poverty in Ireland, including the claim in its first annual report of 1987, that probably over a quarter of Irish people were 'living in some degree of poverty' (Combat Poverty Agency, 1987, p. 5).

2.3.2 Religious Change in the 1970s and 1980s

One of the distinctive features of Ireland[53] in the 1970s and 1980s is the large number of surveys that were conducted into different aspects of religious attitudes and practice (Breslin and Weafer, 1982; Breslin and Weafer, 1985; Fogarty et al., 1984; Inglis, 1979; MacGréil, 1974;

McAllister, 1983; McMahon, 1982; MRBI, 1987; MRBI/*The Irish Times*, 1983; Nic Ghiolla Phádraig, 1976; O'Doherty, 1969; Parfrey, 1976; Power, 1969a; Rose, 1971). Many other 'non-religious' surveys also routinely included questions on religious practice (MacGréil, 1977).[54] One reason for the relatively large number of religious surveys in Ireland was the establishment of the Irish Catholic Bishops' research unit in 1970, which built on sociology's 'early affinities with the Catholic Church' (Conway, 2006, p. 30).

The Irish Bishops' Conference set up a special Research & Development Unit (R&D) within the Catholic Communications Institute, 'to research and report on every aspect of religion in Ireland, with a view to pastoral planning and programming, and to monitor changes in Irish society which impinge on religious belief and practice' (Council for Research & Development, 1981, p. vi). This unit was to the forefront of empirical religious research throughout the 1970s and 1980s, with the result that much more was known about the Irish Catholic towards the end of the eighties than was known in the 1960s. As previously stated in chapter one, the focus of religious research in the 1970s was on the mapping of statistical trends in 'the Church's manpower' (Lennon et al., 1972), including vocations (Newman et al., 1972). These reports were followed by similar statistical projects at regular intervals (Council for Research & Development, 1971–2004; Council for Research & Development, 2007; Hanley, 1995; Hanley, 2000b; MacGréil and Inglis, 1977; Weafer and Breslin, 1983). A second wave of research initiated in the 1970s changed the focus to the measurement of religious belief and practice amongst the laity (Nic Ghiolla Phádraig, 1976).

Another reason for the proliferation of religious research was undoubtedly Ireland's ongoing interest, if not fascination, with religion. The surveys conducted during the 1970s and 1980s indicated that Ireland was a very religious country, especially when compared with other Western countries (Table 2.1).

Table 2.1 Frequency of Mass Attendance, Republic of Ireland, 1970–89
Base: Adult Catholics, 18+ years

Survey	More often than weekly	Once a week	At least once a week (Cumulative)	Less Often	Never
	%	%	%	%	%
R&D* 1973–4 (Nic Ghiolla Phádraig, 1976)	23	68	91	6	3
RTÉ 1974 (RTÉ, 1974)	n/a	n/a	91	n/a	n/a
MacGréil 1977 (MacGréil, 1977)	30	59	90	8	3
EVS 1981 (Fogarty et al., 1984)	30	57	87	13	n/a
R&D 1984 (Breslin and Weafer, 1985)	30	57	87	10	3
MacGréil, 1988–9 (MacGréil, 1996)	15	67	82	16	2.5

*R&D denotes the Irish Bishops' Conference Council for Research & Development.

The authors of the 1974 R&D report, *A Survey of Religious Practice, Attitudes and Beliefs, 1973–4*, summarised the situation in the mid 1970s as follows:

> The general picture of religious practice in the country is a reasonably bright one. Even the most confirmed pessimist or the most biased commentator must acknowledge that a weekly Mass attendance of 91%, a monthly Communion rate of 65.5% and a monthly attendance at Confession of 46.5% to be something exceptional, if not unique, in the mid-20th century.
>
> *Council for Research & Development, 1975, Volume 1, p. 71*

Towards the end of the 1970s, statistics confirmed that Ireland was still 'one of the last remaining countries where the overwhelming majority can be assumed to profess Christian belief both in theory and practice' (Connolly, 1979, p. 757). The predominantly positive picture of Irish Catholicism continued into the 1980s. Fr Liam Ryan concluded his review of faith in Ireland in the early 1980s, with the observation that 'by any standards Ireland is still a pre-eminently religious country' (Ryan, 1983, p. 4). The authors of the *European Values Study* (EVS) expressed similar views: 'every indicator of belief, informal and formal practice and attitudes to the church or churches, shows Irish people, North and South, to be far more inclined to religion than those of other countries in Europe' (Fogarty et al., 1984, p. 8). The 1985 Council for Research & Development (R&D) report, *Religious Beliefs, Practice and Moral Attitudes: A Comparison of Two Irish Surveys, 1974–1984*, also noted that nearly everyone believed in God and the vast majority (87%) of Catholics went to Mass every week (Breslin and Weafer, 1985).

Yet, some commentators were uneasy with the picture that was emerging from the statistics. A report by Fr Joseph Nolan on 'Youth Culture and the Faith' for the Irish Episcopal Conference, for example, stated that while the 1974 research indicated that there is 'no widespread unbelief among the young' nevertheless, there is 'widespread apprehension among parents' as to what is happening to their children in the area of religion (Nolan, 1974, p. 10). The 'Working Party Report' that accompanied the R&D's 1974 national study also observed that 'some problems' were appearing in the 'structure of traditional Irish Catholicism' particularly in the areas of education and family life (Council for Research & Development, 1975). They concluded that the Irish Church was moving from its traditional position which 'attempted a universal embrace of society to a situation where the Church has become a recognised institution alongside other major institutions of the cultural system' (Council for Research & Development, 1975).

The R&D's 1985 report noted a decrease since 1974 in almost all religious indicators, including sacramental participation, moral attitudes, religious beliefs and acceptance of Church teachings (Breslin and Weafer, 1985). Less than half of Irish adults believed in the devil or hell, just over six in ten fully accepted papal infallibility, and over one third said they had difficulty with some aspect of Church teaching. Only one sixth of Irish adults believed that married couples using contraceptives to avoid having children was always wrong, and almost half felt that divorce should be allowed in certain circumstances (Weafer, 1986).[55] These liberal trends were more pronounced for young adults, those living in urban areas, and people with higher levels of formal education. However, in the 1980s, it was more a case of confusion and uncertainty than outright rejection. Jesuit priest Fr Michael Paul Gallagher summarised the predominant portrait of Irish youth which emerged from the major surveys conducted during the 1980s as 'a picture of high practice having little influence on values, of a solid institutional Church fostering little on the level of spiritual experience, and of a younger generation suffering more from confusion over faith than from any definite rebellion against religion' (Gallagher, 1986, p. 36).

The data from social surveys led professor Liam Ryan to observe that the 'essence of religious belief in Ireland today is that conflicting values and beliefs are held by the same person' (Ryan, 1983, p. 5),[56] and he hypothesised the emergence of a 'new' type of Catholic in Ireland, which, 'as yet in the minority, is characterised by an informed appreciation of the value of the supernatural and sacramental life of the Church, but retains an independence of mind largely on moral matters (Ryan, 1983, p. 7). Diverse typologies constructed by other sociologists around this time also proposed the emergence of different types of Catholics and the increasing polarisation of the Church (Nic Ghiolla Phádraig, 1982).[57] The position of the laity evolved slowly during this period, with the introduction of diverse ministries associated with an enhanced participation in the Mass. Lay participation in the Church was also promoted by various organisations, such as *Pobal Dé* (People of God) who described themselves as a 'group of committed and practising Catholics who are concerned about the lack of resolve on the part of the leadership of the Church to empower people to meet the challenges of the world in which we live'.[58]

The relationship between Church and State began to change perceptibly in this period, with 'often acrimonious' debates on issues surrounding contraception, divorce, and abortion (Lane, 2004, p. 72). However, the traditional position of the Church prevailed for much of the 1970s[59] and 1980s. The sale of contraceptives[60] was legalised (but not universally available) in 1979 (Fitzgerald, 1991); the first 'pro-life' amendment to the constitution was passed in 1983; and the first divorce referendum was defeated in 1986. Ireland's problematic relationship with public morality was well illustrated by a number of events that occurred at this time, including the death of a fifteen-year old girl after giving birth in a grotto outside a church.[61] The Catholic Church was most defiant in relation to legislation that sought to legalise divorce[62] and abortion, which resulted in 'bruising national debates' and 'revealed widening gaps between what the Church taught and what significant proportions of the people were willing to accept' (Fahey et al., 2005, p. 33). Individual bishops also voiced their opposition to any change in the law that would permit the sale of contraceptives, abortion, divorce or homosexuality (Newman, 1983). Fr Liam Ryan suggested that the role of the hierarchy in the 1970s could best be described as the 'conscience of society' (Ryan, 1979).[63]

This was a time when the cloak of power of the Irish bishops began to dissolve perceptibly (Inglis, 1998), when the Church decided to confront the State 'in the bedroom' (Inglis, 1986, p. 48) and to restrict the liberal-isation of sexuality. That battle was effectively lost by the early 1990s when the moral authority of the Church was undermined by the disclosures concerning Bishop Casey's affair and by the actions of individual priests who were convicted of sexually abusing young children.

2.3.3 The Papacy of John Paul II (1978–2005)

This period coincided with the first part of the charismatic papacy of John Paul II (*The Sunday Tribune*, 2005). He was one of the most travelled popes and world leaders in the twentieth century, and in September 1979, he visited Ireland. His visit was regarded as 'a truly mythic event' for Ireland's millions of Catholics (Garvin, 2005, p. 263) and, for a short period, it was associated with increased religious practice and vocations to the priesthood. The visit literally 'stopped the country in its tracks' with over a million people attending Mass in the Phoenix Park and other venues. However, its 'effects soon wore off' (Coogan, 1987, p. 74). While some people were 'massively encouraged' by the visit, others saw it as akin to a nation attempting 'to find solace in difficult times harking back to an era when life had seemed much less complex and much less threatening' (Sweeney, 2010, pp. 174–5). In hindsight, it was clear that the Catholic Church was in 'serious trouble' (Donnelly, 2000, p. 12).

Pope John Paul II was one of the most influential leaders in the twentieth century (Weigel, 1999). However, while he was loved and admired by many, he was severely criticised by others for his centralising style of rule that failed to deal appropriately with clerical sexual abuse, and for his opposition to the liberal agenda within the Church (Cornwell, 2004). During his lengthy papacy, he took a strong stance on the sanctity of marriage and he opposed many issues including: women's ordination, married clergy, some elements of liberation theology, and aspects of sexuality morality. He has also been criticised for 'his policy of appointing very conservative bishops, theologically and politically, from outside dioceses, and, more often than not, disregarding the advice of local church leaders' (White, 2002, p. xix). His alleged support for right-wing Church organisations, such as Opus Dei and the Legionaries of Christ, also caused considerable controversy. Conversely, his supporters perceived his papacy as a time of renewal when Vatican II was reinterpreted to reflect Church orthodoxy.

In summary, by the end of the 1980s Ireland was still very much a conservative country, and quite preoccupied with morality[64] and religion in its various forms.[65] Religion continued to be important to most people (Breslin and Weafer, 1985; MRBI, 1987), and sacramental participation was very high when compared with most other Western countries (Fogarty et al., 1984). However, Mass attendance had begun to decline perceptibly, especially among young adults and people with third level education, both groups that were increasing in Ireland. The 'traditional image of Holy Catholic Ireland' was 'beginning to fade' (Inglis, 1985, p. 39) and the legalism of Irish Catholicism was undermined by a moderation of Church laws and regulations following the Second Vatican Council. Ireland was characterised by a large number of people who continued to practice their faith but who increasingly paid less attention to the Church's moral teachings. Some commentators wrote of a 'major crisis' in the Catholic Church due to 'the accelerating decline in religious practice amongst young people, the legalistic motivation of many loyal Catholics, the high number of people who had some difficulty with some aspect of Church teaching, and the increasing irrelevance of religion for many Catholics (Kirby, 1984, p. 36).

However, at the conclusion of this second period in the history of the contemporary Irish Church, Ireland was not yet lost to the secular world. English sociologist Hornsby-Smith made the point, for example, that 'in spite of considerable social turmoil and the religious transformations over the past three decades, it is clear that modernisation processes in Ireland have not been accompanied unambiguously by secularisation' (Hornsby-Smith, 1992, p. 289). This 'fundamental shift' in Ireland's religious culture was to occur in the following decades, when a generation of young adults felt able to adopt behaviour that 'did not conform to the views of previous generations' (Matte, 2007, p. 29).

2.4 THE TURBULENT YEARS OF 'CELTIC TIGER' IRELAND, 1990–2010

By the late twentieth century, Ireland had increasingly become a pluralist, secularist and cosmopolitan society, that exhibited many of the values of Western consumerism (Tuathaigh, 2005, p. 57). This contemporary period in Ireland's history has proven to be quite turbulent for public morality, with referenda on abortion[66] and divorce,[67] the decriminalising of homosexuality,[68] and the holding of numerous tribunals and official government inquiries into areas as diverse as, illicit payments to politicians (The 'Mahon' and 'Moriarty' Tribunals), complaints against Gardaí (The 'Morris' Tribunal) and clerical child sexual abuse (The Laffoy Commission; The Ferns Inquiry). This period was also marked by increased levels of secularisation for large numbers of people and society. However, the final decade of the twentieth century and the first decade of the twenty-first century will undoubtedly be remembered for two phenomena, one economic and the other socio-religious.

2.4.1 The Tiger Economy

Following relatively modest growth in the first years of the decade, both economic growth and employment increased substantially after 1993 (Murphy, 2000a), culminating in what became known as the 'Tiger Economy'. The Irish economy began its rollercoaster ride from a long recession in the 1980s to a buoyant economy in the mid 1990s and early 2000s, before it experienced a 'downturn' and an enduring recession and hardship for many people, which 'is without precedent in Ireland's recorded economic history and has few modern parallels at an international level' (Government of Ireland, 2010, p. 10). Economist David McWilliams summed up the 'new' Ireland at the height of the boom in 2005, as follows:

> Ireland has arrived. We are richer than any of us imagined possible ten years ago. No Irish person has to emigrate, none of us need pay for education and even our universities are free. Unemployment is the lowest in our history. We have more choice than ever, the place is more tolerant and no-one can be legally discriminated against.
>
> *McWilliams, 2005, p. 3*

However, while there is no doubting the economic benefits of the boom years, which gave an impetus to Ireland's 'economic modern-isation' (Fahey et al., 2005, p. 32), nevertheless, there was a price to be paid for what has turned out to be a false boom, including a 'spiritual emptiness' that 'invariably attends the process of modernisation' (Coulter, 2003, p. 25), and the increased marginalisation of poorer sectors of Irish society (Kirby, 2010). Geographers Bartley and Kitchen, writing in the latter part of the Celtic Tiger era, highlighted some features of the 'dark side' of the Celtic Tiger as 'a widening gap between rich and poor; rising crime rates; increased environmental pollution; a large infrastructure deficit; a housing market that excludes many; a huge growth in long-distance commuting; health and welfare systems creaking under pressure; a weakening rural economy with a decline in agricultural income; the continued marginalisation of Travellers; and in Northern Ireland sectarianism is still rife' (Bartley and Kitchen, 2007, pp. 303–4). More than six years following the start of the current recession, the Irish economy is still experiencing the effects of the downturn, with all the misery and prolonged austerity that it entails for many sections of Irish society.

2.4.2 Clerical Sexual Abuse of Children

This contemporary period in Irish history will also live long in Irish memories for the horrendous and seemingly never-ending disclosures surrounding the sexual abuse of children by priests and religious that emerged from various publications, televisions programmes, and a number of Government inquiries (Raftery and O'Sullivan, 1999; Moore, 1995; O'Gorman, 2009; Murphy et al., 2005; Murphy et al., 2009; Murphy et al., 2011). One of the tribunals of inquiry set up by the state in the Dublin Archdiocese, 'The Commission of Investigation Report into the Catholic Archdiocese of Dublin', highlighted the serious nature of their findings as follows:[69]

> The Dublin Archdiocese's pre-occupation in dealing with cases of child sexual abuse, at least until the mid 1990s, were the maintenance of secrecy, the avoidance of scandal, the protection of the reputation of the Church, and the preservation of its assets. All other considerations, including the welfare of children and justice for victims, were subordinated to these priorities. The Archdiocese did not implement its own canon laws and did its best to avoid any application of the law of the State.
>
> *Murphy et al., 2009, p. 4*

The sex scandals began in 1991 with disclosures that Bishop Eamonn Casey had fathered a son when he was Bishop of Kerry (Murphy and de Rosa, 1993). The impact of these revelations was compounded by further revelations that another high profile cleric, Fr Michael Cleary had had a long-term relationship with his housekeeper, with whom he allegedly fathered two sons. However, it was the horrific disclosures[70] surrounding the abuse of children by priests and religious that shook the Catholic Church most of all during the past twenty years (Raftery and O'Sullivan, 1999; Murphy et al., 2005; Murphy et al., 2009). One of the most notorious abusers, serial paedophile priest Fr Brendan Smyth, epitomised the public face of clerical child sexual abuse in the early 1990s. His face, which filled television screens and newspapers throughout Ireland, was, for many people, the face of evil in the Catholic Church. For more than four decades he had abused children in different countries, during which time 'senior clergy within the Catholic church in Ireland turned a blind eye' to his criminal activities (Moore, 1995, p. 15).

The extent of the abuse gradually unfolded during the 1990s and it has continued into the first decades of the twenty-first century when the focus shifted to the alleged activities of diocesan priests. In October 2005, 'The Ferns Report'[71] into the handling of complaints and allegations of clerical child sexual abuse in the diocese of Ferns identified more than one hundred allegations of child sexual abuse made between 1962 and 2002 against twenty-one priests attached to the diocese of Ferns. A second Commission of Investigation into the Archdiocese of Dublin reported in 2009. The Commission 'received information about complaints, suspicions or knowledge of child sexual abuse in respect of 172 named priests and 11 unnamed priests' (The Murphy Report, 2009, p. 171). A third investigation in Cloyne diocese published in 2011, concluded that the response of the diocese of Cloyne was 'inadequate and inappropriate' (Murphy et al., 2011, p. 19). Other abuse cases involving diocesan priests also entered the public arena, serving to keep unwanted[72] attention on the Catholic Church, e.g. allegations surrounding a former president of Maynooth College, Micheál Ledwidth (McCullough, 2005), and the ongoing publication of diocesan audits into individual dioceses' response to abuse allegations by the National Board for Safeguarding Children in the Catholic Church of Ireland (NBSCCCI).[73]

During the past eight years, the Irish Catholic Church has responded in a comprehensive way to protect children from further abuse by priests and religious, and by anyone working with children. They compiled and published various child protection policies and procedures (Irish Catholic Bishops' Advisory Committee on Child Sexual Abuse by Priests and Religious, 1996), followed by the publication of standards and guidance document in 2008 (National Board for Safeguarding Children in the Catholic Church, 2008). However, the value of such measures have been undermined by the 'drip-drip' revelations concerning tardiness by the Irish Church,[74] interference by the Vatican,[75] and a naivety concerning sexual deviancy by some bishops. Priests were, in the opinion of some commentators, portrayed as 'villains' who had 'facilitated' the abuse of children (McCarthy, 2013). A review of the Murphy Commission commissioned by the Association of Catholic priests concluded that 'insofar as the Catholic clerics who were called to testify were concerned, the practices and procedures of the Murphy Commission fell far short of meeting the concerns of the Law Reform Commission and, more importantly, of natural and Constitutional justice' (Sweeney, 2013, p. 39).

The revelations in the Cloyne report were particularly significant in the public deterioration of the relationship between the Irish state and the Vatican. The Taoiseach, Enda Kenny, made the views of his government very clear in a virulent speech in the Dáil on 20 July 2011,[76] as follows:

> It's fair to say that after the Ryan and Murphy reports Ireland is, perhaps, unshockable when it comes to the abuse of children. But Cloyne has proved to be of a different order. Because for the first time in Ireland, a report into child sexual abuse exposes an attempt by the Holy See, to frustrate an inquiry in a sovereign, democratic republic … and in doing so, the Cloyne report excavates the dysfunction, disconnection, elitism – the narcissism – that dominate the culture of the Vatican to this day. The rape and torture of children were downplayed or 'managed' to uphold instead, the primacy of the institution, its power, standing and 'reputation'.
>
> *Kenny, 2011, p. 18*

Former editor of *The Irish Times*, Conor Brady, is one of many commentators who believes that the past decade has witnessed 'the great levelling of the hierarchical Catholic church, as it had operated in Ireland, more or less since the immediate post-Famine era' (Brady, 2005, p. 143). This opinion is also largely supported by the findings of various surveys and public opinion polls commissioned in the 1990s and 2000s, which indicated a significant shift in religious practice and attitudes towards the Church (Council for Research & Development, 1997; Gallup International, 1999; Goode et al., 2003; Greeley and Ward, 2000; Hanley, 2000a; Association of Catholic Priests, 2012; Iona Institute, 2011; *The Irish Times*, 2012; MacGréil, 1996; MacGréil and Rhatigan, 2009; O'Mahony, 2010; RTÉ, 1998; RTÉ, 2003; *The Sunday Tribune*, 2005; Weafer, 1993; Weafer, 2007; Whelan, 1994).[77] In effect, the clerical sex scandals of the 1990s served to further undermine the moral authority of the Church, a process that had begun with the issuing of the encyclical *Humanae Vitae* in 1968. Like other iconic moments in history, the fall from grace by Bishop Casey and the high profile of Church scandals 'marked the Irish psyche for good, like a tag announcing that things would never be the same again' (Matte, 2007, p. 24).

2.4.3 A Polarised Church

In the past, there was effectively only one accepted way of being a Catholic; it is now less clear as to what constitutes a Catholic (McBrien, 2004).[78] Empirical research and anecdotal evidence suggests that the Irish Catholic Church has become increasingly polarised, with different types of Catholics co-existing in Ireland. While a substantial number of Catholics are maintaining a presence on the margins of the Church, without any real sense of loyalty or commitment, others are committed to the Church in varying ways, with some more extreme than others (Inglis, 2007, Ryan, 1983). This trend for cognitive dissonance amongst Irish Catholics, whereby people can hold conflicting views at the same time, was observed by Ryan and other social commentators in the 1980s. Fr Ryan identified the emergence of a 'new' type of Catholic in 1980s Ireland, where religion is important but separate from other areas in their lives, particularly moral issues.

Other sociologists, such as Máire Nic Ghiolla Phádraig (Nic Ghiolla Phádraig, 1982) and Tom Inglis (Inglis, 2007) developed our understanding of Catholicism by constructing different typologies of Catholic identity. Inglis, for example, constructed a typology of Catholic identity on the basis of the *European values Survey* (EVS) and *Contemporary Irish Identities* (CII) study. He proposed the existence of four forms of Catholic identity: *orthodox* Catholics who are loyal and where religion permeates every part of their lives; *creative* Catholics, who choose different beliefs, teachings and practices (similar to the à la carte Catholic) but who also mixes these with non-Catholic beliefs and practices; *cultural* Catholics who identify less with the institutional Church and more with a Catholic heritage and identity; and *individualist* Catholics, who identify themselves as Catholics but who reject some fundamental Church teachings and practices.

It is clear to me and many other commentators that the modern Irish Church is polarised and the conservative-liberal debate that gathered momentum following Vatican II continues unresolved in the contemporary Church. Fr Hoban, for example, is convinced that the 'pendulum has swung very firmly in the direction of the pre-conciliar Church' (Hoban, 2009, p. 348). He cites various examples to support this view: the promulgation of the old Latin Mass, the diminishment of the authority of bishops, and the lifting of the excommunication of the four Lefebvrist bishops without their acceptance of Vatican II.[79] A conservative voice is also well represented in Ireland by prominent lay people and organisations, and a large number of 'ordinary' people whose actions and attitudes reflect their loyalty to Church teachings and its leaders. Conversely, a more liberal stance is promoted by a substantial number of priests, religious and lay people who promote the spirit of Vatican II.[80]

Thus, while some Catholics in contemporary Ireland are liberal, others are conservative; while some are regular church-goers, others rarely if ever go to church. This is not necessarily a bad dynamic for the Catholic Church as it can lead to more creative and authentic ways of being a Catholic. But I believe it is problematic for many priests. A priest is expected to respond to the diverse pastoral needs of different groups in his parish, whilst remaining true to the teachings of the Church and his own personal views. The potential challenge for priests is greatest where a priest's personal views oppose those of some parishioners or the official Church position. For example, a priest who disagrees with the position of *Humanae Vitae* or the stance of the Church towards homosexuality is faced with a dilemma if he is expected to preach on family values. Does he give the Church's position and possibly ignore his own beliefs and those of many of his parishioners, or does he risk the anger of other parishioners and possibly his bishop, by refusing to preach on the topic or by giving a view that does not coincide with the official Church position? The impact of an increasingly polarised Church on the lived experience of priests will be explored further in chapter six.

2.5 A CHURCH IN CRISIS?

I believe that there is sufficient empirical and anecdotal evidence to conclude that the Irish Catholic Church is in crisis, although not necessarily in terminal decline if appropriate change happens in the Church (Coghlan, 2010; O'Hanlon, 2012).[81] The evidence presented in this chapter has shown how Ireland has been transformed from a resilient Catholic country into a society that is increasingly experiencing the effects of secularisation (Dobbelaere, 2005).[82] One obvious sign of the crisis is that churches are progressively emptier and 'grey' on Sundays, with the majority of Catholics increasingly content to be 'cultural' or 'ritual' Catholics, often only using the Church for special occasions, such as marriage and First Holy Communion (Breslin and Weafer, 1985; Inglis, 2007; *The Irish Times*, 2012; Nic Ghiolla Phádraig, 1976; Weafer, 1993). Substantially less people are attending Mass on a regular basis nowadays when compared with the 1960s and 1970s. From a recorded high of 91% weekly or more often Mass attendance in 1973–4, to 85% in 1990, the percentage of adult Catholics in the Republic of Ireland who attend Mass at least once a week has fallen below 40% (Table 2.2, overleaf). Other forms of sacramental participation, such as confession and Holy Communion, have also declined sharply in the past fifty years (MacGréil and Rhatigan, 2009). The decline is especially obvious for young adults (*The Sunday Times*, 2013),[83] many of whom are 'moving towards a cultural attachment to Catholicism' (Andersen, 2010, p. 37).[84]

Table 2.2 Weekly or More Often Mass Attendance, ROI 1973–2012

Year of Research	Study (Base: Catholics, 18+ years)	Weekly & Mass attendance %
1973–4	A Survey of Religious Practice, Attitudes and Beliefs 1973–1974 (R&D) (Nic Ghiolla Phádraig, 1976)	91
1981	The Irish Report of the European Value Systems Study (EVS, Wave 1) (Fogarty et al., 1984)	87
1984	Religious Beliefs, Practice and Moral Attitudes (R&D) (Breslin and Weafer, 1985)	87
1988–9	Prejudice in Ireland Revisited (MacGréil, 1996)	82
1990	Values and Social Change in Ireland (EVS, Wave 2) (Whelan, 1994)	85
1991	International Social Survey Programme (Wave 1) (Greeley and Ward, 2000)	65
1992	Comparison of Three National Surveys, 1974–92 (Weafer, 1993)	78
1997	Religious Confidence Survey (Council for Research & Development, 1997)	67
1998	Religious Confidence Survey (Council for Research & Development, 1997)	60
1998	International Social Survey Programme (Wave 2) (Hanley, 2000a)	63
1999	European values Survey (Wave 3)	65
2002	Royal College of Surgeons of Ireland (Goode et al., 2003)	63
2003	Religious Issues (RTÉ, 2003)	50
2005	Attitudes to Irish Church (*The Sunday Tribune*, 2005)	44
2007	Irish Religious Monitor (Weafer, 2007)	50
2008	European Values Survey (Wave 4) (O'Mahony, 2010)	45
2009	The Challenge of Indifference: A need for Religious Revival in Ireland (MacGréil and Rhatigan, 2009)	43
2011	Attitudes towards the Catholic Church (Iona Institute, 2011)	30
2012	Contemporary Catholic Perspectives (Association of Catholic Priests, 2012)	35
2012	Catholicism Now (*The Irish Times*, 2012)	34
2012	Irish Attitudes and Values Survey (Ipsos MRBI, 2012)	37

As previously stated, there is also considerable evidence to suggest that less people trust the leadership of the Catholic Church (McGreevy, 2010, p. 3). Research commissioned by the Iona Institute,[85] reported that almost half (47%) of Irish adult Catholics have 'unfavourable' views of the Catholic Church. Most of those having an unfavourable attitude cited the scandal over child abuse as the main reason for their negative views (Iona Institute, 2011). Research commissioned by the Association of Catholic Priests[86] in 2012, also noted a lack of trust in the Church, with almost half of adult Catholics (45%) believing that the leaders of the Irish Catholic Church do not understand the challenges faced by Irish Catholics (Association of Catholic Priests, 2012).

Research by *The Irish Times*/MRBI in 2012 found that almost one in ten Irish Catholics (9%) feel Ireland would be a better place in which to live if the Catholic Church withdrew tomorrow, with a further 46% believing it would make no difference one way or the other. It is also the case that less than half (47%) of Irish adults consider themselves to be religious (WIN-Gallup International, 2012), and that many Irish Catholics experience difficulties with Church teachings that affect their daily lives. For example, only one in four (25%) Catholic adults believe that the teachings of the Catholic Church on sexuality are relevant to them or their family (Association of Catholic Priests, 2012), and a majority of adult Catholics disagree with the Church's position on divorce and contraception (RTÉ, 2003; *The Sunday Tribune*, 2005).[87]

In addition to individual secularisation, there is substantial evidence to suggest that Irish society is experiencing 'societal secularisation', which sociologist Peter Berger defines as 'the process by which sectors of society and culture are removed from the domination of religious institutions and symbols' (Berger, 1973, p. 113). This is central to the whole notion of secularisation according to Inglis, who, with reference to French theorist Pierre Bourdieu's concept of social fields, states that 'secularisation is not so much about transformations in the religious field, as about the decline of the importance of religion in social institutions and everyday social life' (Inglis, 2003, p. 48). Inglis contends that the Catholic Church is no longer as dominant in the religious field and its influence in other fields is also decreasing. The Catholic Church has, for the moment at least, lost its absolute symbolic power, whereby it was able to construct a reality that was readily accepted by the laity.

However, this does not mean the Catholic Church has lost all its appeal or influence. Rather, it is now one of a number of influential institutions in Irish society that has to compete for an audience in all the major social fields, such as education, the media, health and politics' (Andersen, 2010, p. 36). Fahey argues that the Irish Catholic Church has effectively become a 'lazy monopoly' (Fahey, 2001) and ill-prepared to counteract competition, with the result that it has gone into decline. However, he believes that there is 'no inevitability to the decline' (Fahey, 2001, p. 45) if the Irish Catholic Church can become more competitive and less complacent. There are some indicators that suggest Ireland has not yet lost its Catholic culture completely. Substantial numbers of Catholics continue to observe their religion and to regard their religion as important in their lives, and most parishes and dioceses have pastoral initiatives in place to promote evangelisation and worship.[88] The impact of Pope Francis on the Church is also an unknown factor that is likely to be positive.

2.6 Concluding Comment

This chapter has demonstrated that the socio-religious landscape within which Irish diocesan priests live and work has changed significantly and often for the worst, during the past fifty years or so. Many of the changes have produced an environment that is less welcoming and more hostile towards the Church, resulting in widening gap between the institutional Church and its people. These changes have also impacted on the lives and ministry of priests. For example, not only do priests have to cope with increasing secularisation and a loss of trust from a diminishing congregation, but they are also faced with competing demands from an increasingly polarised Church. Conversely, anecdotal evidence and empirical research suggests that priests are still highly regarded by some sections of Irish society and that their image has not been as severely tarnished as the institutional Church. The extent to which priests have been affected by the socio-religious changes that occurred in the past fifty years will be explored in chapter four.

Chapter Three

The Changing Profile of an Irish Diocesan Priest, 1960–2010

For years, the parish was run and managed by the priest with a few voluntary lay people. There was a priest at the altar, a priest in the confessional, a priest to bless the rings. There was a priest at the bedside with the oil for anointing, and a priest to trowel the clay over the coffin laid to rest … These days, for the foreseeable future, are gone.

Archbishop Michael Neary, 2003

3.1 INTRODUCTION

The main aim of this chapter is to present a brief profile of the diocesan priest in modern Irish society and to explore how diocesan priesthood has evolved since Vatican II. The literature suggests that the prevailing understanding of priesthood has shifted on two occasions during the past fifty years or so (Hoge and Wenger, 2003). The first shift occurred around Vatican II, when a servant-leader model replaced the prevailing cultic model of priesthood. The second shift occurred in the early 1980s, when a new model of priesthood emerged, which I will refer to as 'neo-orthodox'. This model shares many characteristics of the pre-Vatican II cultic model but it is also different. US sociologists Hoge and Wenger postulated that the first shift occurred largely in response to the significant organisational changes that took place in the Church following Vatican II, while the second shift occurred when younger priests, disillusioned by modern, relativistic society, went 'in search of stability and solidity' in the Church (Hoge and Wenger, 2003, p. 121). The nature of these paradigm shifts and their relevance to Irish diocesan priesthood will be explored in the first section of the chapter, followed by a review of the lived experience of Irish diocesan priests since Vatican II.

This chapter will also explore the notion of a crisis in priesthood. Anecdotal evidence and the opinions of some clerical commentators would suggest that priesthood is in trouble, and that many priests are overworked, lonely, disillusioned, and unsure of their role in the Church (Fitzgibbon, 2010; Hoban, 1990; Flannery, 1997). Some priests are also experiencing low morale, partly due to increasing levels of secularisation in Ireland where their services are taken for granted, and an increasing workload for fewer and ageing priests. Conversely, Irish and international research and some commentators would argue that priests are quite content in their ministry, and that they are generally satisfied with their lives as priests (Lane, 1997; Rossetti, 2005). This chapter will explore this contentious issue from the viewpoint of the literature on this topic.

3.2 A Priest's Identity

A priest's identity, how he sees himself and how others perceive him, is 'the culmination of his vocation journey' (Irish Bishops' Conference, 2006, p. 21) or 'vocational dialogue' (Costello, 2002, p. 10). The Church teaches that a priest is called by God to be holy, to proclaim the gospel, and to be of service to people through his ministry (Congregation for the Clergy, 2002). A priest is called to be a man of faith and to respond to a call of holiness (Danneels; 1993; Brophy, 1960; John Paul II, 1997). A report on Dublin priests in 1996 emphasised the importance of God in the life of a priest when it stated that the Dublin priest is 'first and foremost a man of God' who 'relies on the nearness of God's help, which he experiences through the Mass and his own personal prayer' (Forristal, 1997, p. 27). A vocation is regarded as 'the fruit of being chosen, just as Jesus called the twelve disciples (Luke 6:13–16) to the ministerial priesthood; it is the fruit of a specific vocation' (Congregation for the Clergy, 2002, p. 13). It is a life of service that is based on a special intimacy with Christ. A vocation is a 'call from God' and discerning a vocation is regarded by the Catholic Church as the first step in a priest's vocational journey that may result in ordination.[89] If the call is accepted by the individual and he is deemed worthy by the relevant Church authorities, he will be ordained a priest, and remain a priest until death or laicisation.[90] The importance of God in the life of a priest is formally acknowledged during his ordination when he undertakes to fulfil the duties of a priest 'with the help of God' (International Committee on English in the Liturgy, 1975, p. 13).[91] A priest is also called to fulfil a specific mission within the Church and to be celibate.

At one level, a vocation is a very personal matter between God and the person concerned. However, at another level, a vocation denotes that a person is centrally connected to the structures of the institutional Church. The Church accepts that a vocation has a social dimension that is influenced both by personal and social criteria (Capps, 1970).[92] A religious vocation 'implies action in response to a "call" from a larger social reality' (Weigert and Blasi, 2007, p. 23). It is a choice that occurs within a social context and accordingly can be influenced by societal, organisational, and personal factors (Giordan, 2007). It is an ongoing process which is influenced by a variety of factors, including a priest's family and social background, his seminary training, the clerical culture he joins as a priest, and ongoing training after ordination (John Paul II, 1992). According to the Church, a person's 'vocation journey' (Irish Bishops' Conference, 2006, p. 21) begins in the Christian community, and continues through the influence of other agents of change, and the candidate himself (Irish Bishops' Conference, 2006). In his study of 112 seminarians in Maynooth in 1997, for example, Fr Micheál MacGréil found that the home, school and parish were the three most important places in which their vocations were born and nurtured. The principal motivation for wanting to be a priest was their desire to be close to God or their sense that this was what God wanted from them. Conversely, the most discouraging factors were the negative attitudes of people, the scandals in the Church, and celibacy. For many priests, a vocation is a source of great joy, while, for others, it can be very difficult, particularly if they feel they don't have a vocation to celibacy (Castle, 2009).[93] Irish priest Fr Dunn, for example, believes the life of a priest only makes sense because it is 'all part of the mysterious process called "having a vocation"' (Dunn, 1994, p. 15). The diverse ways in which different generations of priests understand and experience their vocation as priests are considered in chapter six.

3.3 EVOLVING MODELS OF DIOCESAN PRIESTHOOD

During the course of the past fifty years or so, the understanding of priesthood has evolved in the Catholic Church. The cultic model that prevailed before Vatican II was so-called because of the central importance placed on the sacraments, most often Mass and confession (Bacik, 1999, p. 51). The cultic priest is a man set apart who leads 'a distinctive lifestyle by remaining celibate, living in a rectory, and wearing clerical garb' (Bacik, 1999, p. 51). His parishioners typically place him on a pedestal, where he is content to stay, and further to the 'indelible character received at ordination' these priests are effectively 'other Christs' who rule and sanctify the faithful (Bacik, 1999, p. 51). A cultic priest is primarily an 'administrator of the sacraments and teacher of the faith', compared to the servant-leader priest who is 'the spiritual and social leader of the community' (Hoge and Wenger, 2003, p. 59).

The changing theology of the council represented a time of significant change and uncertainty for many priests who had been trained in a cultic Church. Accordingly, the cultic model of priesthood was 'severely challenged' by the servant-leader model, which emerged around Vatican II (Hoge and Wenger, 2003, p. 9). The servant-leader model grew in popularity with the ordination of priests who embraced the spirit of Vatican II, and who are perceived to be more progressive in their outlook than their pre-Vatican II counterparts. They tended to be more supportive of lay involvement, and more critical of some aspects of Church teachings, such as artificial birth control and mandatory celibacy. The servant-leader model emphasised pastoral leadership, flexible Church leadership and structures, creative liturgies, tolerance towards theological differences, and optional celibacy (Hoge and Wenger, 2003). The main features of the cultic and servant-leader models of priesthood are illustrated in Table 3.1.

Table 3.1 The Cultic and Servant-Leader Models of Priesthood
Source: (Hoge and Wenger, 2003, p. 114)

Cultic Model	Areas of Difference	Servant-Leader Model
'Man set apart'	Ontological status of the priest	Pastoral leader
Values strict hierarchy	Attitudes towards the Church magisterium	Values flexible structure
Follows established rules	Liturgy and devotions	Allows creativity
Defends 'orthodoxy'	Theological perspective	Allows for theological differences
Essential to the priesthood	Attitudes towards celibacy	Optional for the priesthood

The polarisation of priests in these two models 'mainly concerns ecclesiology, the theology of priesthood, and the liturgy' (Hoge and Wenger, 2003, p. 114). Conversely, there are also 'many areas of *agreement*' (italics in original) according to Hoge and Wenger. Most priests agreed on 'their love for God's people, desire to serve God's people, love for the Catholic church, and acceptance of celibate homosexual priests' (Hoge and Wenger, 2003, p. 114).

A third paradigm of priesthood emerged in the 1980s, which I refer to as 'neo-orthodox' because the priests that adopt this model of priesthood are committed to the restoration of pre-Vatican II orthodoxy to the Church and an acceptance of some aspects of Vatican II.

> In some ways, this model approximates to the earlier cultic model, but it is also quite different in other respects. The neo-orthodox priest is readily attracted to the more traditional forms of piety, worship, clerical dress, and the neo-scholastic theology that was predominant prior to the Second Vatican Council.
>
> *(Bohr, 2009, p. 160)*

Like their pre-Vatican II counterparts, the younger neo-orthodox priests feel the need to 'gravitate to safe ground and orient their ministry around institutional authority, including faithful adherence to Vatican rules about liturgy, sexual morality, and catechetical teachings' (Hoge and Wenger, 2003, p. 121). Conversely, this 'new type of priest' (Hoge and Wenger, 2003, p. 61) perceive some of the initiatives introduced by Vatican II to be authentic, and their aim is to combine these modern developments with older liturgical forms and symbols.

> Priestly identity for these priests means having a unique and sacred position in the Church, clearly different from (though in principle not better than) the positions of lay people. Clarity about Catholic identity is also important to them, so they reject attitudes that strike them as too Protestant. Being solidly Catholic means following papal authority faithfully and unquestioningly.
>
> *Hoge and Wenger, 2003, p. 61*

The literature suggests that the presence of three models of priesthood in the Catholic Church has led to theological tensions and also some competition between the different generations of priests, as each cohort seeks to establish itself or remain dominant in the religious field. Bacik, for example, believes that there are 'fundamental theological tensions' built into the 'current understanding of priesthood' (Bacik, 1999, p. 54). It is clear to him that 'many recently ordained priests favour the cultic model' and that they see themselves as 'part of a separate clerical caste' who 'resist the more collaborative approaches associated with the reforms of the Second Vatican Council' (Bacik, 1999, p. 54). Thus, while some priests are imbued with reform and the spirit of Vatican II, he believes that others are intent on restoring orthodoxy within the Church. The formation of two priests' associations in Ireland, one liberal and the other more orthodox, is an illustration of the different positions priests hold on the priesthood and the Church (McCarthy, 2014).

The history of the priesthood in the twentieth century suggests that a new model of priesthood will evolve over time, and that it will be influenced by the prevailing culture within the Church and society. It will be interesting to see if and how the neo-orthodox model of priesthood will evolve during the papacy of Pope Francis, particularly if his reforms target traditional elements of the Catholic Church. Although it is still very early days in his papacy, some sociologists have observed a positive impact of the 'Francis effect' on the rise in the number of people attending Mass in Italy and England (Hooper, 2013), although not yet in the Irish or US Church.[94] He has also adopted a relatively tolerant view towards groups that have traditionally been marginalised in the Church. It remains to be seen how much impact the 'Francis effect' will have on the Church in the long-term and specifically, on the ideals and identity of diocesan priests. Anecdotal evidence suggests that Irish diocesan priesthood is divided theologically along the lines found in the US and elsewhere. The life cycle of priesthood has evolved since Vatican II, leaving the servant-leader priests confused and frustrated following the conservative shift in the direction of the Church since Vatican II, and their role as priests in this Church (Hegarty, 2012; Hoban, 2013b). Conversely, younger priests would appear to be enthused by the 'orthodox' vision of John Paul II and Benedict XVI. The changing nature of Irish diocesan priesthood will be explored in this chapter as a precursor to the analysis of the research participants' understanding of priesthood in chapter six.

3.4 THE DIOCESAN PRIEST IN 1960s IRELAND

The early 1960s was a time of relative certainty, continuity and homogeneity for Irish society, the Catholic Church, and diocesan priests. As previously outlined in chapter two, the Catholic Church in the early 1960s shared many of the features of the 1950s triumphalist Church, including a high regard for priests. American Jesuit, Fr B. F. Biever's 1962 study of Catholic culture in Dublin revealed an overwhelming majority of Irish people who expressed support for the Church and its priests. Over two-thirds of his sample 'endorsed the proposition that if one followed a priest's advice, one could not go wrong' (Garvin, 2005, p. 253). It was a 'pleasant life' for many priests (Olden, 2004, p. 336), which often entailed a 'presumption of preference' and an 'assumption of power' (Hoban, 1996). Msgr Michael Olden captures the essence of the Irish priest in 1960s Ireland very well when he describes him as a person who was:

> ... in undisputed charge of his parish, pretty well guaranteed the obedience of the people. Unstressed by criticism of his work or absenteeism from the religious services which he conducts ... largely unaccountable controller of parish finances. His social position and respect in matters other than strictly religious was assured: sporting, recreational, cultural societies and clubs would have had him as chairman or patron. He was indeed a determining figure in the community.
>
> *Olden, 2004, p. 336*

The living standards of priests were 'considerably higher than average' at this time, but they were not 'grudged him by the people' according to some commentators (Olden, 2004, p. 336), because most priests dedicated their lives to the service of people. The priesthood was highly regarded as a career, with many young people considering the possibility of being a priest (Newman et al., 1972; O'Toole, 2010).[95] People in rural communities in particular 'encouraged their daughters to be nuns and delighted in a son who gained the priesthood' (Brody, 1973, p. 177; O'Morain, 2010).[96] This esteem was reflected in the lavish parish celebrations that typically accompanied the ordination of a priest and his first Mass (Flannery, 1999).

One generally knew what to expect from priests in a parish during the first part of the 1960s (Ward, 1965).[97] He was immersed in the cultic model of priesthood. He had a specific mission to fulfil that rarely if ever threatened the established order (Schneider and Zurcher, 1970). Msgr Olden, for example, lists a variety of 'clearly defined demands' that were placed on him and his fellow priests as they left the seminary in the early 1960s, including the demand to 'dress in a special way', to 'pray the breviary every day', to be 'celibate' and never marry, to celebrate the Sacraments 'lawfully and validly', to 'preach the Word of God', to 'celebrate the Eucharist', to 'baptise', to 'pronounce the words of absolution in the Sacrament of Penance', to 'administer the Sacrament of the Sick', to 'conduct weddings', to 'officiate at funerals', and to 'bless people' and things in the name of the Church (Olden, 2008, p. 16). Conversely, the priest also knew what to expect from people in pre-Vatican II Ireland: full churches, busy confessionals, people who obeyed priests without question, and financial support (Hoban, 1996), i.e. people who 'prayed, paid and obeyed'.

While anecdotal evidence suggests that some priests were scrupulous about their observance of Church laws (Hepworth et al., 2010),[98] others were less so. The early 1960s was a time when the lives of priests and seminarians were highly regulated by canon law, diocesan rules[99] and rubrics.[100] Bishops could, and regularly did impose various sanctions[101] on priests, and seminary life was very strict (Dunn, 1994). Seminaries were very difficult places where 'there were rules for the sake of rules' (Brady, 1980, p. 707). Students had to observe solemn silence at night and often during meal times, and they were discouraged from having 'particular friends' or visiting each other's rooms. Furthermore, staff treated students with 'excessive formality' (Brady, 1980, p. 707). The 1960s was a time when seminaries like Maynooth 'wanted rugged men for a rugged life of solitary confinement' (Brady, 1989, p. 11). Unfortunately, this system did not develop students' emotional side (Flannery, 1997).[102]

There was a plentiful supply of priests in the 1960s, which meant that newly ordained priests often had to spend time in another diocese, or in another country, while awaiting a position in their own diocese. Anecdotal evidence suggests that Irish dioceses had first call on young men, leaving others to follow their vocations in a foreign diocese or in a religious order. Some of the larger dioceses, such as Dublin, also accepted students from around the country, although this could present difficulties for the diocese and the student.[103] A priest's status was primarily linked to his seniority within priesthood rather than any specific achievements he may have attained during his career (Peterson and Schoenherr, 1978). Accordingly, priests were usually promoted to the position of parish priest because of their age and seniority in their seminary class.[104]

There were 'glaring inequalities' in the income positions of priests within and between parishes (Brady, 1980, p. 712). Some parishes were considerably richer than other parishes, with the result that some parishes were sought after and others avoided, wherever possible. Within parishes, the parish priest earned substantially more than his curate, and assistants were often paid very poorly. For example, in a parish with one parish priest and three curates, the money taken in at Christmas, Easter and November would usually be divided into five shares, with the parish priest receiving two shares. In many dioceses, the parish priest lived alone, often in a large house, leaving his curates and assistants to find their own accommodation.

A major turning point for the Catholic Church and the priesthood coincided with the convocation of the Second Vatican Council (1962–5) by Pope John XXIII (Hebblethwaite, 1994).[105] As previously stated, prior to the Second Vatican Council, priesthood was defined largely in cultic terms, with an emphasis on the sacramental role of the priest. Following Vatican II, the theology of the priesthood was expanded to include priestly, prophetic and kingly roles. A priest was regarded as more than a dispenser of sacraments or, as described by one of the research participants in my study, 'service station priests who busy themselves dispensing sacraments' (Parish priest, 1960s); he was also commissioned to continue Christ's mission by proclaiming the gospel and celebrating the Eucharist.

However, not all priests welcomed Vatican II to the same extent,[106] and some older priests felt that the priesthood had been devalued (O'Carroll, 1987).[107] Older priests who had been trained in the pre-Vatican II cultic model of priesthood found that they were required to undertake a greater range of duties, leading some of them to resist the 'immense changes in the parameters of priestly service' (Tierney, 1986, p. 41). No longer was it sufficient for a priest to 'say Mass and give Benediction'; now priests had to have the ability 'to communicate the meaning of the liturgy', to have an understanding of Church music, to train lay ministers, and to have the 'skills and talents that go to the establishment and pasturing of the Christian community' and conflict resolution (Tierney, 1986, p. 41).

The confusion was not, however, confined to older priests as some younger priests also found the transition to a Vatican II Church difficult. Fr Ray Brady, for example, described how the newly ordained priests who had also been trained in the pre-Vatican II cultic model of priesthood felt like 'yesterday's men', when the theology they had been taught in the seminary was 'consigned to the dump' following Vatican II. He describes how he felt a 'new kind of anxiety', a loss of 'confidence and security', and 'a sense of alienation' in 'those heady post-Vatican II days' as the 'ground began shifting' under his feet. The result was that he found himself 'marginalized at an alarming rate in the 1970s' (Brady, 1989, pp. 9–10). However, for the most part, the younger priests ordained following Vatican II were most enthusiastic about the council.

To summarise, the 1960s was a time of significant change for Irish diocesan priests. For some, it was a time of hope and positive change following Vatican II, while, for many others who disagreed with the new direction for the Church advocated by the council, it was a period of uncertainty, if not personal crisis. The hope for change in the Church, such as greater lay involvement and more inclusive liturgies, was negated to some extent by a resistance to change by some priests and people, and a decline in ordinations in many Western countries (Lennon et al., 1971; Stark and Finke, 2000). However, the traditional status and position of Irish priests as community leaders endured throughout the 1960s, even in relatively marginalised urban areas (Kenny, 1997, p. 259). In spite of a decline in vocations, the priesthood continued to attract many young men to its ranks and the public support of most Irish people.

3.5 THE DIOCESAN PRIEST IN 1970S AND 1980S IRELAND

The 1970s and 1980s was a period of significant change for the Irish Church and its priests, as the Church came to terms with the organisational changes of Vatican II and increasing levels of secularisation. However, the change was not immediate and the diocesan priest continued to be held in high esteem during this period, reflecting the enduring and strong Catholic identity of most Irish people (Council for Research & Development, 1975). In his study of Dublin adults, Fr Micheál MacGréil found that they had a very positive view of priests (MacGréil,

1977). Priests were welcomed into most people's homes and they were often guests of honour at weddings and various secular activities. They were also chairmen of school boards and, in many rural parishes, the parish priest was automatically elected as chairman of the local GAA club. The general goodwill towards priests was also shown towards bishops, although more so in the 1970s than the 1980s. A national survey conducted in 1974 found that the vast majority (82%) of Irish people felt that their local bishop was 'doing a good job' (Breslin and Weafer, 1985, p. 117). Ten years later, this figure was still relatively high although it had fallen to 65% (Table 3.2).

The conservative nature of many Irish Catholics informed their views of priests, and in spite of the new model of Church that emerged following the Second Vatican Council, many Irish people did not want their priests to change. For example, two national surveys conducted in 1974 and 1984, respectively, found that the majority of Irish people wanted their priests to wear clerical clothes in public (Breslin and Weafer, 1985). A substantial number were also against women priests and married priests. However, the general trend from 1974 to 1984 was away from traditional towards a more liberal perspective on priesthood (Table 3.2).

Table 3.2 Attitudes of Irish Catholic Adults Towards the Role and Work of Priests, 1974–84

Statement (Traditional Church Position)	Agreement with statement	
	1974	1984
	%	%
1. Priests should wear clerical clothes in public (AGREE).	68	64
2. It would be good if priests were allowed to marry (DISAGREE).	54	48
3. Women should be allowed become priests (DISAGREE).	75	57
4. The clergy are too concerned with collecting money (DISAGREE).	51	48
5. Priests in general are not well off (AGREE).	41	48
6. Leaders of the Catholic Church are out of touch with the real needs of its members (DISAGREE).	33	26
7. My own local bishop is doing a good job (AGREE).	82	65

Source: Breslin and Weafer (1985, p. 117)

Irish people's views of what constitutes an 'ideal priest' changed noticeably during this period, with more people wanting a priest to be 'a person who gives an example of Christian living' and less emphasis on 'a person who visits people and helps those in trouble' (Table 3.3).

Table 3.3 Qualities of an Ideal Priest, 1974–84

Priestly Qualities	1974 (N=2,473)	1984 (N=1,005)
	%	%
A spiritual advisor	22.4	20.4
A person who visits people and helps those in trouble	42.7	25.6
A person who gives an example of Christian living	24.5	43.7
A person who conducts religious services	8.0	6.1
All these qualities are important	2.4	4.3

Source: (Breslin and Weafer, 1985, p. 114)

Following Vatican II, an increasing amount of a priest's time was dedicated to pastoral care, liturgy, social and community activities, and administration (Forde, 1987; McVeigh, 2008).[108] New roles emerged for priests, such as a 'youth' priest (Doherty, 1977), and 'vocations directors', amongst others, that sought to respond to the emerging needs of the times. Individual priests became involved in areas such as social justice, community development, adult education, and local politics (Freeney, 1979; Callanan, 1972; Bohan, 2002). Many priests, and especially younger priests, felt energised by the Second Vatican Council (Mulcahy, 1974). They were enthusiastic about the spirit and potential initiatives of the Second Vatican Council, and many priests immersed themselves in pastoral planning with enthusiasm and energy.

Research by Fr Brian Mulcahy in 1974[109] found that 60% of priests believed that the Second Vatican Council had inspired greater interest in the Church and made people think more seriously about it, even if it was also generally agreed that the council had 'left the older generation confused and disturbed'. The survey also found that over half the priests said they would be enthusiastic about experiments in liturgical matters, teaching religion, and in the area of the development of dogma and morals. Nearly three quarters of the priests said the laity should take a more active part in the pastoral work of the Church. Most priests said they would involve the people in the 'traditional' social work of the Church and the administration of parish finances, while all priests agreed that celebrating Mass/Sacraments, personal example, preaching and home visitation were essential priestly work. The reaction of younger priests to parish councils was very positive, although it took many years before they became a reality in most parishes.

During this post-conciliar period, priests had to come to terms with the many liturgical changes that emanated from the Second Vatican Council and the formation of structures and roles in their parish, such as Parish Pastoral Councils and lay ministries, to facilitate greater lay involvement. In some parishes, new forms of evangelisation and collaborative ministry were considered, if not always acted upon (Ryan, 1988b). It was also a time when theologians and people alike began to seriously consider the practical implications of Vatican II for the laity (Birch, 1979). New roles and ministries also emerged for lay people, leading to some discussion on the deployment of priests and lay participation (Ryan, 1988a).[110] For the first time, it appeared as if the Church, clergy and the laity were questioning the 'special' nature of the priest's vocation. Theologians and priests began to view priesthood differently, as the servant-leader model increasingly prevailed in the Irish Church. No longer, in the opinion of some theologians, was the priest a man apart from the people, someone who has the 'sacramental power' to make Christ present in the Mass and confession (Corbett, 1979, p. 456). Rather, there was a growing realisation that the 'layperson and priest are at one within the people of God' and that the priest can 'no longer be identified simply by the sacred actions he performs' or the clerical clothes he wears (Corbett, 1979, p. 455).

The 1980s concluded with priests generally satisfied with their lives, albeit not without some difficulties, with some priests confused about their role and identity.[111] One priest expressed this uncertainty as follows:

> Since the Second Vatican Council many priests have found that their vision – their dream of priesthood – and their understanding of the role of the priest are no longer clear. Emerging new ministries, ever changing

demands, personnel boards, retirement policies and many other factors
have left far too many unsure about their role.

Dalton, 1990, p. 94

By the end of the 1980s, Irish society had changed quite noticeably
and priests were increasingly having to take positions on moral areas,
such as divorce, contraception, sterilisation, and abortion (MacNamara,
1985b). They were also faced with discussions on the nature of morality
and sin in a changing Ireland (Fagan, 1977; Gallagher, 1981), and more
specific debates on the ordination of women, homosexuality, and
married priests (Maloney, 1981). Priesthood was increasingly a 'risky
business' with priests leaving and vocations declining (McDonagh, 2000,
p. 592). This risk was to increase substantially in the following decades.

3.6 THE DIOCESAN PRIEST IN MODERN IRELAND, 1990–2010

The Irish Catholic Church has encountered significant challenges in the
past two decades and it is only to be expected that some or all of these
difficulties would also have affected diocesan priests. Bishop Murray,
for example, captures the uncertainty of priesthood for many of his
colleagues who were ordained in a pre-Vatican II Church, as follows:

> This is not how I imagined it! We are a long way from the world of the
> 1950s when many of us were seminarians. We expected to minister to
> large congregations with lines of penitents outside our confessionals
> every Saturday. We expected the full seminaries in which we were
> trained to educate large numbers of young men to follow us. The
> 'seamless robe' of Catholic life – the rules, the observances, the liturgy –
> which seemed fixed and universal, unravelled. We wanted to serve a
> community, which was waiting for us to lead it in living out its shared
> faith. We didn't expect to find it, and ourselves, so full of questions,
> shocks and uncertainties.

Murray, 1995, p. 607

Irish priests in contemporary Ireland are allegedly more confused,
disillusioned, overworked, and possibly more lonely than previous
generations of priests (Fitzgibbon, 2010; Flannery, 1999). Priesthood has
become a subject of satire in television programmes, and public criticism
of priests is at a level that that would have been unthinkable fifty years
ago (Council for Research & Development, 1997). Some commentators

believe that the clerical world in which many priests were trained and worked is 'falling apart' (Hoban, 1992, p. 495) and that many priests are 'confused and demoralised' (O'Donohue, 1998, p. 323). The relationship between priests and people has deteriorated as a result of public disclosures concerning clerical sexual abuse, although less than might have been expected, with many people still supporting their local clergy and bishop (Council for Research & Development, 1997; Hanley, 1998; RTÉ, 2003).[112] There are also indications that the relationship between priests and their bishops is increasingly strained (Duffy, 2006). Other aspects of priestly life, such as clericalism,[113] and the ongoing disclosures concerning clerical child sex abuse, continue to damage the Church and its priests (Doherty, 2013). No longer is it the situation that priests are automatically regarded as 'the key men' in the local areas, 'obeyed without question' (Draper, 2001, p. 349). All this suggests that priesthood is in trouble, though not necessarily in crisis.

3.7 DIOCESAN PRIESTHOOD IN CRISIS?

A number of commentators believe that Irish diocesan priesthood is in crisis, or at least on the cusp of a crisis. Different dimensions of the crisis have been identified including, a crisis of ministry, a crisis of morale, a crisis of intimacy, a crisis of leadership, and a crisis of identity (Fitzgibbon, 2010). Conversely, other evidence suggests that many priests are quite content in their priesthood, even if they experience difficulties from time to time. The nature of the alleged crisis is discussed briefly below.

3.7.1 A Crisis in Ministry?

One of the most visible symptoms of the alleged crisis affecting priesthood is the ageing profile and the diminishing numbers of diocesan priests in Ireland, resulting in a perceived crisis to ministry (Dalton, 1990)[114] and a threat to the provision of the Eucharist (Association of Catholic Priests, 2012; Duffy, 2010a; Duffy, 2012; Fitzgibbon, 2010; Hoban, 2013b).[115] It is argued that the decline in vocations will inevitably mean that 'traditional structures and ways of ministering are no longer sustainable' (Fitzgibbon, 2010, pp. 162–3), and that 'forms of pastoral ministry and parish life that were such staples of the Catholic Church in

Ireland for generations will no longer be possible' (Duffy, 2010b, p. 7). Not only is the number of priests and vocations declining (O'Mahony, 2011),[116] but those in active ministry are ageing (Moloney, 2007; Myers, 2001). Of the 1,965 priests assigned to parish ministry in 2011, just over one third (37%) were over sixty-five years of age, with only one seventh (14%) less than forty-five years of age. Fitzgibbon and others argue that if there is no reduction in the number of Masses and other priestly duties, priests will inevitably become more stressed and exhausted as they 'continue to valiantly expend themselves in traditional pastoral practices, such as parish visitation, leading the prayers at the funeral home, visiting the school classes, receiving the remains of the deceased' (Fitzgibbon, 2010, p. 163).

Commentators tend to emphasise different causes of this alleged crisis in ministry, with some people arguing that it has as much to do with managerial style as it has with declining vocations. The experience of 'being pulled in a number of different directions simultaneously' is a common theme in Irish priesthood (Ryan, 2008, p. 340). Some priests find that they are expected to work too much, particularly in areas that have more to do with administration than spirituality or preaching the gospel (Brady, 1991; Forde, 1987; O'Meara, 1996). For example, priests often find they are sidetracked into areas of work that 'have little to do with being a priest' and where they have 'little skill and competence', such as 'chasing the Department to get the new extension done' (O'Meara, 1996, p. 159). Other priests are stressed because they find themselves 'struggling with methods of ministry that worked well a generation ago' but are no longer suitable for the post-Vatican II Church (O'Driscoll, 1988, p. 26). Thus, while some priests are undoubtedly overworked, some commentators believe that part of the problem lies with the inability of priests to delegate work that could be done by others in the parish. Draper (2001), for example, questions the need for priests to be constantly running around doing things, while McGuane believes that priests run around in circles chasing their own tails creating a 'myth of busyness' because they will not delegate due to personal insecurity and a lack of trust (McGuane, 2008, p. 558). Accordingly, some dedicated priests, whilst doing substantial amounts of work, effectively adopt a 'one-man-band approach to ministry' and are unable to delegate work to others in the parish (Whiteside, 1988, p. 348).

If the number of priests continues to decline and vocations do not increase, then Irish priesthood and the Irish Church will face a crisis in the near future.[117] If the demographic trends continue to decline, it represents a significant threat to the Eucharist and priests will increasingly be required to work longer hours. Some possible solutions to this impending crisis include the employment of priests from other countries where vocations are more plentiful, an increase in the number of married permanent deacons, and the reinstatement of former priests into active ministry. I am aware that these suggestions are not new (Hoban, 2013b) and neither do they include more radical ideas, such as the ordination of married men, allowing priests to marry, or the ordination of women to the diaconate or priesthood. Some US dioceses are also looking to older men for potential vocations, while the power of prayer cannot be discounted. What is clear is that given the certainty of old age and death, a prompt and relatively radical solution to the decline in the number of priests in Irish parishes is required.

3.7.2 A Crisis of Morale?

Anecdotal evidence and some research suggests that Irish priests are experiencing low morale (Duffy, 2002; Lane, 1997; Lane, 2004). Fr Dermot Lane, for example, believes that the scandals in the Church since 1992 and in particular the abuse of children by a small number of priests 'have deeply affected the morale of most diocesan and religious priests' (Lane, 2004, p. 76). Some priests feel scapegoated by the activities of a minority of their counterparts (McGarry, 2013a).[118] Fr Eugene Duffy wrote of a 'real cry from the heart' from most priests in the West of Ireland when they articulated their need for ongoing formation in areas such as prayer, scripture, spiritual renewal, and a clearer understanding of the theology of priestly ministry (Duffy, 2002, p. 536). Other commentators believe that Irish priests are experiencing a growing sense of disillusionment when faced with an increasing number of 'ritual Catholics' who no longer practice their faith or trust the institutional Church but who, nevertheless, turn to the Church for the sacraments. A survey of Dublin priests in 1997 found that 'coping with the perceived irrelevance of the Church/the faith' was deemed to be the most significant challenge facing priests (Breen, 1997, p. 62).

Fitzgibbon argues that priests are increasingly demoralised when people use the Church for rituals, such as First Holy Communion and weddings, without any sense of 'faith conviction', which in turn grates upon 'the deeply and passionately held faith convictions of the priest' (Fitzgibbon, 2010, p. 164).[119] He believes that some priests are experiencing a sense of 'pain' and loss in 'relinquishing that which may have been formerly enjoyed' (Fitzgibbon, 2010, p. 167). Gone is the certainty of priesthood, leaving the priest without the 'special status' that characterised priesthood for much of the twentieth century (Fogarty, 1988). Fr Brendan Hoban, a priest in the diocese of Killala, argues that the clergy are 'in truth a demoralised force', where the media have declared 'open season' on priests and where they are presented 'variously as a motley band of power-hungry semi-politicians, manipulators of civil legislation, self-appointed policemen, and latterly, closet sexual deviants' (Hoban, 1992, p. 495). Some priests are also disillusioned with the direction taken by the Church following Vatican II (Standún, 1993), leading to the formation of the Association of Catholic Priests in 2010 (Hoban, 2010).

However, the evidence is inconclusive and other research suggests that many priests experience joy in their lives and fulfilment in their ministry. Msgr Olden, for example, found work in his parish 'very satisfying and very hard' (Olden, 2004, p. 341), while Fr Patrick O'Brien, admits to 'a sense of life as joy' (O'Brien, 1995, p. 15). Furthermore, most surveys conducted in Ireland (Lane, 1997) and in the US (Rossetti, 2005, Hoge and Wenger, 2003) have consistently found that, in spite of many difficulties and disappointments, priests are often fulfilled and happy men. One of the 'best kept secrets' in the Church today, according to Fr Stephen Rossetti, is that priests are 'happy and satisfied men' (Rossetti, 2008, p. 461). Thus, while low morale is a problem for some priests, further research is required to establish to what extent Irish diocesan priests are consistently experiencing poor morale, or if the perceived low morale amongst Irish priests may have more to do with public perception than reality (Ryan, 2008).

3.7.3 A Crisis of Intimacy?
Loneliness is not a condition of priesthood but anecdotal evidence suggests that it is a feature of many priests' lives, especially those who find celibacy difficult and who live alone (Harding, 2013). The perceived

causes of clerical loneliness are many, including the oppressive nature of clericalism (Hoban, 1996), the shortage of priests, which results in more priests living alone, and the demands of mandatory celibacy, which prohibit a priest from forming a long-term sexual relationship with an adult partner (Fitzgibbon, 1996). Loneliness is not a new feature of priesthood and various writers have identified loneliness and isolation as one of the causes of priests developing 'drinking habits' (Hoban, 2013a). Some commentators believe that celibacy is more difficult for priests nowadays than in the past, when priests had better 'life-support systems' and they lived in a small community based around their presbytery, comprising of fellow priests, a housekeeper, a gardener, and local people who had business with the Church (Hoban, 2013a).

Nowadays, according to Bishop Walsh, many priests live alone and in need of 'human intimacy', which he defines as a 'safe place' where priests can be themselves, where they are valued and loved for who they are, and where they can share their joys and sorrows 'with others and equally share in their joys and sorrows' (Walsh, 2002, p. 529). Vincentian priest Pat Collins argues that the dangers associated with a heterosexual relationship outweigh the 'difficulties and dangers associated with a life of isolation, devoid of intimacy' (Collins, 1990, p. 611). The evidence for a crisis of intimacy is inconclusive. While some priests find support from each other as a 'band of brothers' (Greeley, 2004), and the stories of individual priests suggest that chaste love 'is possible and desirable' (D'Arcy, 2006, p. 202), others 'find themselves living lives of increasing isolation with few skills for developing true and appropriate intimacy' (Fitzgibbon, 2010, p. 175). Furthermore, it is clear that many thousands of priests and seminarians have left the priesthood because of celibacy. The extent to which the research participants are experiencing a crisis of intimacy in their lives will be explored in chapter four.

3.7.4 A Crisis of Authority?
Anecdotal evidence suggests that Irish diocesan priests are typically loyal to their bishops and obedient to the laws and teachings of the Church. For the most part, they would appear to have a good working relationship with their bishops and Rome, with very few priests receiving public sanctions or dismissal from the priesthood. The Church

is fundamentally hierarchical and it would appear that most priests know their position within this structure. However, there are indications that some priests are less than satisfied with the support given by leadership in their diocese and that many of them find Church leadership to be an important source of stress (Lane, 1997). It is also apparent that a substantial number of priests disagree with the Vatican on fundamental aspects of priesthood, such as mandatory celibacy and women priests (*The Irish Catholic*, 2004). Some priests are also critical of the way their bishops handled the child clerical abuse cases and their tendency to abandon priests accused of abuse (Duffy, 2006). The formation of the Association of Catholic Priests would suggest that a relatively large number of priests are less than satisfied with some aspects of Church leadership. Overall, I believe that the evidence suggests a shift but not a rupture or crisis in the traditional relationship between priests and Church leadership. The issue of authority will be explored in chapter five, within a broader discussion of clerical obedience.

3.7.5 A Crisis of Identity?

A distinctive symptom of a crisis in priesthood is an alleged crisis in identity, where some commentators believe that many priests 'feel threatened and diminished as they struggle to maintain a distinct identity and role' (Fitzgibbon, 2010, p. 173). Some US commentators perceive the crisis in priesthood to be a 'crisis of confidence' (Bacik, 2006, p. 44) or a crisis of 'identity' (Wood, 2006, p. 3). Irish priest Fr Thomas McGovern believes that there is substantial evidence to suggest that Catholic priests are experiencing an identity crisis, some symptoms of which include 'defections from the priesthood and a serious decline in vocations' (McGovern, 2002, p. 7). Theologian Avery Dulles (1997) believes that 'one contributing cause' for the crisis of priesthood in Western Europe and North America 'has been the uncertainty about the role and identity of the priest arising from the introduction of new theological paradigms' (Dulles, 1997, p. 1).

Many commentators believe that the crisis of identity has its origins in Vatican II (Greeley, 1991), which they believe has led to a confused identity for priesthood due to an 'increased status and profile of lay ministry' (Fitzgibbon, 2010, p. 172), and a lack of 'any clear direction for priesthood' since this time (Fitzgibbon, 2010, p. 168). They argue that there was no corresponding clarification of the role of priests in the council's documents, to match the attention given to the laity. The council's *Presbyterorum Ordinis* (*Decree on the Ministry and Life of Priests*) 'disappointed many because it lacked a clear theology of the priesthood' and many priests 'felt confused, since their earlier role and their secure status were lost' (Hoge and Wenger, 2003, p. 9). Following the introduction of various lay ministries, the Mass or the altar were no longer perceived to belong exclusively to ordained priests (Philibert, 2005). Consequently, confusion was generated surrounding the role and understanding of ordained priesthood and the 'common priesthood' of lay people, leading to a perceived diminishment of the ordained priesthood (Wood, 2006). The 'proliferation of lay ministers and the restoration of the permanent diaconate in the years following the council also added to the confusion in the minds of many priests trained in a pre-conciliar, neo-scholastic theology' (Bohr, 2009, p. 4). Consequently, 'the image of the priesthood and the priest's own self-image were thrown into confusion. The mirror was broken' (Bohr, 2009, p. 5).

In the US, Fr Greeley wrote that Vatican II was 'a severe blow to morale, the self-esteem, the self-confidence, and the self-respect of priests' (Greeley, 1991, p. 122). In Ireland, theologian Fr Michael Drumm wrote that the Second Vatican Council document on priests, *Presbyterorum Ordinis* (*Decree on the Ministry and Life of Priests*), did not have the 'same cutting edge' as the renewed focus on episcopal ministry, the role of the laity, and those who live under religious vows (Drumm, 1999, p. 589). This, he believes, has led to 'tension, misunderstanding and downright hostility' as 'priests ceaselessly ask themselves: who are we? and what is our role? what is the new relationship with the laity? what are the priorities in ministry? what exactly should one do from day to day?' These are questions to which Vatican II 'did not give theologically significant answers' (Drumm, 1999, p. 590). The result is that many priests 'feel threatened and diminished as they struggle to maintain a distinct identity and role' (Fitzgibbon, 2010, p. 173). The confusion is compounded by varying interpretations of the Vatican II documents, such as the following key sentence from the *Dogmatic Constitution of the Church* (*Lumen Gentium*): 'Though they differ essentially and not only in degree, the common priesthood of the faithful and the ministerial or hierarchical priesthood are none the less interrelated; each in its own way shares in the one priesthood of Christ' (Flannery, 1996, p. 14). While some theologians believe this sentence 'is mainly concerned with affirming a close connection between the two, and merely assumes the essential difference' (Ryan, 1988b, p. 63), others disagree and place the emphasis on difference (Irish Bishops' Conference, 2006).[120]

A second aspect of the alleged identity crisis in priesthood concerns the nature of priesthood itself. Those who are committed to the spirit of Vatican II believe that a priestly ministry 'that has a purely sacramental focus is a distortion' (Fitzgibbon, 2010, p. 172). Priesthood, according to Fitzgibbon, 'can never be adequately understood on a purely cultic or liturgical basis; if the sacramental aspect is divorced from the other aspects of ministry, such as preaching or pastoral care, it is a reduced and marginalised ministry which will become increasingly irrelevant in the lives of people' (Fitzgibbon, 2010, p. 172). Irish theologian Fr Eugene Duffy believes that an emphasis on the cultic priesthood is not in accord with 'the image of priesthood put forward by Vatican II, especially in its decree *Presbyterorum Ordinis*, which 'speaks of presbyters rather than priests, suggesting a shift away from a cultic understanding of ministry. It speaks more of a service of leadership within the Christian community' (Duffy, 1993, p. 210).

Conversely, other prominent theologians and Church leaders, including Pope John Paul II and Pope Benedict XVI, believe that 'the distinction between the priesthood of the baptized and that of the ordained' has been blurred (Bohr, 2009, p. 3) following 'the errant attempts by some theologians to reinterpret Vatican II's more elaborative teaching on the nature and mission of the Church and ordained ministry' (Bohr, 2009, p. 1). Pope Benedict XVI placed emphasis on traditional iconic aspects of the priesthood, such as ritual, liturgy, and clerical dress, and an orthodox interpretation of Vatican II. In his final address to the clergy of Rome, he was critical of interests who trivialised 'the idea of the Council' in their interpretation of the liturgy and the People of God (Benedict XVI, 2013). The support given by the Vatican to the neo-orthodox model of priesthood has heightened the sense of unease in priests who believe that a servant-leader model is more authentic and relevant.

I believe that the crisis in priestly identity reflects the tension between two paradigms of priesthood, servant-leader and neo-orthodox, with both models seeking to assert themselves in the Irish Church. A similar development took place following Vatican II, when the servant-leader model challenged and ultimately replaced the cultic model, leaving many priests and people disillusioned and in apparent crisis. The issue of priestly identity will be explored in chapter six.

3.8 CONCLUDING COMMENT

This brief profile of Irish diocesan priesthood suggests that the life of a diocesan has changed substantially since Vatican II, and that many priests' lives are increasingly uncertain and stressed. In the early 1960s, a priest knew what to expect and how to act; his life was highly regulated by canon law, rubrics, diocesan rules, the vigilance of his parishioners, and his personal view of what priesthood constituted. There was essentially only one paradigm of priesthood, the cultic model, to be found in the Irish Church. A priest was very highly regarded in his parish and rarely questioned or criticised in public. He was one of many priests, with a plentiful supply of young men entering the seminary. Fifty years later, and the lived experience of Irish diocesan priesthood has changed fundamentally. While he is still highly regarded in Irish society, a priest's life is much less certain and his status has diminished. The environment in which he operates is more secularised and polarised, with increasing levels of anti-Church and anti-clerical sentiment evident, particularly, but not exclusively, amongst young adults. The evolving nature of priesthood has resulted in theological tensions and social divisions between different paradigms of priesthood. Lay involvement in the parish and on the altar is increasingly the norm, albeit still subject to the authority of parish clergy.

One group of commentators believes that priesthood is in crisis, with priests perceived to be increasingly feeling overworked, lacking intimacy, demoralised, and living with confused identities as priests. Conversely, others believe that most priests are quite satisfied with their lives, and that while some priests have difficulties with one or more aspects of their lives, relatively few are experiencing all or even most of the symptoms that would confirm the existence or otherwise of a crisis in priesthood. Furthermore, it may be argued that priests are no different to the lay population, some of whom are lonely, dissatisfied with their working conditions, disillusioned with life, and suffering from poor mental health well-being (Eurofound, 2012). The reality is that no one knows to what extent priests are experiencing a crisis because there is insufficient evidence to make an informed view. I hope that the evidence from my research will shed light on this problematic issue by exploring different aspects of the research participants' lives: celibacy, obedience and identity.

SECTION II

THE LIVED EXPERIENCE OF THIRTY-THREE
IRISH DIOCESAN PRIESTS AND FORMER PRIESTS

Chapter Four

The Celibacy Continuum

Celibacy is an ideal and a challenge. It is an ideal to be striven for, an ideal which we may never achieve as we seek to actualise our human potential, an ideal that cannot be achieved without God's grace. It is not only an ideal, however; it is also a challenge. To live celibate love incarnationally day by day in a secular world amid an alien value system is not easy and borders on the heroic.

Goergen, 1974, p. 226

4.1 INTRODUCTION

Sexuality is 'a central aspect of being human throughout life', which is 'experienced and expressed in thoughts, fantasies, desires, beliefs, attitudes, values, behaviours, practices, roles and relationships' (World Health Organisation, 2006, p. 5). It is a complex concept which, in addition to sex, 'encompasses gender identities and roles, sexual orientation, eroticism, pleasure, intimacy and reproduction' (World Health Organisation, 2006, p. 5). It is a condition of humanity that affects everyone, including some groups that might mistakenly have been regarded by some people as virtually asexual, such as the elderly, people with intellectual disabilities, and Catholic priests. However, research and common sense suggests otherwise (Drummond, 2006; Lindau et al., 2007; Rice, 1990; Taylor and Gosney, 2011). This chapter focuses on one relatively rare expression of sexuality, celibacy, where a person decides to remain unmarried and to abstain from sexual intercourse, often for economic or religious reasons (Fahey, 1999). The primary aim of this chapter is to explore and understand how the thirty-three research participants understand and experience celibacy in their day-to-day lives.[121]

Sexuality has traditionally been a relatively taboo subject in Irish society and, until 'comparatively recently, discussions on sexuality and public policy regarding sexual behaviour occurred within a cultural framework that was significantly influenced by Catholic social and moral teaching' (Layte et al., 2006, p. 9). Even today, the topic continues to generate controversy as Irish society grapples with the implications of same-sex marriage and abortion. Furthermore, sexuality has been 'conspicuous by its absence in the research agenda of Irish sociology' (Inglis, 1997, p. 23). This agenda is, however, changing and research indicates that Irish attitudes have become 'increasingly liberal on issues such as sex outside marriage, homosexuality and abortion' (Layte et al., 2006, p. 280). Conversely, some commentators believe that sexuality remains a problem for many Irish priests and seminarians, and that the problem that is compounded by its secretive nature and an inadequate theology of sexuality (Keenan, 2012).

While the 'juxtaposition' of the two words 'sex' and 'clergy' may appear to be an oxymoron, there is a 'long historical thread of confluence of sex and the clergy' (McCall, 2002, p. 89). A growing body of literature has drawn attention to the stress priests face when they struggle with their sexuality and the deficiency of intimacy in their lives. Fr Patrick McDevitt, for example, makes the point that priests 'are challenged with the same psychological challenges as other adult males in regards to sexual development' and that they have 'the same need for under-standing, healing, and therapeutic support as males in the general population' (McDevitt, 2012, p. 213). He concludes that if their needs are not met, the challenges of intimacy and sexuality 'can leave priests feeling hopeless, despairing, and angry' (McDevitt, 2012).

Two central themes will be explored in the chapter. First, the literature[122] indicates that priests throughout the world experience personal difficulties with celibacy (Anderson, 2005; Hoenkamp-Bisschops; 1992, Sipe, 1995), and that a minority of priests consistently fail to live up to the ideal of their priesthood. However, it is not a black and white situation, with the majority of priests living celibate lives most of the time (Bordisso, 2011). Second, the literature suggests that Irish diocesan priests understand celibacy in diverse ways, with some priests in favour of mandatory celibacy and others against it (Dorr, 2004). International research further suggests that a generational difference exists within priesthood, with younger post-Vatican II priests most likely to embrace the ideal of celibacy, while their older Vatican II counterparts experience most difficulties with the lived experience of mandatory celibacy (Hoge and Wenger, 2003).

It is hoped that by exploring the stories of thirty-three priests and former priests, the study will address these two themes and challenge the myth of an asexual priesthood. It will also challenge the notion of a highly sexualised priesthood that may have emerged following the disclosures of child sexual abuse by priests and religious. The reality, as is the case with most of life, lies somewhere in between both of these extremes. The first section of the chapter will review the literature on celibacy, including the experience of priestly celibacy in Ireland. This will be followed by a discussion of the research findings from my study, which explores how the research participants understand and experience celibacy in their day-to-day lives.

4.2 PRIESTLY CELIBACY

To be celibate is to be 'unmarried' (O'Malley, 2002, p. 8), although within the context of the Catholic priesthood it has come to mean being unmarried and 'the abstinence from sexual activity' (Sipe, 2007, p. 545). According to the *Catechism of the Catholic Church* (Libreria Editrice Vaticana, 1994) every Catholic is called to be chaste.[123] Accordingly, clerical celibacy is essentially 'celibate chastity' (Sammon, 1993). It is the 'key organizational condition distinguishing the Catholic priesthood from all other Christian ministries (Schoenherr, 2002, p. 19). Allowing for some rare exceptions,[124] all Roman Catholic bishops, priests and transitional deacons[125] are expected to refrain from sexual activity and marriage. It is an ecclesiastical discipline that is governed by Church law, as laid down in canon 277 of the new *Code of Canon Law*.

> Clerics are obliged to observe perfect and perpetual continence for the sake of the kingdom of heaven and therefore are bound to observe celibacy which is a special gift of God by which sacred ministers can adhere more easily to Christ with an undivided heart and can more freely dedicate themselves to the service of God and human kind.
>
> *Vatican, 1983, Canon 277, Code of Canon Law*

Celibacy is not simply the opposite or absence of marriage or the exclusion of sexual activity from a person's life. Rather, as various commentators have highlighted, sexuality and intimacy need to be embodied into an authentic understanding of celibacy (McDevitt, 2012). Thus, an increasing number of commentators believe that a celibate masculine-feminine friendship is possible if the individuals are prudent (Conner, 1979). US theologian Fr Donal Goergen, for example, wrote his classic book, *The Sexual Celibate* 'upon the growing conviction that friendship is not detrimental but central to celibate living' and a belief that 'celibate persons are also sexual persons' (Goergen, 1974). Similar views on the nature of celibacy gained momentum in the decades following Vatican II, spurred on by an increasing realisation that the Church was not going to introduce optional celibacy (Greeley, 1972),[126] and the reality that many priests were leaving the priesthood in search of marriage and intimacy (Carey, 1972; Rice, 1990; Schoenherr, 2002; Schoenherr and Young, 1990; Stark and Finke, 2000; Verdieck et al., 1988).

The importance of integrating sexuality into celibacy and the dangers of trying to live a life without emotional support was subsequently echoed by many clerical writers (Holmes, 1996).[127] Irish theologian Fr Enda McDonagh believes that 'the stabilising influence of some intimate relationships in both his personal and ministerial life' are essential for the celibate priest if he is to counter the 'isolation and superiority surrounding priesthood' (McDonagh, 2000, p. 596). US theologian Fr Donald Cozzens wrote that while 'the witness of celibate friendship is counter-cultural to the indulgence and radical individualism typical of Western society' it is possible for priests to develop intimate and chaste friendships with women or men (Cozzens, 2006, pp. 403–4). A priest, according to English academic Fr Bob Whiteside, is called to 'experience life as a warm, sensuous, and passionate' person rather than a 'cold, clinical, and distant' person (Whiteside, 1988, p. 348). Writer and former nun, Kathleen Norris wrote of celibate men and women who 'express their sexuality in a celibate way' which means that 'they manage to sublimate their sexual energies towards another purpose than sexual intercourse and procreation' (Norris, 1996, p. 117). A life of celibate chastity is just 'one way of being a sexual person' (Sammon, 1993, p. 4) according to US Marist Sean Sammon, who believes that intimacy is possible and desirable for priests provided it has roots in the spiritual life and it does not involve 'sexual union or genital expression' (Sammon, 1993, p. 40).

A number of surveys in the US have shown that priests often live fulfilled lives as celibate priests and that many priests value their celibacy as an essential part of their priesthood (Greeley, 1972; Rossetti, 2005).[128] Other research indicates that priests can experience enhanced professional opportunities and spiritual benefits from their celibate lifestyle (Manuel, 1989). Furthermore, it is acknowledged that many priests struggle, more or less successfully, with the demands of celibacy (Sipe, 1995), and that it is possible to lead a happy and fulfilled life as a truly celibate parish priest, particularly if the choice is made voluntarily (Hoenkamp-Bisschops, 1992, p. 335).

Conversely, there is substantial research and opinion which indicates that many priests find celibacy to be a challenging, if not impossible, ideal resulting in many priests leaving to get married (Rice, 1990; Walker, 2008), while many others have remained in priesthood, living lives that are 'emotionally sterile and lacking in intimacy' (Whiteside, 1988, p. 347). Others lead double lives as celibate priests and sexually intimate individuals (Bordisso, 2011; Holmes, 1996). The problem is not with celibacy *per se*, since many opponents of celibacy see a value in celibacy for the priesthood (Dorr, 2004; Hoban, 1989),[129] but with mandatory celibacy. Many individuals who oppose mandatory celibacy value celibacy 'as a freely chosen option' (Dorr, 2004, p. 138) and believe that there 'is no doubting the value and the witness of a voluntarily assumed celibate commitment' (Hoban, 1989, p. 196).

4.2.1 The Duality of Celibacy: Church Discipline and a Gift from God

Compulsory celibacy is one of the most contentious disciplines in the Catholic Church and 'the pros and cons of the practice have been debated for nearly two millennia' (Swenson, 1998, p. 37). While the apostolic origins of celibacy are disputed (Dorr, 2011; Sipe, 2007),[130] advocates of mandatory celibacy, such as Cardinal Stickler, argue that 'there was never toleration for marriage after major orders had been conferred; and candidates who were already married were forbidden to continue their conjugal life after ordination' (Stickler, 1972, p. 593). Celibacy is regarded to be a Church discipline and a way of life that is highly valued by the Church as a 'positive choice of the single life for the sake of Christ in response to the call of God' (Goergen, 1974, p. 228). It is a distinctive part of a countercultural lifestyle that is 'part of the special logic of priestly life' and which can only be understood within the larger context of priesthood (Bleichner, 2004, p. 108).

Following hundreds of years when clerical celibacy and chastity were widely ignored[131] (De Rosa, 1988; O'Malley, 2002; Parish, 2010; Laven, 2001), and during which the celibate ideal had 'become one of the principal liabilities of the Catholic church' (Laven, 2001, p. 866), the Catholic Church sought to impose order in relation to clerical celibacy in the Third and Fourth Lateran Councils (in 1179 and 1215, respectively), the Council of Trent (1545–63),[132] and ultimately through canon law.[133] The Second Vatican Council confirmed the importance of celibacy as an inherent part of the priesthood, although celibacy was not included in the agenda of the Second Vatican Council (O'Malley, 2008).[134] The Vatican II document *Lumen Gentium* ('Dogmatic Constitution on the Church'), states that 'the church's holiness is fostered in a special way' by those who 'devote themselves to God alone more easily with an undivided heart in virginity or celibacy' (Flannery, 1996, p. 64).

Since the Church regards celibacy as 'a special gift from God', in theory, it only ordains those who have 'received' the charism (O'Malley, 2002, p. 8). However, since celibacy is acknowledged to be a 'rare charism' that is 'bestowed upon relatively few men and women' (Cozzens, 2006, p. 404), the Church teaches that a priest who accepts the 'obligation of celibacy' will be 'given the grace to live a faithful celibate life' (Cozzens, 2006, p. 407). Roman Catholic priests are expected to accept celibacy willingly as a sign of their service to 'God and men' (Libreria Editrice Vaticana, 1994, p. 354, No. 1579).

Pope John Paul II affirmed the Church's commitment to the celibacy of priests on a number of occasions during his relatively long reign (1978–2005). In 1992, he published an apostolic exhortation *Pastores Dabo Vobis*, which concerned the formation of priests (John Paul II, 1992). In this document, he stated that 'priestly celibacy should not be considered just as a legal norm or as a totally external condition for admission to ordination, but rather as a value that is profoundly connected with ordination, whereby a man takes on the likeness of Jesus Christ, the good shepherd and spouse of the Church' (John Paul II, 1992, No. 50). It is a gift, which will enable the priest to 'fulfil better his ministry on behalf of the People of God' (John Paul II, 1992). His successor, Pope Benedict XVI, also affirmed the importance of priestly celibacy

(Landsberg, 2010), and in 2012, he criticised priests who questioned the Church's teaching on celibacy during his *Holy Thursday* sermon. Conversely, this Church tradition may be under threat during the papacy of Pope Francis following some tentative comments from the Vatican's secretary of state, who said that priestly celibacy is not a church dogma and therefore open to discussion (F. Brinley Bruton, 2013).

4.2.2 Opposition to Mandatory Celibacy

Opposition to mandatory celibacy gathered momentum shortly after the Second Vatican Council from many different sources,[135] prompting a response from Pope Paul VI in his encyclical on celibacy, '*Sacerdotalis Coelibatus*' (Paul VI, 1967).[136] The encyclical determined that 'the present law of celibacy should today continue to be linked to the ecclesiastical ministry' (Paul VI, 1967, No. 14). Critics, such as Swiss theologian Hans Küng, argued that the encyclical and the leaders of the Roman Catholic Church 'twisted what, according to the gospel, was a completely free vocation to celibacy into a law which oppressed freedom' (Küng, 2001, p. 198). Others also disputed the encyclical's interpretation of the gospels. They pointed out that gospel accounts suggest that the gift of celibacy is given only to a minority of people, those who can control their sexual urges outside of marriage (Mt 19:11; 1 Cor 7:7). Thus, while St Paul 'holds up virginity, continence and celibacy as Christian ideals' (O'Malley, 2002, p. 9),[137] priestly celibacy is neither tacitly pre-supposed nor expressly commanded' in the New Testament (Auer, 1967, p. 299).

In spite of the endorsement of celibacy for priesthood from various popes and other Church leaders, opposition to mandatory celibacy is found widely in the contemporary Catholic Church. Dr Edward Daly, the former Bishop of Derry, in the second instalment of his memoirs, *A Troubled See*, questions the value of mandatory celibacy when he writes:

> I ask myself, more and more, why celibacy should be the great sacred and unyielding arbiter, the paradigm of diocesan priesthood. Why not prayerfulness, conviction in the faith, knowledge of the faith, ability to communicate in the modern age, honesty, integrity, humility, a commitment to social justice, a work ethic, respect for others, compassion and caring? Surely many of these qualities are at least as important in a diocesan priest as celibacy – yet celibacy seems to be perceived as the predominant obligation, the *sine qua non*.
>
> Daly, 2011, p. 267

Many opponents of mandatory celibacy argue that celibacy is 'an ecclesiastical discipline, a ruling by the church for the church' (Sipe, 2007, p. 552). Accordingly, they believe that as a discipline, 'the requirement of celibacy is something that can change, has changed, and might in the future change' (O'Malley, 2002, p. 8), particularly if circumstances demonstrate that it is having a negative impact on the Church. There are many practical reasons for supporting the intro-duction of optional celibacy. For example, many studies suggest a link between mandatory celibacy and decreases in priestly recruitment and retention (Rice, 1990; Schoenherr, 2002; Cutié, 2011). They suggest that celibacy is a key negative factor for people considering religious life (Stark and Finke, 2000; Schoenherr and Greeley, 1974; Verdieck et al., 1988). It is also a principal consideration for many priests in determining whether they withdraw or continue in the active ministerial priesthood, and, sometimes, the Catholic faith (Cooney, 2008; Cutié, 2011).

In his study of priests who left the priesthood, former priest David Rice estimated that more than 100,000 priests left the formal ministry within twenty years of the Second Vatican Council and that many of these priests subsequently married (Rice, 1990). Conversely, other studies have found that celibacy is just one of a number of inter-related factors that can lead to a priest resigning his priesthood (Association of Irish Priests, 1972; Hoge, 2002; Carey, 1972; Schoenherr and Greeley, 1974). Some commentators also believe that the decline in the number of priests constitutes a threat to the celebration of the Mass (Duffy, 2010c; Hoban, 2013b; Schoenherr and Young, 1993). It is also perceived to be a challenge to the priesthood, with four in ten priests in the US reporting that loneliness is a problem (Gautier et al., 2012). US priest Fr Albert Cutié, for example, left the priesthood because of celibacy and redefined his relationship with God to become a husband, father, and Anglican priest (Cutié, 2011). Irish priest, Fr Dermot Dunne followed a similar path when he left the Catholic priesthood to marry and become an Anglican minister (Cooney, 2008).

It is clear from the literature that mandatory celibacy is difficult for many priests (Anderson, 2005; Bordisso, 2011; Forristal, 1997; Hoenkamp-Bisschops, 1992; Hoge, 2002; Keenan, 2012; Sipe, 1995). In his study of more than 1,500 priests in the US, for example, former Benedictine monk-priest, therapist and sociologist Richard Sipe estimated that only half of priests practice celibacy, sometimes with an 'occasional lapse' (Sipe, 1995, p. 69).[138] Of the remainder, one in five priests (20%) were involved in sexual relationships with women, with the remainder involved in some form of sexual behaviour, such as homosexual behaviour and sexual experimentation. In her study of approximately 50 priests in Australia, anthropologist Jane Anderson tells the stories of priests 'with friends' who had formed long-term, intimate sexual relationships (Anderson, 2005; Anderson, 2007).

In the US, Bardisso concluded from his research of 59 Roman Catholic priests regarding celibacy, genital-sexual activity, and priesthood, and a follow-up study, that 'there is a huge disconnect between the reality of celibate chastity in the life of a priest and the legal, theological, and spiritual ideals of holy Mother Church' (Bordisso, 2011, p. 4). Some of the priests he interviewed who were in a sexual relationship justified it as their way of coping with loneliness and a natural need for sexual intimacy. Others felt the law of celibacy was a 'foolish law' (Bordisso, 2011, p. 15) that goes against their human needs. One of his informants, Fr Frank, for example, believes that he has 'a right as a person to healthy expression' and to express his love genitally as long as he is 'prudent' so that his 'loving actions' do not cause scandal (Bordisso, 2011, p. 16). Others wrote of falling in love, their desire for long-term sexual relationships, their needs as gay men, and how they had first experimented with sexuality in the seminary. Conversely, other priests told of how they had lived a celibate life since ordination. Some priests regarded celibacy as a 'cross to bear' (Bordisso, 2011, p. 31) that caused an unhealthy attitude towards women and which can cause 'selfishness, oddity, and a desire to control others through power' (Bordisso, 2011, p. 32). They had chosen celibacy because of their love of ministry and they had learnt different ways of coping with this unwanted lifestyle. He concluded that celibacy is best regarded as a continuum rather than an absolute, ranging from total abstinence to regular sexual activity.

In the Netherlands, psychologist, Anne Hoenkamp-Bisschops, conducted extended personal interviews with 24 priests. She constructed a typology of priesthood based on how they responded to the demands of celibacy, i.e. living a life without a sexually intimate relationship. She identified three main ways in which these priests dealt with their celibate obligation. First, she found there are priests who reject the discipline of celibacy and who, at one point in their lives, have chosen to have a 'long-term, exclusive, and sexually intimate relationship,' whilst living apart from their partner (Hoenkamp-Bisschops, 1992, p. 328). This type of priest justifies his behaviour on the grounds that his relationship makes him a better person and ultimately, a better pastor. Second, there are priests who find celibacy relatively easy because of their psychological make-up. They value the benefits of greater availability that their celibate lifestyle allows. Having made a 'free choice for celibacy does not, however, mean that he has no problems at all with it' (Hoenkamp-Bisschops, 1992, p. 331). This priest can fall in love or feel lonely but 'since celibacy is what he really wants, this means he just has to go through this often painful experience, and so he does' (Hoenkamp-Bisschops, 1992, p. 331).

Third, there are priests who struggle between the demands of celibacy and their need for sexual intimacy. He accepts celibacy as part of priesthood, even if he occasionally lapses due to loneliness or falling in love. On a conscious level, 'he wants to comply with the rules and live up to the expectation of others' (Hoenkamp-Bisschops, 1992, p. 331). She concludes that 'under certain conditions it is possible to lead a happy and fulfilled life as a truly celibate parish priest, particularly where the priest has made the choice freely' (Hoenkamp-Bisschops, 1992, p. 335). However, due to the restrictive nature of their seminary training, whereby a student's education in celibacy and sexuality typically consisted of a strict prohibition against personal friendships, she concludes the traditional education towards celibate priesthood 'often only thwarted the personal development of the students, thus diminishing the capacity to choose freely' (Hoenkamp-Bisschops, 1992, p. 333).

Some researchers suggest that the celibate lifestyle, when it is imposed on an individual, may be detrimental to the physical, psycho-logical and spiritual health of priests, leading to sexual immaturity and possible disorder (Flannery, 1999, p. 75; Adams, 2003; Doyle, 2006; Holmes, 1996). Canon lawyer Thomas Doyle argues that there is a 'definite relationship between celibacy, the clericalist mystique, and the emotional health of priests' (Doyle, 2006, p. 195). Others believe that the priest's sense of loneliness is made worse by having to live alone due to there being less priests in the modern Church (Yamane, 2002), with a consequent decrease in traditional support structures for priests

(Virginia, 1998).[139] The loneliness is accentuated when priests no longer socialise with each other as much as they did in the past (Gautier et al., 2012).[140] Conversely, other commentators believe that a support structure exists for priests. US sociologist Fr Greeley, for example, describes a strong support network for and by priests, a 'band of brothers' if you will, which is a consequence of spending years together in the seminary, spending vacations together, taking days off together, eating dinners together, speaking the same kind of 'clerical lingo', sharing the same jokes, and sharing the same gossip (Greeley, 2004, p. 105).

4.2.3 Clerical Celibacy in Ireland

Clerical sexuality in Ireland has been surrounded by a 'conspiracy of secrecy' (Keenan, 2012, p. 30), where celibacy has rarely been acknowledged or discussed (Tierney, 2010). Most Irish priests have grown up in a society where Irish Catholic sexuality was 'built on purity, chastity, virginity, modesty, and piety,' which left the 'Irish psyche with a sense of shame and embarrassment about sexual practices, feelings, and emotions' (Keenan, 2012, p. 149). People were accustomed to the Church controlling their sexual desires[141] and celibacy was traditionally held in high esteem in Irish society (Inglis, 1987). This was reinforced for seminarians, where their sexual education was minimal and 'only too often consisted of a strict prohibition against personal friendships' and a strict regulation of most aspects of their lives (Hoenkamp-Bisschops, 1992, p. 333).

Prior to the Second Vatican Council, and for many years afterwards, sex or celibacy was rarely if ever discussed in Irish seminaries (Hederman, 2010; Tierney, 2010).[142] Dublin priest Fr Martin Tierney remarked that when he was in the seminary in the 1960s, celibacy was 'seldom a topic of chat or debate among seminarians' and that he could 'only recall two talks on celibacy' during his six years in Clonliffe (Tierney, 2010, p. 39). He regarded sex to be like a 'nuclear cauldron, within which lay explosive possibilities for sinning' (Tierney, 2010, p. 39). However, in spite of a lack of overt attention given to celibacy and sexuality, some measures were nevertheless put in place to control the sexual behaviour of seminarians.[143] Students' potential homosexual behaviour was controlled through rules that strictly forbade students from entering other students' rooms, or developing 'personal friend-ships' with other students. Seminaries were also divided into junior and senior divisions, which kept younger and older students apart, thereby minimising the risk of sexual contact or abuse. These rules were not unusual for seminarians, many of whom had attended boarding schools where they had similar routines and rules.

The ban on sexual activity continued after Vatican II, however, there were fewer restrictions on students visiting each other's rooms or socialising outside the seminary with lay people, male and female.[144] In the post-Vatican II period friendships with females became more common, resulting in students and priests continuing to leave the seminary and priesthood in search of sexual and emotional intimacy. One positive development in recent years has been the introduction of personal development courses into seminaries, and specifically, the Clinical Pastoral Education (CPE) programme. However, anecdotally, more remains to be done if this key area of human development is to receive adequate attention by priests.

The evidence on clerical celibacy in Ireland is largely anecdotal, backed up by some empirical research and individual biographies. On the one hand, some Irish priests have written about celibacy in a positive way. Msgr O'Callaghan, for example, is grateful that celibacy did not become a 'personal problem' even though he admits to 'a mutual sexual attraction' with close women friends (O'Callaghan, 2007, pp 106–7). In his autobiography, *Steps on My Pilgrim Journey*, Cardinal Cahal Daly indicated that he found celibacy to be 'a joy and a blessing', which 'brought an ease and a freedom' to his 'relationships and my friend-ships, particularly with women, which otherwise would have been missing' from his life (Daly, 1998, p. 270). Fr McVeigh believes a 'sense of fraternity and friendship' exists among 'the ordinary priests in the diocese' (McVeigh, 2008 p. 95), which is an important aspect of many priests' support networks, even if some priests are more 'aloof' or 'reserved' than others (McVeigh, 2008, p. 96).

Conversely, other priests have drawn attention to the adverse effects of priests living alone, with limited support from their fellow clergy (Hoban, 2013a). O'Callaghan, for example, believes that the traditional social practices engaged in by priests, such as playing cards and watching TV together are less frequent nowadays where 'priests across the generations may hardly know one another' and where in general 'we see one another only at funerals and at formal meetings of official diocesan committees' (O'Callaghan, 2007, p. 196).[145] Some priests have written that the priesthood can be a very lonely place, where they can experience a 'terrible sense of isolation and loneliness', where 'keeping going' and surviving on 'resignation and tenacity' does for most of the time (Hoban, 1996, pp. 659–60).

It is a loneliness that has been captured by novelists, priests and researchers alike (Power, 1969b; O'Connor, 1993; Harding, 1986; Harding, 2013).[146] Former priest and novelist Michael Harding wrote that he was isolated by his priesthood and especially his celibacy, which he regarded as 'a declaration' that he would 'remain without a lover for life, without all the consequent tenderness and intimacy that family ties nurture in a human being' (Harding, 2013, p. 48). Journalist and agony-aunt Angela MacNamara wrote that she had seen 'the breakdown of celibacy in terms of bitter, lonely men' and men who 'nibble at intimate relationships with women' (MacNamara, 1985a, p. 240). Irish Redemptorist priest Tony Flannery captured the feeling of loss and isolation that he believes illustrates the celibate lives of some priests, as follows:

> A frequent case I meet is of the curate in his forties. He is a friendly man, sensitive, warm and with a real care for his people. He is devoted to his ministry and works hard. He lives on his own in what is often a large old house and a woman comes in about three days a week to do some basic cleaning. It is a lonely house and he is a lonely man; his loneliness accentuated by his very humanity and the intensity with which he responds to the problems of his parishioners. A drink at the end of the day enables him to unwind and what begins as a means of relaxation can enslave him as the years go on.
>
> *Flannery, 1995, p. 624*

Fr Joe McVeigh wrote that while 'the rule of celibacy made some sense' within the context of 'making a sacrifice for a special cause', as the years went by, he 'began to question the whole idea of compulsory celibacy' and to discover that 'the longing for intimacy and friendship did not go away' (McVeigh, 2008, pp 70–1). Others have made known the difficulties they encountered as a result of falling in love but surviving to stay in priesthood (Fitzgibbon, 1996). Different religious order priests have made similar comments on celibacy. Fr Brian D'Arcy, for example, wrote of his experience of celibacy where he admits to knowing 'what it is to love another human being who also loved' him but 'he has never known sexual love' (D'Arcy, 2006, p. 202).

In conclusion, it would appear that most Irish priests would favour the option of marriage, although not all would avail of the opportunity. The majority of Irish priests (57%) that responded to an *Irish Catholic* survey of Irish diocesan priests in 2004 said that the compulsory celibacy rule for priests should be changed. Furthermore, a substantial number of Dublin priests surveyed in 1996 found loneliness and celibacy to be stressful (Lane, 1997).[147]

4.2.4 The Gay Celibate

The literature is vague on the question of gay celibates, with some commentators highlighting the difficulties of their vocation because they are gay priests (Murray, 2008), and others suggesting gay priests lead a more active sex life than their heterosexual counterparts (Bordisso, 2011). Homosexuality is largely hidden in Irish society and within the Catholic Church, with the threat of serious criminal and disciplinary consequences for anyone found violating this moral code (Doyle, 2006).[148] Intimacy can be difficult for many people but it is possibly more difficult when your sexual orientation must remain hidden (O'Brien, 1995; Anonymous, 2008).[149] It is an area that is surrounded in secrecy (Sipe, 2004) and to some extent this is understandable, since intimate sexual behaviour by priests is prohibited. This would appear to be particularly the case for homosexual priests, with sensationalist disclosures of gay activity by priests in the media (Agnew, 2010). Unlike their heterosexual counterparts, gay priests have also to consider the implications of their 'coming out' at some stage in their lives. They must also carve out identities, which are contradictory to Church teaching but which nevertheless allows them to reconcile their sexual orientation with Church teachings and their desire to be priests. US Jesuit priest Fr Thomas Brennan, for example, writes of his coming out that was informed by 'at least two identities', his being gay and being a Catholic priest (Brennan, 2004).

According to US sociologist, Dean Hoge, 'Homosexual men have been in the priesthood since time immemorial, even if this is not publicly acknowledged (Hoge and Wenger, 2003, p. 13). His research amongst

US priests suggests that a homosexual subculture does exist and that it is most problematic in the seminary, where some priests 'expressed concerns about promiscuity, a predatory attitude towards young seminarians, and an unwillingness to acknowledge or address these issues on the part of seminary faculty' (Hoge and Wenger, 2003, p. 110).[150] However, he also found that homosexual subcultures pose few problems for priests in dioceses.

The Catholic Church has made very few official statements on priests' sexuality, and its theology of sexuality is deemed by some experts to be 'inadequate for modern conditions' (Keenan, 2012, p. 30). A generation ago, according to Irish theologian Fr Raphael Gallagher, homosexuality in the priesthood was not 'publicly acknowledged' and accordingly, 'if it did not exist there was no need to discuss it' (Gallagher and Hannon, 2006, p. 67). However, even though it is now accepted that there are homosexual priests in the Catholic Church, and possibly quite a large number of priests (Cozzens, 2000), there is nothing 'explicit' in canon law on the matter (Gallagher and Hannon, 2006, p. 68), and very few official statements have been made on priests' sexuality generally (Keenan, 2012). Accordingly, the publication of an official document on homosexuality in 2005, *Instruction Concerning the Criteria for the Discernment of Vocations with regard to Persons with Homosexual Tendencies in view of their Admission to the Seminary and to Holy Orders*, represented a significant departure from tradition in one sense, but not in its core message by Benedict XVI. This document stated that the Church 'cannot admit to the seminary or holy orders those who practice homosexuality, present deep-seated homosexual tendencies or support the so-called 'gay culture' (Congregation for Catholic Education, 2005). In this document, Pope Benedict XVI wrote that homosexuality was 'a strong tendency ordered toward an intrinsic moral evil' and an 'objective disorder'. However, Irish theologian Fr Hannon believes it would be a 'mistake to read the document as excluding all homosexual men from the priesthood', as the *Instruction* 'can hardly wish to say that no homosexual person is capable of right relationships with other men and women' (Gallagher and Hannon, 2006, p. 79). A more compassionate and open stance towards gay priests was evident in some remarks by Pope Francis, although he did not challenge current Church teaching regarding the sinfulness of homosexual acts (Donadio, 2013).

Irish people have an ambivalent attitude towards homosexuality and priesthood, with less than three in ten Irish adults supportive of the ordination of sexually active gay men (RTÉ, 2003): 28% disagreed and 55% agreed with the statement, 'Sexually active men should not be ordained as Catholic priests.' While this represents a more tolerant stance towards homosexuality, there is still substantial anti-homosexual sentiment in Ireland. Almost half of Irish adults (45%) believe that 'Homosexual acts are morally wrong' and also that 'Gay couples should not be allowed to marry in a Catholic Church'. The actual number of priests who are gay is unknown, although various studies have estimated that the percentage may lie somewhere between 10% and 60% (Cozzens, 2000), with 'most experts' estimating between 25% and 40% (Plante, 2007, p. 495). However, the level of sexual activity is possibly less than suggested by these figures, as it is unlikely that all gay priests, no more than their heterosexual counterparts, are in sexual relationships. Irish gay priest Fr Bernard Lynch says, for example, that homosexuality was not 'rampant' in the seminary because 'close physical contact was forbidden' and everyone had to be 'on their guard' (Lynch, 1993, p. 19). Conversely, studies in the US suggest that the number of men applying to religious life who are 'homosexual in orientation is significantly higher than in the general population of men and that these men are as well adjusted as, and not significantly different in their psychological profiles from, heterosexual men' (Plante, 2007, p. 498).

4.2.5 The Politics of Celibacy

The sublimation of one's sexuality is somewhat of a conundrum in modern society where the majority of adults engage in sexual behaviour (Ferriter, 2009; Layte et al., 2006). While many priests accept it willingly as part of their priesthood, it would appear that a substantial number of priests only accept celibacy reluctantly, even when it is detrimental to their emotional and physical health (Anderson, 2005). Yet, apart from the exodus of priests who cannot live a celibate life, and some opposition from individual priests and commentators, most priests would appear to accept celibacy with minimal dissent. The question addressed in this section is why priests continue to accept celibacy as a requirement of their priesthood. Four possible explanations are hypothesised, although the reality may be a combination of all four.

First, and most simply, it may be that priests 'accept' celibacy because it is a condition of priesthood and a prerequisite of priestly ministry. Second, it may be that mandatory celibacy continues to exist because it is of benefit to the institutional Church. Some commentators believe that celibacy has more to do with 'the politics of control and the question of Church finance' than with spirituality or asceticism (O'Donohue, 1998, p. 334). They believe that celibacy gives power to the Church through its priests. Clinical psychiatrist Walker argues that sexual regulation is central to Catholic teaching because the more central sexuality became, 'the more power a sexually pure clergy had over the economy of sin and salvation' (Walker, 2008, p. 251). Celibacy is perceived to be a sign of organisational loyalty that can also help to 'ensure the control of wealth' (Qirko, 2002, p. 322). In the Middle Ages, for example, the universal imposition of a celibacy rule on priests enabled the Church to counteract the power of priestly dynasties that virtually neutered papal power (Mackey, 2010). Some commentators believe that celibacy continues to be mandatory in the modern Church because it enables the institutional Church to control the activities of its priests more easily, and it eliminates potential disputes over the ownership of Church property (Keenan, 2011). A celibate priesthood also represents a 'key economic resource and power elite of the hierarchical Church', which the Church is reluctant to change in case it leads to changes in other areas of its political and economic structures (Schoenherr and Young, 1993, p. 353). According to this argument, the Vatican is able to impose and sustain mandatory celibacy on its priests because, further to French social theorist Pierre Bourdieu, the Vatican occupies the dominant position within the Catholic field, where it can set the 'rules of the game' for its own benefit (Bourdieu, 1991; Thomson, 2008). Australian anthropologist Anderson argues priests are effectively muzzled in their opposition to celibacy because 'the papacy demands uncritical support of, and passive obedience to, its rigid belief system' (Anderson, 2005, p. 199). She perceives the imposition of mandatory celibacy as an 'abuse of power' which is centralised in the Vatican (Anderson, 2005, p. 199). By concentrating 'leadership and decision-making power in a church bureaucracy distant from the life and ministry of priests' she argues that the pope and his curia are 'well placed' to promote the belief that 'celibacy is the one and only true way for a priest to serve God' and to imbed this belief into Church law (Anderson, 2005, p. 12). The Church is able to control both the rhetoric on celibacy and the resources available to priests that could potentially be used to instigate change. Furthermore, priests are aware of the sanctions that could be imposed on them for violating a rule of the Church and they are naturally reluctant to do so, at least not publically.

A third possible reason why priests are willing to accept a celibate life is that they know their superiors will not impose sanctions of any real consequence provided they are discreet. Anecdotal evidence suggests that, similar to the manner in which Irish people resisted the demands of sexual morality imposed on them by the Catholic Church through 'clandestine and illicit sexual behaviour' (Ferriter, 2009, p. 546), some priests resist the imperative of celibacy by discreetly engaging in sexually intimate behaviour from time to time. To my knowledge, very few priests or bishops, other than the high profile case of Bishop Casey, have been dismissed or publicly sanctioned for violating their promise of celibacy in recent years. While this could mean that priests rarely or never engage in sexual activity, it could also mean that those that do engage in sexual activities do so within acceptable limits.

Fourth, it may be that priests accept mandatory celibacy as an intrinsic part of their priesthood because of its ascetic and spiritual qualities. For example, the majority of diocesan priests interviewed by Hoge and Wenger in the US in 2001 said they would 'certainly' not (41%) or 'probably' not (31%) marry if celibacy for priests became optional. There were no noteworthy differences by age to this question. Similar findings were reported in other US surveys (Greeley, 1972, Rossetti, 2005) and the *Irish Catholic* survey of Irish priests in 2004. According to this argument, priests are prepared to accept and even embrace celibacy as part of their vocation to the priesthood.

To conclude, celibacy, as a consciously chosen lifestyle, is very rare and something of an anomaly in modern society (Central Statistics Office, 2012; Layte et al., 2006). From an evolutionary perspective, with a primary emphasis on reproduction, it 'should not exist' except in very extraordinary circumstances (Qirko, 2002, p. 322). Yet, celibacy, or lifelong sexual abstinence, clearly exists and has been practiced by various religious groups for thousands of years. However, this situation is changing and the 'social construction of sexuality in modern society and in the post-Second Vatican Council Church has greatly reduced the positive motivation previously attached to celibacy' (Schoenherr, 2002, p. 21). The views and experiences of celibacy for the thirty-three priests and former priests are reviewed in the following pages.

THE RESEARCH FINDINGS: PRIESTLY CELIBACY
4.3 PRE-VATICAN II PRIESTS[151] UNDERSTANDING AND EXPERIENCE OF MANDATORY CELIBACY

Most of the pre-Vatican II research participants are in their seventies, with two priests in their early eighties. At 'this stage of their lives', the sexual side of celibacy is effectively a non-issue for most, but not all, of these priests (Retired, 1950s). For the most part, they said they had learnt to live with the physical demands of celibacy. Four pre-Vatican II priests saw themselves as 'natural' celibates[152] who had 'never' wished to marry and neither had they experienced any 'serious' problems with celibacy: 'priesthood and celibacy was like a doddle really, like a duck getting into water' (Semi-retired priest, 1960s).[153] Two pre-Vatican II priests regard themselves to be 'confirmed bachelors' (Retired, 1950; Semi-retired, 1960s), although this had not always been the case, and they now believe they are too old and set in their ways to change their lifestyle. Similar to older people in the wider population, this group of pre-Vatican II priests has less interest in sexual intimacy than when they were younger men, and they are now more concerned with the absence of social intimacy they would have expected in a marriage (Taylor and Gosney, 2011). Conversely, three pre-Vatican II priests said that they are 'not dead yet' and they are still attracted to women, 'thank God'. However, it has been some time since their priesthood was 'threatened' by an 'inappropriate relationship'. One pre-Vatican II priest summarised his views on celibate intimacy, as follows:

> Intimacy is not confined to the physical. When married people can no longer have the physical side, their intimacy can still exist and thrive. People can be intimate without being physically involved and being physically involved is no guarantee of intimacy. Intimacy involves trust and confidence in someone else with whom we can share our inmost feelings and thoughts, someone with whom we relate without fear or worry that we will be betrayed or rejected.
>
> *Parish priest, 1960s*

Two pre-Vatican II priests made veiled comments that suggested they had homosexual tendencies, but they said that they had 'never acted' on their impulses. One priest admitted to a 'certain attraction' to other students in the seminary, although he joked that this was probably because there were no females 'to take your mind of other attractive seminarians' (Retired, 1950s). Another priest said that he had 'never been attracted to women' (Semi-retired priest, 1960s). While all of these pre-Vatican II priests said they were unaware of any homosexual activity amongst their peers in the seminary and following ordination, some comments suggest otherwise.

> Priests are just human beings and two priests in (parish x) were just inseparable. It was a love match between them and they went on holidays together.
>
> *Parish priest, 1960s*

One priest, who accepted he had 'inappropriate sexual feelings' for most of his priesthood was nevertheless 'shocked' when he heard that two priests of his diocese, whom he knew quite well and with whom he sometimes went on holiday, were accused and subsequently convicted of multiple sexual abuses against young boys. While he could understand their feelings and sexual urges, he could not understand why they could not control themselves. He was more mystified than angry by their actions.

> It seems that a paedophile is like an alcoholic. His genes are upside down and he can't do a damn thing about the bloody yoke. It is an awful situation. I don't know why someone has to go that far with children but they must have an awful weird kind of mind to bring in young chaps and to expose them and to do all sorts of dreadful things with them. I suppose they had urges and that was it.
>
> *Semi-retired priest, 1960s*

Four pre-Vatican II priests regarded celibacy as a practical blessing to their ministries because it has allowed them to work in different ministries and locations, including foreign countries, which, they believe would probably not have been possible for a married man with a family.

> I think it has been a blessing to my ministry. In order to give yourself to your people it is better that you are celibate.
>
> *Retired priest, 1950s*

Conversely, six pre-Vatican II priests said they had found celibacy to be difficult and five of them said they would like to have married. Celibacy has been particularly difficult for three of these priests, leaving them wondering what they had 'missed' by not having a wife and family. Their experience of celibacy changed over time, and, if anything, they found celibacy to be more difficult as they became older, when sexual attraction was effectively replaced by 'a certain loneliness' in living alone sometimes in relatively isolated areas (Parish priest, 1960s). One pre-Vatican II priest referred to celibacy as 'a curse' he had 'endured' for 'too many years' and he still regarded it as an 'awful trial' (Curate, 1960s). He yearned for a family life he would 'never have'.

> I suppose I wanted to be a family man at times in my middle years when you see your friends married with families, and coming back to this house on your own. You would miss that, even more than when I was younger and full of enthusiasm and energy.
>
> *Parish priest, 1960s*

Vatican II was a significant factor in the way three pre-Vatican II priests came to understand and experience celibacy. One priest who had travelled abroad for further education after ordination was 'almost overcome' by the freedom he had when compared to the closed environment in Maynooth (Parish priest, 1960s). The theology was 'so different' and the experience was a 'real liberation' for him, and it was only in this foreign country that he 'encountered ladies for the first time'. However, while the 'thought did strike him', he was 'very committed to the priesthood then' and he has continued as a priest for the past fifty years, albeit not without some difficulty.

A former priest who regarded himself to be an 'extremely conservative person' and 'very cut away from life, with little experience' travelled on holiday to America with two priest friends shortly after his ordination in the 1960s. He 'came of age' when he met a beautiful American girl.

> I went with two friends to America. I was a pioneer and I had absolutely no experience of women's company or anything like that. Over there, we visited friends and cousins of my priest friends, and there was a glamorous girl there, and I couldn't believe it when she danced with me and wrote a big note to me afterwards. I was very infatuated with her but it blew over.
>
> *Former priest, 1960s*

99

The 1960s and early 1970s was a time when 'things were beginning to change in the Irish Church and a lot of his priest friends were beginning to mix in female company, having dinners and that kind of thing' (Former priest, 1960s). However, while this former priest 'got looser and looser', it was only when he met the woman he would eventually marry that he realised he could not live a celibate lifestyle and remain true to his vocation as a Catholic priest. Conversely, he knew other priests who were able to lead a double life, and he spoke of how some of his colleagues 'were in and out of relationships' and that one priest had 'destroyed two girls by long relationships'. Many of these men are still priests in senior positions and while he is reluctant to condemn them, neither is he at ease with their actions.

Initially, five pre-Vatican II priests spoke of celibacy as a 'choice' they had made in order to become a diocesan priest. For them, it was 'just another condition of diocesan priesthood' that everyone had to accept if they wished to be ordained.

> You make your choice and you have to live with it and see it through. You can't hanker after every alternative. I suppose I would like to have been married but I would like to have been a farmer too. I can see the reasons behind mandatory celibacy and I am prepared to accept those reasons. I don't think it would be wise to try and change it.
>
> *Retired priest, 1950s*

However, for most of them, it was a choice constrained by circumstances. Upon reflection, most of them accepted that they had little option in agreeing to celibacy, and that, in hindsight, it was not a 'free' choice. There was 'nothing' that could be done about it because it was 'a rule of the Church' (Parish priest, 1960s). They had been so caught up in the attraction and fascination of priesthood, that few of them had given much time or consideration to the implications of celibacy. After all, it was not something they could change and all of them knew priests who lived celibate lives and 'if they could do it, why not them?' (Parish priest, 1960s). One priest who was ordained almost fifty years ago, for example, said he knew he had to accept celibacy because he wanted to be a priest.

> When I hear them say celibacy is a gift and the presumption by the Church is that if a man has a vocation to the priesthood he gets the gift

of celibacy. I just don't believe that. I would quite honestly say that I wasn't meant to be celibate, but I am sure that I was meant to be a priest.

Parish priest, 1960s

One former pre-Vatican II priest in this age cohort said that he had entered the seminary and become a priest 'in order to do good for others'. He had a 'deep faith' and he accepted celibacy 'freely' and 'wholeheartedly' (Former priest, 1960s). He stayed in Maynooth, even when some of his friends left, because he 'knew' that priesthood 'was for him'. However, he accepts that his vision of marriage was somewhat idyllic and when he saw couples heading home after Mass, he often thought of how 'happy they must be and how great their sexual lives were together'. Ultimately, he left the priesthood because of love.

> The big factor in my leaving was falling in love. I couldn't bear leaving this woman. We had done our best to break off contact. We tried but it was too powerful for me. The freedom of the 1960s and my growing confidence mixing with women also wore down the edges.
>
> *Former priest, 1960s*

Another former priest, who had left the priesthood for different reasons, subsequently 'discovered the joy of marriage', although he had not been particularly lonely as a priest and he had not left the priesthood because of celibacy (Former priest, 1960s).

Four pre-Vatican II priests felt that mandatory celibacy had endured in the Catholic priesthood because it enabled Church authorities to 'crack the whip' over priests and to give the Church 'total control over guys' (Semi-retired priest, 1960s). Without celibacy, one priest said he felt that it would not be possible for the Church to have 'the same level of control over priests at all'. Another priest perceived celibacy as being 'part of the game' priests played with Church authorities and 'you just had to get on with it' (Curate, 1960s). It is a 'game' that is controlled by Church authorities.

> The people at the top seem to have excluded any discussion of celibacy, which is totally contrary to the world we live in. We should be open to different forms of priesthood but that is not possible with the present administration. The ordination of women priests is probably too much for the Church to swallow but there should be more discussion of it and also married priests.
>
> *Parish priest, 1960s*

101

While all of these priests could see some value in celibacy, nine of the ten priests in the pre-Vatican II cohort disagree with mandatory celibacy because they do not believe it is intrinsic to priesthood, and because they believe that 'a lot of good men are lost to the church because of celibacy' (Curate, 1960s). One priest gave examples of priests he knew who had endured lives of loneliness and bouts of alcoholism because of mandatory celibacy. Others spoke of priests who had 'hidden themselves away' or been 'left to their own devices' because they were regarded as 'odd'.

None of these priests felt they would have any problems working with married priests, and most of them said they would be tolerant towards 'lapses' in celibacy, provided the violations were not too many or too public (Retired priest, 1950s). They believe that celibacy should be optional, even if they themselves are too old to change their ways.

> I would say there is no reason it shouldn't be optional for students to declare one way or the other. It shouldn't be made a condition for priesthood. It wasn't a condition in Our Lord's time. It is only a law of the Church and it was for reasons to cut out nepotism. But you have married priests in the Orthodox Church and the Uniate church. I would be quite open to married priests. I don't see why celibacy should be made a condition for priesthood.
>
> *Retired priest, 1950s*

For the most part, they did not believe that mandatory celibacy could be justified on practical or spiritual grounds. Three pre-Vatican II priests dismissed the potential disadvantages for priests having to rear a family and 'do some work as well'. After all, they argued that 'this is what most people have to do' (Parish priest, 1960s). Others questioned the alleged gospel foundation of celibacy. Interestingly, given the relatively homophobic nature of Irish society and the Catholic Church, most of these pre-Vatican II priests would have no problem working with a homosexual priest 'provided he was celibate' or at least 'tried his best'. Two of the older priests had some misgivings about working with a homosexual priest but this did not reflect any specific or deeply held views on homosexuality.

In summary, the views and experiences of pre-Vatican II priests indicate that celibacy has been and continues to be a blessing for some priests and a difficulty for most. Their stories confirm that sexuality is a life-long condition and that they are not asexual or sexual predators. They came across as normal men with healthy sexual interests, which they have suppressed for the sake of an ideology. Most of these pre-Vatican II priests said they were sexually attracted to women at different times of their lives, and that they would like to have had the opportunity to marry and have children. Conversely, four priests said they had never wished to marry and that they were content to live celibate lives. Over the years their desire for sexual intimacy has effectively been replaced by a need for emotional support. Most of them now see themselves as either natural celibates or confirmed bachelors who are too old to change their ways.

Most of the pre-Vatican II research participants understand celibacy to be a restricted 'choice' that was enforced on them because they wished to become diocesan priests. Half of them believe that mandatory celibacy has endured because it enables Church leadership to control priests. While all of them can see a value in celibacy for the priesthood, and none of them would realistically consider marriage at this time of their lives, nine out of ten priests in this cohort disagree with mandatory celibacy. Furthermore, they believe that the value and potential practical advantages of celibacy are often outweighed by unrealistic expectations and the damage done to priests and the priesthood. For example, some of them said that there is no guarantee that a celibate priest would be more available than his married counterpart. They also believe that the introduction of married priests would 'probably enrich priesthood' (Parish priest, 1960s) and it 'would provide a real choice' for priests (Retired priest, 1950s). Only one priest disagreed with this sentiment and instead argued that he and his fellow priests had ample opportunity to consider the implications of celibacy: 'You can't be everything. You have to choose' (Retired priest, 1950s).

4.4 VATICAN II PRIESTS'[154] UNDERSTANDING AND EXPERIENCE OF MANDATORY CELIBACY

Most of the Vatican II research participants are in their late forties and fifties, and unlike most of their older counterparts, many of this group readily admitted to ongoing difficulties in their personal struggle with sexual attraction and the physical side of celibacy. Most of them had been 'in difficult situations' with women or men, leading some of them to leave the priesthood. For some priests, sexual intimacy is the main problem, while for others, the main issue is loneliness.

> Sexuality has always been a problem. It is not something you can dismiss or ignore but that is what we are expected to do. At times you would have fallen in love, or maybe been infatuated with a girl, and sometimes it would have been a toss up whether to stay or go, but I felt I was called to the priesthood and I would have felt guilty if I had left.
>
> *Parish priest, 1980s*

For the most part, these Vatican II priests see celibacy as a discipline that has been imposed on them by the Church and one which they have no choice other than to accept if they wish to be priests. Conversely, none of them would have serious problems if they or one of their colleagues did not live up to the ideal of celibacy, provided it did not lead to scandal. For most, it is just another part of being a priest, and less serious than many other sins. Two priests believe that while falling in love is not ideal for a priest, it is something many priests have to cope with during the course of their lives. One priest believes it only becomes serious if, for example, a child is conceived and a priest is responsible for a life.

Three Vatican II priests were somewhat embarrassed to say that they left their radios or lights on when they left their houses, so that they wouldn't feel quite so alone when they returned home. One priest said that while sexuality was more important to him when he was younger, he could cope with celibacy then because of 'the newness of priesthood' (Parish priest, 1980s). Three others agreed with this sentiment. Two priests admitted to feeling a 'deep deprivation' and an 'emptiness' in not having a special person that 'has laid down their lives for you in a continuous ongoing life-supporting way' (Parish priest, 1970s). Having said that, five Vatican II priests said they are unlikely to marry even if the rule changes because it is 'too late' for them (Parish priest, 1960s). Conversely, one gay priest, who is in a long-term sexual relationship, said he is 'just waiting for the right time' to marry his partner secretly (Parish priest, 1980s), while another gay priest said he would 'consider the equivalent of marriage if it was a real option'.

Celibacy is very much a live issue for this group of Vatican II priests, and while most of them said they have 'come to terms' with celibacy as 'part of the package of priesthood' (Parish priest, 1970s), they continue to struggle and to 'compartmentalise the demands of sexuality' (Parish priest, 1970s). One priest who admitted to loving 'women's company' considered celibacy to be a 'barrier' to the development of relationships with his female parishioners (Parish priest, 1970s), while another priest felt he used it as a 'defence mechanism' for avoiding relationships (Parish priest, 1980s). Three Vatican II priests said they fear the danger of becoming 'cosy old bachelors' that are content 'to settle for the comfortable life' without the balance a partner brings into a person's life (Parish priests, 1970s). Another priest believes that priests are largely 'incorrectable' and because of celibacy, there is 'a real danger of becoming odd and isolated' (Parish priest, 1970s).

One priest believes that he lacks an understanding of women, which he feels a married man and father would have. He sometimes feels a gap in his understanding of women, especially when giving sermons on topics that 'fundamentally relate to women as mothers, wives and young women' (Parish priest, 1970s).

> I think I would have been as good, if not better, a priest if I was married. I have had to work hard to learn the insights of relationships and marriage. I know what it is to be male but I had to listen to women to know what it is like to be a woman. If you were married you would have a lot more insights and have learnt their psychology, their moods, their needs, their affections – things that matter to them. It is difficult for a celibate priest to understand how two women can spend a whole afternoon looking at a dress or buying shoes. They are a mystery really.
>
> *Parish priest, 1970s*

Vatican II has had a significant impact on their priesthood, with most of these priests embracing the progressive spirit of the Second Vatican Council, including doubts concerning the value and future of mandatory celibacy. Unlike many of their friends and colleagues who left the seminary and priesthood because of celibacy, this group of Vatican II priests believes celibacy has a value for the priesthood, but that it also entails some personal difficulties.

> Celibacy has been both a blessing and a hindrance for me. A hindrance because it has always been a struggle for me. It has brought me and others pain because of relationships I have been in or am still in. That is the pain that goes with celibacy. The other side is that it has helped me

grow through the pain and difficulties, falling down and getting up again. It gives me the time to devote to my priesthood and my own spiritual life that would not be possible if I was married. I have to believe it is a virtue and a help to my pastoral ministry and priesthood but the compulsory thing is crazy.

Parish priest, 1980s

Only one priest in this age cohort is in favour of mandatory celibacy. He believes that marriage would be a 'distraction' to his priesthood and that celibacy is a blessing that represents the ideal way of being a priest (Parish priest, 1980s). He also believes that a celibate lifestyle is consistent with the gospels and Church teaching, and that it is a lifestyle that enables a priest to be more available to his people. Conversely, the other thirteen Vatican II priests and former priests believe that celibacy should be a free choice, and that diocesan priests should have the option of getting married. While most of them highlighted the practical benefits of celibacy for their ministry – 'I see a value in being available and relatively free' (Parish priest, 1980s) – and others mentioned the 'sign' value of celibacy, all felt somewhat uneasy about their celibate lifestyle. One priest felt it was 'a very unnatural life' that obliged him to live alone without the company of anyone (Parish priest, 1970s). Another priest believes that the 'supposed' benefits of celibacy are often used by 'bachelor priests' as an excuse to play golf or play cards, rather than working in their ministry (Parish priest, 1970s).

One priest spoke of how he occasionally invited in homeless people to share his home because 'it is nice to have someone in the house' (Parish priest, 1980s).

I suppose celibacy has been a blessing in that it has allowed me freedom. I don't have responsibilities and commitments, which has allowed me to work in missionary countries. But it is a very unnatural life. I work in one of the most dysfunctional parishes in the country and sometimes you go through the most extraordinary of experiences with people and you go home at night with no one to talk to. A homeless man sometimes shares my home and that can be nice. I remember another man of the roads who used to visit me once or twice a year. I might be out and come in when he is in bed but there was a different energy in the house. It is not just about celibacy, it is about sharing a house with someone else; it is about relationships.

Parish priest, 1970s

These Vatican II priests do not believe that celibacy is an inseparable part of priesthood or that it is grounded in the gospels.[155] Consequently, while all of this group believes they have a vocation to the priesthood, many of them have questioned their vocation to a celibate priesthood. One priest was aggrieved that he had to 'sacrifice' his wish to be married because of his desire to celebrate the Eucharist.

> I have never accepted that to celebrate the Eucharist, you had to be a celibate male, but I accepted the huge imposition of celibacy at twenty-one and now because I wanted to be a priest so much. I believe it is wrong but I really want to give my life as a priest.
>
> *Parish priest, 1980s*

Another priest, who is happy with his life as a celibate priest and considers himself too old to ever get married, nevertheless has an 'open mind' to married priests and feels that optional celibacy would 'provide a real choice and probably enrich priesthood' (Parish priest, 1970s).

This group of priests also believes that mandatory celibacy is a key contributory factor in priests' loneliness and that it constitutes a threat to the Eucharist through its impact on declining vocations and priests leaving the priesthood. Six priests found it difficult to see any positive side to celibacy and three of them, including one priest who is homosexual, resent not being able to marry and have families. Because of a Church law that is a 'kind of a deformity' (Parish priest, 1970s), they feel they now lack the support that other men receive from their wives and families. It is an unnecessarily lonely life that some of them have coped with through humour. One priest spoke of 'running away' from a widow in his parish when she showed too much interest in him (Parish priest, 1970s). Another was so 'terrified' of the stories of ghosts of dead priests when he moved into a large old country house as a young curate that he ran from room to room at night for most of his first year in the parish (Parish priest, 1980s).

Five Vatican II priests suggested that celibacy is essentially an issue of Church power over priests. They felt that celibacy was mandatory because it suited the Church authorities and the clerical lifestyle. One priest said that Church authorities can more easily move celibate priests to a different parish or ministry with minimal or no consultation. He argued that a married priesthood would create problems related to property and inheritance. Other priests, including some of the pre-Vatican II cohort, also made a similar point.

> I think one of the big reasons for celibacy is that it is easier to control me. I have been moved five times in my life and if I had a wife, the bishop would not have had that freedom. The property thing is also big. If I was a married priest and I died, what would happen to my wife and where would she live? So, it is more about control and that is a bad thing. It should definitely be optional. Why can't there be part-time priests? Why does it have to take over your life?
>
> *Parish priest, 1980s*

One priest felt that the Church used celibacy to promote sexual desire in a negative way, as 'a weakness' that was to be controlled rather than embraced (Parish priest, 1980s). It was, he argued, used to 'keep women in their place' by treating them as second-class citizens. Celibacy was 'more about power' than anything else. The story of a former Vatican II priest, Fr Dave,[156] illustrates the adverse impact of celibacy on a priest who was otherwise committed to his priesthood.

Fr Dave's Story of Celibacy

Fr Dave is a heterosexual male who was ordained in the 1980s. He describes his life as a young priest as 'frantic, phonetic and extra-ordinarily busy, with very little time for reflection'. He 'lived hard and he played hard', combining his busy ministry with a hectic social life. However, he was always committed to the priesthood and he felt 'privileged' to have a 'huge and profound access to people's struggles and pains' that would not have been possible in any other profession. He still misses the 'seamlessness of life' that enabled him to 'do something important for people he valued'. He was one of the young priests that was 'cutting a dash' in many Irish dioceses at that time as they sought to change the direction of the Church to meet the needs of young people. However, he felt that some of the older priests treated him and others like him 'as if they were not real priests at all' because they had missed the 'glory days of the 1940s and 1950s, when churches were full and there was a rosary said in every home. The younger priests like him were seen as 'johnny-come-latelies' or 'Gay Byrne' priests, who were part of the problem facing the Church, whereas the goal of the older priests was to 'get the Church back to the authoritarian model' where everyone obeyed priests, rather than moving things on.

Eventually, he 'cracked' and sought support from a female friend he had known for many years in college. There was 'no drama' about their meeting, but 'for the first time' he realised that there was 'more' to their relationship than neither of them was willing to admit. She was sensitive to his situation and ultimately filled a 'void' in his life through love and marriage. He believes that celibacy/sexuality is the principal reason he left the priesthood and that if he had been 'able to integrate celibacy into a spirituality and, in some way, make it meaningful to the core' of what he was, he would have stayed and been a 'very good priest'.

> I think celibacy is a disaster, an absolute bloody disaster. I took celibacy as part of a package, like saying the breviary or saying Mass without ever thinking seriously about it. Like most young lads growing up, you think that any issues you have around sexuality are a phase that will pass and you will grow out of. We always looked to the older guys and thought they were over it but you don't [get over it], and so it was like a cancer constantly eating away there. Perhaps it was inevitable that I would leave but had I been able to embrace celibacy and make it a meaningful part of my life, that would have been very important to me. I would say celibacy and sexuality, the whole thing, were the reasons I left.

He believes that celibacy is just another form of control that the Church exerts over priests and people. This contrasts with his vision of priesthood, which is to serve and be with the people at their most important and often vulnerable times. Just as he was controlled as a priest, he sees his children being 'moulded and controlled' as they are taught what to believe and how to live their lives. However, ironically, it was a lack of control that probably contributed to his decision to leave: 'I came from a very controlled environment in Maynooth and suddenly I was given the keys of a car, the run of a parish, thousands of pounds in cheque books, and I was expected to get on with things.' The pressure to stay a priest, although intense, was also less than in previous generations. While some family members, parishioners and priests showed their disapproval at his decision to leave, most people were supportive. He feels that he was 'culturally conditioned' and although he struggled with celibacy for many years, he 'swallowed it' until he left.

Fr Dave is now happily married with children. He considers himself more of a cultural Catholic, and he doesn't always go to Sunday Mass. It took him many years to stop dreaming about saying Mass and to come to terms with his new life. At one stage, he considered becoming a minister in the Church of Ireland, because he thought it would allow him to continue his ministry as a married man in a Church that he considers to be 'basically the same as the Catholic Church'. Ultimately, he decided against this route because of the 'historical thing'. His priesthood ended with the 'silent scratching' of names on paper, which, he felt, was in sharp contrast to the 'pomp and ceremony' of his ordination. He has not returned to Maynooth since leaving the priesthood but feels he will, someday.

In summary, the views expressed by the Vatican II priests on celibacy are quite similar to their older pre-Vatican II colleagues. Most of them disagree with mandatory celibacy. While many of them can see a value in celibacy for the priesthood and the Church, they do not believe that it is an inherent part of priesthood. For the most part, these priests see celibacy as a discipline that has been imposed on them by the Church and one which they have no choice other than to accept if they wish to remain priests. They believe that it is a symbol of Church power over priests and people, and that it has restricted their relationships with, and their understanding of, women. Furthermore, they suggest that the value of celibacy is often counterbalanced by the many difficulties caused to priests by a celibate lifestyle. Many of them have experienced personal difficulties with celibacy, with most of them admitting to ongoing difficulties in their personal struggle with the physical side of celibacy. For some priests, sexual intimacy is the main problem, while for others the main issue is loneliness. A number of them said they feared turning into a cosy old bachelor, with no one to challenge them. While all of them believe they have a vocation to the priesthood, many of them have questioned their vocation to a celibate priesthood.

4.5 POST-VATICAN II PRIESTS'[157] UNDERSTANDING AND EXPERIENCE OF MANDATORY CELIBACY

The younger post-Vatican II priests embrace the ideal of celibacy, which they feel is central to the identity of priesthood. They regard celibacy as a blessing to their ministry, and an inherent part of their vocation to the priesthood. Conversely, few of them would oppose optional celibacy if the Church permitted it, and none of them would find it difficult to work or live with a married priest if this became necessary. However, they believe they would never marry even if given an opportunity to do so. While some of them struggle with celibacy more than others, all of them regard their personal struggles as a challenge that is worthwhile and part of their priesthood.

Celibacy is a discipline, which this group of post-Vatican II priests believes 'makes sense' for a variety of ideological and practical reasons. They believe that celibacy gives a counter-cultural 'sign value' of Christ's love and presence in a consumerist, secular world (Curate, 2000s). They also believe that it is grounded in the gospels and consistent with Church tradition, even if it is not always explicitly stated. Two priests referred to the gospel of Matthew in support of their position. One priest referred to Matthew 6 ('No one can be the slave of two masters') while another referred to Matthew 19 ('... there are eunuchs who have made themselves that way for the sake of the kingdom of heaven').

> Trying to live a married life and raise a family is a bit like trying to serve two masters and, as the Lord says in Matthew 6, you cannot serve two masters. It is either one or the other because one is going to be compromised by the other. It is all about the total availability that we see in Christ's life when he saw it fit to lay down his own life for his flock.
>
> *Curate, 2000s*

While not all of them are totally against optional celibacy for other priests in 'exceptional circumstances' (Curate, 2000s), such as saving the priesthood from an extreme shortage of priests, all of them embrace celibacy as an inherent part of their personal vocation to the priesthood. It is a part of a priesthood that they are 'tied into' and which is a core part of 'who they are' as priests. In the words of one priest, it is 'a part of priesthood now whether we like it or not and it is probably intrinsic to it' (Curate, 2000s). It is regarded as a 'blessing' to them personally, a 'gift' to their ministry and the Church, and a way of life that is consistent with the life of a priest. Furthermore, a number of these priests felt that celibacy was a choice they and other priests had freely made when they were ordained and that it would be wrong to turn their backs on this decision. It is a Church discipline that is part of the 'package' of priesthood and, as such, it should be 'honoured and respected'. Life is comprised of many decisions and celibacy is one of these choices.

All of them have chosen celibacy freely and they continue to choose it freely: 'I am happy with my decision to be celibate. I don't feel that celibacy is being pushed onto me. I can live my priesthood any way I want, and I want celibacy for myself' (Curate, 2000s). Although celibacy is an ecclesiastical discipline, and thus a requirement for priests, five of them said they would definitely have made the choice to be celibate even if it had been optional. Their vocation is to a celibate priesthood and they would be uneasy if a married priesthood were introduced. One priest felt that the introduction of a married priesthood would have adversely affected his decision to study for the priesthood in the first place.

> I don't feel that celibacy is being pushed onto me. I can live my priesthood any way I want, and I want celibacy for myself. If celibacy wasn't there in the first place or if it wasn't an option, I might not be a priest. I might not have been called to be a priest. For me, it would change it. If married priests came in, I would not leave. It wouldn't change my priesthood now but I would not have come in if celibacy wasn't there in the first place.
>
> *Curate, 2000s*

Another priest felt that to 'turn back' on the promise he made during his diaconate would be a betrayal of his priesthood: 'I have my hand on the plough and that is what I am going to do' (Curate, 2000s).[158]

For the most part, the post-Vatican II priests do not spend much time thinking about celibacy or its consequences for their lives. Rather, it is 'just another part of life', which 'neither dominates nor detracts' (Curate, 1990s). However, when asked to discuss celibacy, most of them were adamant of its importance to priesthood and their lives as priests. Most importantly, they felt it 'enriched' their lives as priests and enhanced their spiritual lives: 'Celibacy has deepened my relationship with Christ profoundly because it makes me more like Christ' (Curate, 2000s). Another priest said it helps keep 'the ideal of priesthood more in focus' for him (Curate, 1990s), while another said that celibacy means that 'people know I am a priest and I know I am a priest' (Curate, 2000s).

Celibacy has been an absolute blessing for me and my ministry. It has given me a freedom to live a life of service that I wouldn't have through marriage. It has been a personal enrichment and I would like to think, an enrichment to other people as well. I think it is an ecclesiastical discipline that makes sense and that it has led to an enrichment of the Church even though there have been some who have found it very, very difficult.

Curate, 2000s

Celibacy is also perceived to have a number of practical benefits for these post-Vatican II priests including, the greater freedom it is perceived to give them for their ministry, making them more available to their parishioners: 'It has enabled me to live in the midst of many families in the parish, and it has given me the freedom to serve and to live a life of service that I wouldn't have through marriage' (Curate, 2000s). Conversely, another priest felt that this claim of greater availability was often overstated:

It is a nonsense saying I am more available to people, that's bullshit. I know a Church of Ireland pastor who is married and who does far more work than I do. I can play far more golf because I am single and my car is better because I don't have kids.

Curate, 1990s

Two priests gave examples of married priests they knew from other faiths who were often lonely. Others felt that marriage to a priest would 'be asking an awful lot from a woman'.

I know a Presbyterian minister who is married and he told me that it gets very lonely in ministry because he has to leave so much of it behind him when he goes home. If Mrs B is giving him grief he can't go home and tell his wife because she might tell Mrs B where to go! That opened my mind.

Curate, 2000s

Most of these post-Vatican II priests felt that they were personally responsible for setting boundaries in their relationships with women, and while this can prove 'messy' at times, the challenge is deemed to be worth it (Curate, 1990s). One priest said that he doesn't 'feel racked with guilt' if boundaries occasionally get blurred. He doesn't spend the entire day 'lamenting' the fact that he cannot get married (Curate, 2000s). Furthermore, while he believes that priests should endeavour to avoid 'inappropriate relationships', he feels that a sexual encounter need not wreck a person's priesthood: 'If it happens, just forget it, bury it, and get on with it' (Curate, 2000s). Another young priest described his ongoing struggle with celibacy as follows:

> If I fall in love and get into a situation with somebody, that is obviously wrong, but I can still see celibacy as a very good quality within priesthood despite my failing. If a man falls in love, ok that is not what the Church would want or the man himself might want but that's what happens.
>
> *Curate, 1990s*

The reality of celibacy for one priest is that 'I go to bed on my own and wake up on my own' (Curate, 1990s). Another priest expressed a similar sentiment but, on balance, he feels that it is worth 'the hassle' because it provides him with the 'headspace to reflect' and work as a priest:

> Celibacy is part of my life as a priest. It is real and sometimes difficult but it is part of my faith response to God. I am enjoying my priesthood but that doesn't mean that there are not plenty of nights when I am going to bed when I say, what am I doing? There are plenty of moments like that.
>
> *Curate, 2000s*

For the most part, the post-Vatican II priests do not see a difference between heterosexual and homosexual priests, provided they live celibate lives. They believe that a priest who is in a sexual relationship 'compromises' himself and his priesthood and while 'there are probably many priests in relationships or who are alcoholics and they may function perfectly well as priests', this double standard is unacceptable for this group (Curate, 2000s).

> If you have signed up to a life of celibacy, you have made the same commitment as anyone else, regardless of your sexual orientation. As a young man, you have to ask yourself if you can stand up in front of people if you are in a relationship, heterosexual or homosexual. I have no issue with gay priests provided lads are trying to practice morally what they know they should do. If in conscience you can do that in a relationship, then ok but I couldn't.
>
> *Curate, 2000s*

While celibacy is not particularly difficult for most of these younger priests, they acknowledged that celibacy could be difficult for some priests, particularly where they lacked a support network. One respondent suggested that the heavy drinking of some priests is understandable, if not excusable, because 'it is very hard for lads if they are crippled with loneliness' (Curate, 1990s). Others suggested that it is in a priest's own hands how he copes with loneliness:

> As a priest in the parish, you could end up sitting alone in your own room. You could just go to the church and say Mass, then come back and not stir out for the rest of the day, or you could say to yourself it is only right that I go out. It would be an awful lot easier for me to just close the door. It is really up to ourselves.
>
> *Curate, 2000s*

They acknowledge that they are fortunate to have the support of their families and particularly the friendship of other priests, since they believe that non-priests can never understand the life of a priest. A number of these priests spontaneously contrasted celibacy with marriage. They pointed out that marriage is not always easy and that married people can be lonely and that they have to make choices too. One priest suggested that 'everything would change' if celibacy was not mandatory because, amongst the many changes that would be required, 'priests would have to be paid an awful lot more and (we) couldn't all be lumped into parochial houses together' (Curate, 2000s). He felt that a married priest would face difficulties not currently encountered by celibate priests. In effect, 'it is easier to be a priest and celibate' and the way priests live nowadays would not be possible if they were married.

A number of the younger priests indicated that they or some of their colleagues had been sexually active with females during their studies and following ordination. Three priests admitted having a 'few girlfriends' in the seminary and that they felt that it was accepted by Church authorities (informally) that students could 'see girls' (Former priest, 2000s), but only during holidays as part of their discernment process where they 'learnt what celibacy meant in practice'. This freedom contrasts sharply with the secrecy surrounding sexuality in earlier decades. One priest, who was ordained in the 1950s, for example, suggested that by prohibiting close personal friendships and ensuring students did not visit each other's rooms, the college authorities 'somehow succeeded in preventing homosexual activity' (Retired priest, 1950s). To this day, he is not sure if 'it' ever existed.

In summary, this group of young, idealistic post-Vatican II priests believes that celibacy is central to priesthood and that it is embodied into their lives as priests. They perceive their celibacy to be a 'privilege', a 'joy', 'a challenge', and a freely chosen 'duty' of their priesthood. It is both counter-cultural and of practical benefit to priesthood. While it can be difficult at times, it is not perceived to be a sacrifice or a significant loss in their lives. Many of them said that celibacy helps define their identity as priests for themselves and others. Most of them said they receive support from other priests and especially friends from the seminary, 'a band of brothers'. While they feel they would never marry if given the opportunity to do so, they would not stand in the way of other priests marrying.

4.6 THE IRISH GAY CELIBATE

Sexuality is a taboo subject in seminaries, particularly the area of homosexuality, which is ignored by virtually everyone. Most of the research participants said that there was little or no provision for personal development, celibacy or sexuality when they were in the seminary, although this has improved in recent years. They were also unaware of a homosexual culture in the seminary or the wider Church. Conversely, many of them said they were aware of some students who were 'in relationship' with girls. While most of these students eventually left the seminary or ended their relationships, others continued 'to socialise with women' following their ordinations. The implication was that some of these relationships may have been inappropriate but, if so, that was left unsaid.

According to all of the research participants, the topic of homo-sexuality was never discussed in the seminary, even hypothetically. Students were very fearful and reluctant to trust anyone 'even when everyone knew they were gay' (Parish priest, gay). A number of the research participants were responsible for student discipline in different seminaries, and while they accepted that some students must have been sexually active, or that they 'had suspicions about fellows', they believed that 'there wasn't much of it' or 'guys were good at keeping it secret' (Dean, 1960s). They did, however, accept that sexual activity between consenting adults 'wouldn't come to light unless they were caught in the act or the other fellow would tell' (Dean, 1970s). Thus, they argued that while students were branded in various ways, such as the 'Jaffa Cake' group in one seminary, there was nothing to say that students who were more effeminate than others were also homosexual.

Conversely, one priest spoke of the 'gay thing' being strong in his seminary during the 1980s, and that he knew students who used to meet in private in an apartment rented by one student in close proximity to the seminary (Parish priest, 1980s). However, while this went on for an extended period of time, no one in the college ever said anything about it, even after the students had been 'fired because of their homosexual activities' (Parish priest, 1980s).[159] Three priests who had been on the staff of different seminaries, including the one referred to above, said that they knew 'nothing for certain' about homosexuality in the seminary. One former Vatican II priest told of how he got a 'terrible fright' when he was sexually assaulted by a priest on the seminary staff, but that nothing had happened when he reported the priest to his spiritual director. He was simply told that the priest concerned had 'gone a little cracked'.[160]

One Vatican II priest knew of a student in his class who used to combine pastoral work with 'more personal encounters' but that he had no idea of the nature of these activities at the time. A former priest also said he knew 'loads of fellows who were gay or bi-sexual', and while it was never talked about in the seminary, 'it was inferred'. One gay priest said the authorities or students in his seminary never acknowledged that homosexuality existed, even students he knew were gay, including himself. Students joked about it and the college authorities tried to avoid it. However, it was only a 'firing offence' if a student was caught in the act or another student reported 'being interfered with' (Parish priest, 1980s).

> There was a group of gay men in the college and we would have gravitated towards each other, but we couldn't talk amongst ourselves or ever say we were gay.
>
> *Parish priest, 1980s*

In spite of the Church's traditional stance on homosexuality, most of the research participants would have no difficulty working or living with a priest who is homosexual provided he is celibate. The stories of three gay priests who participated in the study are presented in order to illustrate the challenges celibacy posed to a gay man in the priesthood. Fr G is a priest who has ongoing struggles with sexuality, without engaging in sexually intimate behaviour with another party; Fr L left the priesthood because he was unwilling to lead a double life as a sexually active celibate; and Fr C is a priest in active ministry who is in a long-term sexual relationship.

Fr G's Story of Homosexuality
Fr G was ordained in the 1980s. He is a homosexual priest who is very discreet about his sexual inclinations. While some of his close friends know he is gay, most people are not aware of his sexual orientation. In fact, he was not aware himself until quite recently, and it was only when he was in his forties that he came to realise he was gay. I had not been aware of his sexual orientation until he disclosed it during the interview, without any prompting on my part. He has struggled with celibacy for many years and particularly the loneliness of his life as a diocesan priest and the negative attitude of the Church towards homosexuality. Through the medium of dreams and discussions with a counsellor he came to 'understand that sexuality is far more than having sex or necessarily being in an individual relationship'. However, this cerebral understanding did not make his physical desires any the less, although to date, he said that he has managed to maintain a celibate life without physical intimacy. While he received some education on sexuality in the seminary, there was 'very little direct talk on homosexuality' and students dealt with it by 'making jokes'. If given a choice, he would like to be in a relationship and would consider the 'equivalent of marriage' if it were allowed and a 'real alternative'. However, he does not believe the Church will change its laws any time in the near future and he is unlikely to break his vows because of the 'scandal' it would cause. He would also find it difficult, but not impossible, to live a double life as a sexually-active priest. So, for the moment, Fr G is an example of a gay priest who disagrees with the mandatory nature of celibacy but who is willing to accept it for the sake of his priesthood, at least for the foreseeable future.

Fr L's Story of Homosexuality

Fr L was ordained in the 1990s. At that stage, he was aware of his 'attractions to men' but he did not consider himself to be gay. Before he entered the seminary he had 'never done anything about it'. It was only in his third year at the seminary, when someone 'made a pass' at him that really 'freaked him out' and it 'scared the life out of him'. But when he mentioned his feelings to the spiritual director (and subsequent spiritual directors), he was always told to 'pray about it'. Another encounter with a different student some years later resulted in 'kisses' but nothing more. It was only when he was ordained that he finally ended up 'sleeping' with another priest.

> The year before ordination I had a few drinks with another student and he ended up kissing me. I found that uncomfortable but also exciting. I got ordained and ended up sleeping with a priest a year later. Although we both vowed it would never happen again, it did and I was really very confused.

At this stage, he was still uncomfortable, if somewhat excited, with his emerging homosexual identity. He always thought he could be a celibate priest, and following some counselling, he resolved to remain celibate. However, when he ended up in bed 'fumbling around' with another priest, he was 'even more confused'. He eventually decided to try the gay scene and found it 'very daunting' meeting people. He was surprised at the number of married men who were on the gay scene but, unlike other gay men, he felt some empathy for them because they, like him, had 'a lot to lose' if they were discovered: 'At that stage, there was a whole underbelly of gay life I hadn't known before. I found out about cruising, where gay men would go to pick someone up. I tried that a few times when I was a priest and it really upset me.'

Like many of his peers, he resorted to copious amounts of drink to summon up courage before dating. However, he still believed he could continue to be a priest if he 'tried hard enough to fight his sexual urges'. A turning point came when he went on holiday with another priest and had his 'first real gay experience' with a non-priest, and he 'really loved it'. During nearly three years of counselling, he had never mentioned the word gay, but when he returned from holiday, he finally said the words to his counsellor and family, 'I think I am gay.'

He discovered a strong clerical gay scene in Ireland, although it was not easy to access because of their need to be even more secretive than non-priests. He believes that there are 'quite a lot of gay guys in the priesthood' and on one occasion when he went into a gay bar in Dublin, he recognised at least nine priests in the bar. On another occasion, in the same bar, a deacon who was due to be ordained the following month 'chatted him up' before Fr L realised who he was. He was also friends with two priests in his diocese and it later transpired that they were gay. They told him stories of long weekends and holidays abroad, which he found exciting. They were sexual but not with him and he 'lived a fairytale life through their stories'.

Ultimately, he decided to leave the priesthood because he did not wish to celibate and neither did he wish to live a double life. He could not be dishonest, like some other priests he knew. He also panicked when he read about a priest who was found dead in a sauna following a heart attack.

> I don't think a priest has to be celibate but neither should they be giving it away to everybody either. I couldn't balance it but maybe others can. I know some priests who are doing it and it works for them. My wish would have been to be celibate and I really admire those priests who really live celibacy. However, celibacy is not a natural thing and I wanted to be loved and to be in a relationship with someone who loves me. I realised that this was not going to happen in priesthood. I wanted to be honest, so living a double life, I just couldn't see myself doing it.

On one occasion, when he was 'picked up' in a gay cruising place in Dublin, he accidentally discovered the man was a priest and 'a barrier came down'. He got out of the car and refused to engage in sex because of the priest's dishonesty. He also has a 'big issue' with the Church's negative stance towards homosexuality, although he never experienced any hostility from other priests, probably because no one would have known his 'secret'.

Fr C's Story of Homosexuality

Fr C became a priest in the 1980s 'out of a sense of wanting to help people'. He wasn't overly religious but his faith was a 'motivational factor' in his decision to become a priest. He 'hated' the seminary and he found the first few years of his priesthood to be very difficult, with two parish priests who would 'not give him any space at all'. He is now in charge of his own parish and enjoying it. He has always felt somewhat marginalised from the 'clericalist talk shops', with the result that most of his friends are lay people. He also believes that his homosexual orientation has marginalised him from other priests, although he keeps this part of his life hidden. While he believes that 'well over half' of his class in the seminary were gay, the subject was 'never touched upon' by the college authorities and only rarely by students. It was as if homosexuality would cease to exist if it wasn't discussed.

> There was only one form of sexuality recognised by the system, heterosexuality. How incredible. It was such a taboo subject that even amongst ourselves, we didn't acknowledge it. We knew who the other gay ones were, you can tell at fifty paces who is and who isn't, but we couldn't discuss what it is like to be a gay man in that environment. The word was anathema and you couldn't say it because if you were known to be gay, that was a ticket out the door. The authorities will remain in denial until they die. So it took many years and well after ordination before I came out to anybody.

He joined a national clergy support group for priests who are gay, including many priests who had not yet 'come out'. They had to be very careful in case the media discovered its existence, so they used a secret name for their group that was known only to them. He believes that 'a lot of priests found support' through this group, especially those who had never come out to anyone before. There were a 'lot of recovering addicts' which was their way of 'dealing with it' and he is very proud that they helped so many priests to 'restore some balance' into their lives.

He was always comfortable with his sexuality, although he struggled for many years with the dating scene. There was no shortage of sexual liaisons and although he was in his thirties, it was like 'going through his adolescence'. Following many sexual encounters, he eventually decided to look for 'something more stable', which was based on more than sex. He wanted that too but not only sex. He finally met his current long-term partner through the Internet and both of them are very happy together. He is very much at ease with this relationship and he does not see any inconsistency between his lifestyle and his promise to be a celibate priest.

> I don't see any difficulties reconciling my life as a celibate priest and a lover in a long-term gay relationship. I figured that God made me a gay man and God was good enough to send another man into my life, and thank you God! Why should I have any guilt about it and I find it is such a wonderful support to have someone, a partner who cares about me. When civil partnership comes in and if we could do it on the quiet, we would in the morning.[161]

He has chosen to remain in priesthood as a sexually-active celibate because of his love of ministry and a belief that celibacy should not be mandatory. He 'knows' that there are 'lots of gay guys' in the priesthood doing the same as himself. For example, he knows of one priest in another diocese who lived with his male partner in the same house for seven years and it was never an issue for anyone, parishioners or the bishop. This man is still a priest, although now with a different partner. Fr C believes that he was called to the priesthood and that, provided he is careful, he will continue to be a priest for another few years.

> To have someone that cares and supports, someone who I can go to who will understand and accept me totally. It is fabulous! I feel very blessed and lucky, I couldn't have asked for anything more. When I was younger I prayed to God to make me straight like everybody else. To me, straight people were all happy and they didn't have problems. Now I have gone the full circle ... I got comfortable with myself and went through the phase of cruising and looking for sex, and getting over that. I thank God for making me gay and for giving me a partner. Life couldn't be better.

He believes that his life is not much different to other priests he knows who are in long-term relationships with women.

4.7 Priests' Support Networks

The literature suggests that clerical friendships constitute an important source of intimacy and support for celibate priests. US research, for example, suggests that most priests receive support from other priests, and that they are likely to be less lonely when they interact with other priests (Gautier et al., 2012). Conversely, when priests live as 'lone rangers', they are often lonely and liable to being demoralised (Fitzgibbon, 2010). In this section, I will demonstrate that while priests value the support of family and friends, most of the research participants believe that only priests can truly understand the lives of other priests.

The Priest's Housekeeper

In the past, a priest's housekeeper was central to his well-being and mental health. She/he[162] would look after the priest's domestic arrangements, and often act as the first line of defence in deciding who got to speak with 'Father'. She was his housekeeper and often a friend/life companion. She 'lit fires, put out the ashes, tidied the house, put food on the table and hot-water jars in the bed' (Hoban, 2013a). One older priest summarised the value of his housekeeper as follows:

> A woman makes the home. I have a live-in housekeeper and I couldn't envisage her not being here. Part of making priesthood palpable is having a life-in housekeeper who you can trust. If you want a hot meal, get a housekeeper. We have not all been gifted as being good cooks. Women are home-makers and men aren't, let's face it!
>
> *Retired priest, 1950s*

Most of the older priests agreed with this sentiment, although they also acknowledged that it is more difficult nowadays to get a 'woman who is willing to dedicate her life to you' as a live-in housekeeper (Retired priest, 1950s). A live-in housekeeper can also cause difficulties for a priest, if for example, parishioners take a dislike to the housekeeper. One priest was reported to his bishop because he brought his former housekeeper (and her young children) with him when he changed parish. This, it appeared, breached an unspoken tradition of employing local women for the job and the 'unacceptable sight' of 'children in nappies' running around the presbytery (Semi-retired priest, 1960s). However, the report to the bishop suggested her presence was inappropriate for 'other reasons' and he was told to discontinue the arrangement, which he eventually did. As previously mentioned, some middle-aged priests highlighted the gap in their lives coming home to an empty house, with a radio playing or a light left on to give the impression that 'you are not alone' (Parish priest, 1970s).

The Support of Family and Friends

Most priests emphasised the importance of their families and friends in encouraging their vocations and sustaining them during difficult periods of their lives. For example, one priest meets up with a group of walkers from his parish every Sunday because he finds the walk 'socially and physically beneficial' (Parish priest, 1980s). Another priest enjoys the 'warmth and camaraderie' he experiences when playing football with 'guys he knew in school' (Curate, 1990s). Other priests spoke of the support they received from family members, parishioners, and people they socialised with from time to time. However, most priests also said that no matter how close they are, lay people cannot fully understand a priest's life: 'The best supports would be other priests' (Curate, 2000s).

The Support of Other Priests

A number of priests believe that a bond exists between priests that is loosely based on the realisation that they are 'doing something, which is not the nor' (Curate, 2000s).

> I know there are friends outside of priesthood I could go to at the drop of a hat. There are good people around but largely it is the sort of stuff that only people on the inside can understand ... so you kind of keep it within that.
>
> *Curate, 1990s*

Most priests socialise in small groups of like-minded priests, particularly those of a similar age: 'My support network is mainly other priests. I have a few very good friends amongst priests. I can talk with them about most things that I am feeling or thinking. I play golf and cards and I mix with a wide circle of priests' (Parish priest, 1970s).

> A priest from my diocese is my brother. A priest from another diocese is a colleague. You would naturally feel inclined towards your own and outside your diocese is foreign territory.
>
> *Curate, 2000s*

Much of the networking revolves around golf, cards, and class reunions. A number of priests play golf or cards together on a regular basis, sometimes in 'exclusive' clerical clubs, where only priests that 'can play cards' are allowed in ('Serie A'). Less exclusive arrangements are available for 'amateur' priests who simply wished to socialise ('Serie B'). Others meet for walks and conversation, and it is also not unusual for priests to go on holidays together: 'I got on very well in Maynooth and I made good friends there. We have had our reunions down through the years. If we didn't get to go out, we played cards in the clubhouse or something. We would take every Monday off' (Retired priest, 1950s).

The strongest bonds between priests are based on the friendships formed in the seminary: 'In the seminary you are forged as a class and it is not unusual for classmates to be lifelong friends' (Parish priest, 1960s). The bonds between former classmates are strong and enduring, and they regard themselves as 'just like brothers, a band of brothers really, looking out for each other' (Curate, 2000s). They bounce things off their friends from the seminary, with the result that their friends from Maynooth are 'probably the only ones who would have some sense' of their frustrations (Curate, 2000s). In one diocese, the younger priests meet a number of times each year to 'drink a few beers, eat pizza and chat about things that are important to us' (Curate, 1990s). One priest compared the support he receives from his clerical friends with the closeness of a married couple:

> I am lucky that there are lads I get on very well with and can share anything with. You absolutely need that support. To be able to go to someone, like other people in relationships, husband and wife or partners, you need someone to open up to and really say what is going on and that is what I do with these lads.
>
> *Curate, 1990s*

Many of the research participants mentioned instances where a colleague had helped them in their ministry, particularly when they were starting out, or who had 'stood by them' in difficult times (Semi-retired priest, 1960s). Some of these older priests 'looked out for each other' (Retired priest, 1950s), with due recognition of their colleague's human frailties. One priest told a story of being appointed to a parish when he was a young man and he was advised that he might find things 'trí na chéile' (upside down) and 'books that might not be up to date' (Retired priest, 1950s). He was also advised to do his own driving although he was not told the reason for this advice. He subsequently learnt that his elderly PP was such a bad driver that 'he had killed nearly every dog and cat in the place'. However, rather than confronting his PP and embarrassing him, this young curate 'decommissioned' the PP's car by putting a rag up the exhaust and only telling the bishop afterwards.

Conversely, some said that priests could be hurtful in the way they bullied and marginalised other priests, sometimes just because they could or because 'they knew no different' (Curate, 1990s). One young priest, for example, said that he and other priests were treated as 'outsiders' because they held more orthodox theological views than other priests in his diocese. Many others of all ages spoke of how they had been bullied by their parish priests or ignored by their bishop. One priest felt that 'priests don't share that much, except with a couple of guys, and that priests can be hard on each other, often laughing at guys and making fun of them' (Parish priest, 1970s). Others spoke of how their parish priests had curtailed their freedom and authority in the parish, especially if the parish priest suspected his curate was more popular than him.[163] Some priests felt that they 'never really belonged to the diocese' (Former priest, 1980s) or that they 'never had many priest friends' (Semi-retired priest, 1960s).

Priesthood can be lonely for some priests, especially if they do not play golf or cards, or when they are living or working with another priest that is much younger or older. Some priests felt excluded by clerical gossip or by being effectively barred from some activities, such as diocesan card games. While support from their fellow priests is generally 'ok', some priests felt it could be much better.

> Being a priest nowadays is certainly a lonely life in the sense of isolation. You would wish there was more warmth amongst the priests themselves, more support. The relationship between priests in a parish can be difficult and we live very separate lives, even though we get on well. The age gap is huge and that doesn't help. As you get older, there is something odd about a fifty something year old man living with a man who is just thirty.
>
> *Parish priest, 1960s*

When asked if the image of a lone ranger captured the reality of diocesan priesthood in Ireland, a number of priests agreed. They felt that the image of a lone ranger was 'sad' but one that encapsulated the lives of some priests they knew, with little shared intimacy or friendship. A former priest, who is gay, suggested the image of 'batman' was more appropriate because 'a lot of priests are in disguise and afraid to show emotion or who they really are' (Former priest, 1990s). Support from other priests was most often achieved in small groups. One priest said, that while 'you can be friendly with everyone, you know where the boundaries are with others'.

> The banter is good when we get together as a group but you would know the parameters of what not to cross with certain guys. There would be certain fellows you would normally gravitate towards, guys you would go on holiday with or be friends, and then there are others you would avoid.
>
> *Parish priest, 1970s*

In summary, priests get most emotional support from other priests, their 'band of brothers', who understand what it is like to be a diocesan priest. Most of these 'brothers' were in the seminary at the same time as the research participants. However, while most priests receive support from their fellow priests, they are often excluded or ignored by others.

4.8 CONCLUDING COMMENT

The stories of the thirty-three research participants suggest a number of salient findings on clerical celibacy. First, that Irish diocesan priests share similar emotions and sexual desires to those of their lay counterparts. They enjoy the company of women and men, and the majority of them would like to have married and had children. The principal difference between these priests and their lay counterparts is that most of the research participants do not usually act on their sexual desires because of their commitment to priesthood and their promise to remain celibate.

Second, the research findings suggest that a life of celibacy can be both rewarding and difficult for Irish diocesan priests. For some individuals, it is an inherent part of priesthood, a blessing for ministry, and it represents a traditional way of life that is highly regarded in the Church. However, it can also be a difficult life and many of the research participants said that they found celibacy problematic, if not impossible at times. This is illustrated by the stories of former priests who left the priesthood in search of intimacy, and active priests who have engaged in illicit affairs or sexually intimate behaviour. Over the years, however, many priests have found that their desire for sexual intimacy has evolved and gradually, if not completely, been replaced by a need for emotional intimacy and support.

Third, while most of the research participants could see the practical and ideological value of celibacy for the priesthood, most of them disagreed with the imposition of mandatory celibacy. Instead, they argued that priests should be given the option of marrying, if they so wished. Some of them felt that the positive features of celibacy were often overshadowed by its potentially negative effects, including the threat it poses to the priesthood and the Eucharist if vocations and the number of active priests continue to decline. While most of them disagree with mandatory celibacy, and some of them feel lonely and isolated from time to time, they have learnt to cope with celibacy, and they are prepared to accept this lifestyle because it is a requirement of priesthood.

Fourth, the study highlighted inter-generational differences in the way priests understand and experience celibacy. In general, the younger priests came across as most idealistic and supportive of celibacy in the priesthood, with the middle-aged and elderly priests most critical of this discipline. The younger priests were also most likely to say that they would not get married if given an opportunity to do so. They believe that celibacy is central to their priesthood and they perceive their celibacy to be a privilege, a challenge, and a freely chosen duty that helps define their identity as priests for themselves and others. Conversely, they would not oppose the introduction of optional celibacy for other priests, if this became necessary for the good of the Church or the priesthood, although their preference is for celibacy to remain an essential part of priesthood. Whether this difference is a reflection of youthful idealism or a more fundamental shift in the priestly paradigm remains to be seen in the years ahead.

Fifth, the research confirmed the presence of gay priests in the Irish Church and in Irish diocesan seminaries. It is a little sad, but understandable, that so few of the research participants said they knew any gay students in the seminary or any gay priests in their diocese. It may be that their apparent lack of knowledge stems from a concern to protect the privacy of their colleagues and the reputation of priesthood, or a genuine lack of awareness and contact with gay colleagues. For the most part, the research suggests that the need for intimacy transcends sexual orientation and that there is little difference in the attitudes and experiences of homosexual and heterosexual priests towards celibacy. While most homosexual and heterosexual priests are 'compliant celibates', a minority from both groups are either 'natural celibates' or 'celibacy rejecters'. Furthermore, both groups included individuals who felt they had to leave the priesthood in search of love and physical intimacy. Perhaps the main difference between both groups is the Church's traditional negative stance towards homosexuality, and the added complexity of gay priests coming to terms with their homo-sexuality and priesthood. Further research is required into this sensitive and controversial area.

Sixth, the findings suggest that the lived experience of celibacy is best portrayed as a continuum, ranging from complete acceptance to total rejection, with most priests in the middle. The model proposed by Dutch psychologist Hoenkamp-Bisschops (Hoenkamp-Bisschops, 1992) earlier in the chapter is a reasonable illustration of priestly celibacy in Ireland. The priests who find celibacy relatively easy, and those who reject the discipline in favour of a long-term sexually intimate relationship, are relatively few in number. Most priests struggle between the demands of celibacy and a need for intimacy, which is partly provided by their fellow priests, friends and families. Those priests who have freely chosen celibacy are probably most likely to live a happy and fulfilled life, albeit not without some difficulty. I can recall an elderly priest speaking on the priesthood many years ago, who advocated that all priests should be prepared to fall in love at least five times in their lives. This, apparently, was his total 'so far'. Unfortunately, he was not forthcoming on the details of his 'celibate love' and he died soon afterwards, outwardly a happy and contented priest.

In conclusion, while celibacy is perceived to be a gift by some priests, it is a burden for many others, and a duty for all. It is not an easy life, especially for the many priests who feel they do not have the gift of celibacy, and who live lonely and isolated lives. It is difficult for those priests who would like to have married and had a family, and others who would like to have had a long-term relationship to support them in their priesthood. The personal trauma associated with celibacy is perhaps most obvious in the stories and angst of former priests who could not pursue their dream of priesthood because of their inability or reluctance to live a celibate life. It is also apparent in the stories of priests who are challenged by the demands of celibacy and their desire to live authentic lives as priests. However, most of the research participants have chosen to remain in priesthood, suggesting that celibacy and intimacy are challenges to be overcome rather than fatal problems for priesthood.

Chapter Five

The Politics of Clerical Obedience in the Irish Catholic Church

Clerics are bound by a special obligation to show reverence and obedience
to the Supreme Pontiff and their own ordinary.[164]

Canon 273, The Code of Canon Law, 1983

5.1 INTRODUCTION

Obedience, or rather disobedience, is not a major issue in the literature on
Irish diocesan priests, and there is little empirical evidence of individual
diocesan priests speaking out in public against Church policy or practices.
Neither, it should be said, is there evidence of many priests, or indeed
bishops, speaking out in favour of the Church's position on controversial
issues such as *Humanae Vitae*, homosexuality, married priests, women
priests, or abortion. As suggested in chapter two, the 'voice' of the Irish
Catholic Church on such matters is increasingly expressed through the
medium of prominent individuals and organisations with a relatively
conservative agenda. While individual priests and theologians have
publicly challenged the Church on various issues (McDonagh, 2009;
Riegel, 2011; Hoban, 2012; Moloney, 2012),[165] they would appear to have
done so in ways that are acceptable to Church leadership, as suggested by
the fact that very few diocesan priests have been subject to public sanction
(Hegarty, 2012).

Exceptions to this general observation during the past fifty years or
so include the prominent cases of Fr James Good, Fr Kevin Hegarty, and
Bishop Brendan Comiskey. Fr James Good was allegedly banned from
preaching and hearing confession in the Cork diocese when he refused
to withdraw his public criticism of the papal encyclical *Humanae Vitae*
in 1968.[166] The Irish Bishops also allegedly sacked Fr Kevin Hegarty,

editor of *Intercom*, a Catholic Church magazine, from his editorial post in 1994 for raising issues of clerical sexual abuse, and questioning compulsory celibacy and the issue of women priests.[167] In 1995, the then bishop of Ferns, Bishop Brendan Comiskey was admonished and called to Rome to explain himself when he suggested that the celibacy requirement for priests should be relaxed (Ferriter, 2009, p. 533). Three other Irish bishops were also reprimanded by Rome around this time for their views on celibacy.

The voice of Irish diocesan priests is sometimes expressed by representative organisations, albeit not always successfully. The Association of Irish Priests (AIP) was established in 1971 and the National Conference of Irish Priests (NCPI) was formed in 1977. However, the response of Church leaders to these associations was largely dismissive and both associations eventually floundered.[168] Fr Brendan Hoban, for example, tells the story of Fr Seamus Ryan who, as president of the National Council of Priests in Ireland (NCPI) was called to an interview with the papal nuncio, only to be told 'he was a nobody, representing nobodies' (Hoban, 2009, p. 351). A third association of priests, the Association of Catholic Priests (ACP), was established in 2010. One of the ACP's objectives is to provide a voice for Irish Catholic priests at a time when that voice is 'largely silent and needs to be expressed' (Hoban, 2010, p. 485). Their wish is to have their voice heard within the Church rather than outside. Thus, while they may question some teachings and the failure of the Church to implement the spirit of Vatican II, and in spite of some opinions to the contrary,[169] the ACP see themselves as being loyal priests.[170] They believe that priests' views are 'largely silent', thereby suggesting that little has changed for Irish diocesan priests in recent decades (www.associationofcatholicpriests.ie). At the time of writing, another priest's association was in the process of being established (The Irish Confraternity of Catholic Clergy [ICCC]). While this new association of priests would appear to represent a more traditional, orthodox view of priesthood and a response to the more liberal ACP, this has been denied by its leadership who say that the ICCC is about 'mutual support' of priests in 'living the priestly life' (McCarthy, 2014, p. 6). Interestingly, unlike the ACP, the leaders of this new association are young diocesan priests (www.confraternity.ie).

The Vatican's strict position on clerical dissent gathered momentum in the Irish public arena in 2010 and again in 2012 when it silenced six Irish religious order priests[171] for challenging certain aspects of the magisterium of the Church. For example, Redemptorist priest Fr Tony Flannery was allegedly silenced by the Vatican because of his views on contraception, celibacy and women's ordination (McGarry and Agnew, 2012; Flannery, 2013), while Capuchin priest Fr O'Sullivan was allegedly banned by the Vatican from publishing any more of his writings after he suggested homosexuality is 'simply a facet of the human condition' (McGarry, 2010). The Vatican's increasingly tough position on obedience is also evident in the summary report of the *Apostolic Visitation in Ireland*, where it noted a 'certain tendency' that was 'fairly widespread among priests, religious and laity, to hold theological opinions at variance with the teachings of the magisterium'. The response of the visitators to this phenomenon was that it must be 'stressed that dissent from the fundamental teachings of the Church is not the authentic path towards renewal' (Vatican, 2013). Unlike the case of Australian priest, Fr Greg Reynolds, no Irish priest has yet been excommunicated by the Vatican for disobedience in the modern Church (Agnew, 2013).[172]

The focus of this chapter on clerical obedience is on the relationship between individual diocesan priests and the 'institutional Church'.[173] Its primary aim is to explore if the thirty-three priests and former priests who participated in this study have the capacity to act and think independently in a large, complex organisation. Anecdotal evidence suggests that while Irish diocesan priests are constrained in many ways by a highly structured and strictly hierarchical Church, they also have the capacity to exercise agency in certain circumstances, and that many of them do so routinely in their day-to-day lives. The chapter will also explore how different generations of Irish diocesan priests understand and practice clerical obedience in their day-to-day lives. International research and anecdotal evidence suggests that priests ordained in the immediate decades following Vatican II tend to be most critical of Church authority and the Church's hierarchical structures, while younger priests tend to value these structures as an inherent part of their priesthood and Catholicism (Hoge and Wenger, 2003).

5.2 CLERICAL OBEDIENCE

Clerical obedience is underpinned by a number of factors, including: canon law, seminary training, the promise each priest makes to his bishop during ordination, and the threat of diverse sanctions that may be imposed on priests who violate Church norms or teachings.

Canon Law

Priestly obedience is a long-standing tradition in the Catholic Church that is grounded in canon law and framed within a strictly hierarchical Catholic Church. While all Catholics are expected to accept Church teachings and to practice their faith in accordance with the rules and regulations set down in the *Catechism of the Catholic Church*, priests are bound by a 'special obligation' to obey the teachings and rules of the Church (Lynch, 2000, p. 344). The *Code of Canon Law* lists a number of clerical obligations that are 'binding' and valid for the whole Latin Church (Lynch, 2000), including canon 273 quoted above, and canon 274 below:

> *Canon 274/2* – Unless a legitimate impediment excuses them, clerics are bound to undertake and fulfil faithfully a function, which their ordinary has entrusted to them.
>
> *The Code of Canon Law, 1983*

A diocesan priest is allowed to exercise ministry 'only in dependence on the bishop and in communion with him'. He receives 'faculties' or legal permission to administer the sacraments of the Church from his bishop, and this permission is usually confined to his own diocese (*Catechism of the Catholic Church*, 1994, No. 1567).

Seminary Training

Prior to the Second Vatican Council, a strict adherence to rules and respect for the hierarchical Church permeated the Church, and priests were expected to obey their bishop's and parish priest's instructions without question. This legalistic view of obedience was formed in the seminary, with its monastic-style environment and strict timetable of prayer, study, recreation, and sleep. Dublin priest Fr Joe Dunn refers to the climate of fear and strict observance of rules that depicted the life of a seminary in the 1950s and 1960s (Dunn, 1994). A fellow Dublin priest,

Fr Martin Tierney, referred to Clonliffe as a 'desert', a regime which 'left comparatively few things to one's own decision' and where all 'decisions were made for us and were embedded in the rule' (Tierney, 2010, p. 33). Msgr Michael Olden wrote about seminary life in the 1950s that 'individuality and lack of conformity, creativity and innovation, were positively discouraged' (Olden, 2008, p. 13). Anecdotal evidence suggests that seminary life is much less regimented nowadays, although they are still places that are governed by rules and timetables.

Seminaries were places where 'absolute conformity to superiors' was promoted and gossip was endemic, leading to paranoia and superficial relationships (Keenan, 2012, p. 176). According to a priest interviewed by Marie Keenan, 'Speaking one's mind was the thing most likely to have somebody told they were unsuitable for the priesthood' (Keenan, 2012, p. 177). Priests learnt to be 'obsequious' in the presence of seminary authorities and, in some cases, they continued this practice towards their bishop following priesthood (Tierney, 2010, p. 33). Seminarians and priests learnt to 'play the system in order to survive' (Keenan, 2012, p. 177), to keep their heads down and to do whatever was necessary to get through the seminary and to survive life with an intolerant parish priest or bishop (Tierney, 2010). Fr Brady describes his pre-Vatican II seminary days in a semi-monastic Maynooth as follows:

> We were overprotected and underestimated as persons. There were too many rules of the niggling type, rules for the sake of rules. Initiative was frowned upon. The system tended to produce a cautious, safe, middle-of-the-road type of person and what we sometimes called an 'eye-server', one who obeys the rules only when the authorities are around.
>
> *Brady, 1980, p. 707*

A number of prominent social commentators have drawn attention to the formative influence of seminary life on priests. Erving Goffman in his 1961 book, *Asylums*, for example, argues that the function of institutions, such as Catholic seminaries, is to mould inmates into socially approved individuals, i.e. a priest that conforms to the identity of priesthood held by Church authorities. He argued that seminaries are places where students and administrators compete with each other, leading, in extreme cases, to a 'total institutionalisation', which he defines as 'a place of residence and work where a large number of like-situated individuals, cut off from the wider society for an appreciable period of time, together lead an enclosed, formally administered round of life' (Goffman, 1968, p. 11). Inmates come to the institution with a 'presenting culture', which is a 'way of life' they would have 'taken for granted' until their admission to the institution (Goffman, 1968, p. 23). Upon admission to the institution, which includes prisons, mental institutions, and Catholic seminaries, amongst others, an inmate undergoes a process of 'mortification' (Goffman, 1968, p. 24), which consists of identity change, the provision of a uniform form of dress, rules concerning visitors, and the imposition of house rules that are tightly regulated. The end result, according to Goffman, is a priest that conforms to the image held by Church authorities. The formal purpose of a seminary, according to Fr Liam Ryan, is 'to educate, to train the mind and character of the seminarian for his calling as a priest' (Ryan, 1972, p. 61).[174] The hypothesised influence of the seminary on a priest's formation is consistent with research on identity formation in professionals, which suggests that most professional identities are formed in educational settings 'during a process that requires professionals and students preparing for those professions to engage and immerse considerable parts of their individualities in the practices, techniques, and values of the pre-service education and professional practice' (Krejsler, 2005, pp. 336–7).

The Ordination Promise
Following his seven years in a seminary, a diocesan priest is asked to promise 'respect and obedience' to his bishop during his ordination (International Committee on English in the Liturgy, 1975, p. 14). With this promise, the priest is firmly positioned within the formal hierarchical structure of the Catholic Church. Thus, by virtue of his ordination, he is publicly declaring his commitment to the Church and his bishop.

Sanctions
Conversely, should a priest's idealism wane or his circumstances change, the loyalty of a priest is sustained by a variety of sanctions, which are generally imposed by people higher up the Church hierarchy on those lower down, although this is not always easy or possible (Murphy et al., 2005, p. 254). For example, in some situations, the pope

can silence or dismiss priests from the clerical state if they are deemed to have seriously breached Church teaching or norms (McGarry, 2013b).[175] The pope can also admonish bishops for inappropriate views or behaviour. A bishop can forbid a priest in his diocese from saying Mass in public or hearing confession in certain circumstances. He may also sanction a priest by appointing him to a less desirable parish, or by delaying his appointment to parish priest (PP).[176] Until recently, parish priests (PPs) earned considerably more than their curates[177] and they still retain the power to impose a range of sanctions over their curates, such as insisting they undertake some unpalatable aspect of ministry.

5.3 COMPANY MEN 'WITH ATTITUDE'

The positioning of the priest within a strictly hierarchical Church and highly structured Church suggests that a diocesan priest is fundamentally a 'company man'. This view is supported by the absence of overt public dissent by diocesan priests, and the 'service delivery' nature of priests' ministries, whereby they are primarily responsible for the delivery of religious services in a parish. In this regard, a priest shares many of the qualities of Max Weber's 'official' (Weber, 1968, p. 958): a man whose power derives from his position in the Church bureaucracy; a person who is loyal to his 'vocation' within the organisation, and who conforms to its norms in order to pursue his career. However, there is also some anecdotal evidence to suggest that priests do not always give unswerving loyalty to their bishop and the pope, and that they can act independently in some areas of their day-to-day lives. Consequently, for a number of reasons, outlined below, I believe that it would be more accurate to describe Irish diocesan priests as company men 'with attitude'.

First, as previously mentioned, although the Catholic Church is strictly hierarchical, a priest is relatively autonomous within his parish. This was evident, for example, in the inquiry into clerical child sexual abuse in the diocese of Ferns where it identified 'a serious difficulty' for two bishops 'in dealing with Fr Sean Fortune when he refused to comply with the direction of his bishop' and step aside from active ministry (Murphy et al., 2005, p. 254). Similarly, attempts by Archbishop Connell to defrock a priest known to have abused hundreds of children were thwarted by the Vatican for five years when the priest in question appealed to Rome to remain in the priesthood (McGarry, 2013b).

Second, while most priests who have publicly criticised the Church in Ireland and other parts of the world belong to religious orders (Fox, 2011), Irish diocesan priests, and sometimes bishops, have been quite critical of Church leadership and the institutional Church. For example, the former Bishop of Derry, Edward Daly, publicly questioned the value of mandatory celibacy in his memoirs, *A Troubled See* (Daly, 2011). A former Dublin auxiliary bishop, Dermot O'Mahony, criticised Archbishop Martin for his perceived failure to support priests in the Dublin diocese following publication of the Murphy report into clerical child sexual abuse (Smyth, 2010). Some commentators believe that the relationship between priests and their bishops has deteriorated following the perceived mishandling of clerical sexual abuse cases (Duffy, 2006), while others believe that some priests have 'lost complete confidence' in the present system of Episcopal appointments, with bishops 'effectively appointing their colleagues from a gene pool of those deemed loyal to Rome' (Hoban, 2009, p. 345). However, the evidence is relatively scarce and less than compelling, with some research suggesting that the majority of Irish priests believe that they 'enjoy a good relationship' with their bishop (*The Irish Catholic*, 2004).

Third, the literature suggests that there are different ways of being a priest, just as there are different, legitimate ways of being a Catholic, and that priests can choose which model of priesthood best suits their temperament and position. International research and some Irish commentators suggest that different generations of priests exist in the Catholic Church, each with their own defining qualities (Gautier et al., 2012; Hoge and Wenger, 2003). While younger priests are most likely to embrace mandatory celibacy, orthodoxy, and hierarchy, their older counterparts tend to have a more flexible view of the Church and their priesthood (chapter six). Thus, a priest can, within limits, decide the type of priest he wishes to be; whether, for example, he wishes to emphasise the sacramental (cultic) or service nature of priesthood. A priest can also choose how to live celibacy, provided he is discreet (chapter four).

Fourth, while priests share various qualities by virtue of their priesthood,[178] it is clear that priests are not all the same. They have different personalities, talents, ideologies, ambitions and family backgrounds, to name some of the more obvious characteristics. While some priests have the gift of preaching or healing, others are more gifted as administrators or fundraisers. Irish diocesan priests also differ in their attitudes towards some Church teachings and practices. For example, a priest who does not agree with the Church's position on the use of artificial contraception or homosexuality may decide not to preach on these controversial topics, preferring instead to adopt a more liberal/pastoral approach. Conversely, another priest may decide to exclude people from Holy Communion because of their lifestyle or attitudes towards abortion.

In conclusion, this brief review of literature and anecdotal evidence suggests that Irish diocesan priests are generally loyal and obedient to their superiors, partly because of their vocation and sense of duty, encapsulated in the promise they made to their bishop during their ordination ceremony, and partly because of their relatively subordinate position in the Church hierarchy. Yet, it would also appear from anecdotal evidence that many priests are pastorally pragmatic and, in certain circumstances, capable of acting and thinking independently, even if this results in acts of disobedience. This chapter seeks to move beyond anecdotal evidence and explore how the research participants negotiate their priesthood within a highly structured and strictly hierarchical Church. I will argue that they are enabled to act independently within their parishes because of the symbiotic relationship that exists between priests and the institutional Church.

THE RESEARCH FINDINGS: CLERICAL OBEDIENCE
5.4 PRE-VATICAN II PRIESTS' UNDERSTANDING
AND EXPERIENCE OF OBEDIENCE[179]

The pre-Vatican II research participants were formed in a Church that was very legalistic, strictly hierarchical, and dominant within Irish society. The Catholic way of understanding at this time was so strong in Ireland that very few people, priests or laity, would ever consider challenging Church policies or practices (Inglis, 2005). Obedience was regarded as a virtue that permeated Irish society and the life of the Church. However, as discussed earlier, anecdotal evidence suggests that while priests from this era were overtly obedient, they were not necessarily subservient, and some priests learnt how to survive in the seminary and in priesthood by 'keeping their heads down' and 'playing the game'. The views and experiences of the pre-Vatican II research participants are summarised under three headings: the pre-Vatican II Church, seminary life, and the lived experience of clerical obedience.

5.4.1 How Pre-Vatican II Priests Recalled the Pre-Vatican II Church
The three oldest priests in this cohort recalled the pre-Vatican II Church with a sense of nostalgia; however, they also remembered it as being very regimented and legalistic, with too many 'pernickety rules' (Curate, 1960s).[180] At the time, they took this for granted since many aspects of Irish society were also strictly controlled: 'The Church was very regimented but, in those days, life was regimented too. It was no bed of roses anywhere' (Retired priest, 1950s). Ireland was 'a very different world altogether to what we are used to now. It was very tough in many ways. There was no electricity or running water in the countryside' (Retired priest, 1950s). Two of the older priests recalled how it was a hard time for many people, with few employment opportunities for anyone unless they had the financial means to attend university. They also recalled the pre-Vatican II Church as a time of fear, when priests and people were 'very conscious of sin' and 'eternal damnation' (Retired priest, 1960s). There were many occasions of sin in day-to-day life, such as eating meat on a Friday and not observing a fast before receiving Holy Communion. They learnt the *Penny Catechism* by rote in school, which clearly set out the basic tenets of the Catholic faith and the many occasions in which it was possible to commit sins. Some dioceses also had their own moral laws (reserved sins), which could only be heard by the bishop in confession. While two priests felt 'there was something to be said' for these diocesan laws, they also said that it was 'too much for them to be binding under the pain of mortal sin' (Retired priests, 1950s). They were also regarded as 'unworkable' and 'unpractical' in situations where, for example, young people circumvented the law by simply going to dances outside diocesan boundaries where dancing after midnight was not regarded as a sin.

Priests were not exempt from the threat of mortal sin. Some dioceses forbade priests from attending the theatre, going to the races, or hunting.

Others forbade priests from drinking in public or drinking poteen at any time, and gambling. Some scrupulous priests considered it a mortal sin if they didn't say their breviary in full or if they didn't strictly follow the many liturgical rubrics when saying Mass. However, while some of the research participants were conscious of the seriousness of violating 'fussy' Church rules, most of them recalled being much less concerned.

> You had scrupulous priests scraping the corporal trying to get the last fragment of the host. I will never forget when a host fell to the ground and the whole Mass had to be stopped like a train in mid flight and the brakes were put on. The altar boy had to bring out water and the priest had to get down on his knees to clean everything three times and then everything had to be put into a special washing machine.
>
> *Curate, 1960s*

Two priests felt they were often treated like 'children' when they had to ask permission from their bishop or parish priest to do relatively mundane activities (Curate and parish priest, 1960s). One priest told of how he was refused permission by his parish priest to go on pilgrimage because the parish priest was being 'awkward' for the sake of it, even though the curate had found a replacement priest for the time he planned to be away (Curate, 1960s). Another priest described Church discipline as 'contradictory to God's love' (Curate, 1960s). For him, the way people and priests were treated by Church authorities was 'dictatorial' and 'condemnatory', and 'everything was designed to conform to the law' and 'catch people out' (Curate, 1960s).

5.4.2 Pre-Vatican II Priests' Views of Seminary Life[181]

Most of these pre-Vatican II priests were critical of the formation they had received in the seminary, largely because of its regimented nature, which they felt reflected the pre-Vatican Church and the way seminaries operated at this time. As a group, they condemned seminaries for being too 'regimented', 'rigid', 'soulless', 'secretive', 'places where students were groomed and brainwashed', 'blinking jails', 'dictatorial', and 'totally lacking in compassion or vision'. One priest who was ordained more than fifty years ago told of how he and some of his counterparts 'still hate' the college they had attended and the people who ran it 'to this very day' (Curate, 1960s). The following quotes are typical of the emotive and negative feelings expressed by pre-Vatican II priests towards their time in the seminary:

> There were a lot of rules and looking back now, I am inclined to say they were the worst years of my life. It was so drab, especially going back after Christmas and you knew you wouldn't be coming out again until the middle of June. It was very enclosed and you weren't challenged enough. I suppose it was a test of your vocation and we just got through it.
>
> *Parish priest, 1960s*

> Maynooth was like a prison and it was hard to get out in those days. It set out to destroy your individuality and make fellows comply; to regiment them and make everyone the same but it failed. The whole system was geared towards getting rid of fellows that didn't fit in. It didn't scar me, like many others guys, and I remember saying that I just had to survive this place. Fear was everywhere and some bullying too.
>
> *Retired priest, 1960s*

> Clonliffe was absolutely appalling. The staff were arrogant and remote. It was very rigid and very structured. The rooms were freezing and the rules were ridiculous. We weren't allowed into other students' rooms but we were never told why. The dean was a bit of a policeman and once he got us all together and told us there was going to be a reign of terror in Senior House. It was a dreadful place. You had to wear your biretta[182] all the time, day and night, eating your dinner, going up the stairs and you had to take it off before a priest or before the crucifix or a picture of the Sacred Heart or Our Lady. It was so infantile, you might as well have been in a kindergarten.
>
> *Semi-retired priest, 1960s*

When in the seminary, the pre-Vatican II research participants felt they had no choice but to accept the many rules that were imposed on them, including early rising and lights out; observing strict timetables during the day; wearing appropriate religious garb at all times; observing solemn silence at night, during meal times, and during retreats; not visiting other students in their rooms; and not leaving the grounds of the seminary without specific permission from the president of the college. This latter rule was particularly harsh for students who were not allowed out to play in their parish or county teams, even in Provincial or All-Ireland finals.[183] One student, who subsequently became a government minister, was allegedly 'fired' for leaving the seminary to play in an All-Ireland final without permission. Letters were routinely censored, visitors were monitored, and newspapers were only allowed towards the end of the 1950s. Their lives were controlled by bells and monitored by staff inside the college. Some priests spoke of how they were taught etiquette, such as how to peal a potato or top an egg, and what type of present a priest could give a woman: 'A nice bottle of perfume usually did the job' (Curate, 1960s). If they did anything incorrectly they would be 'put out to the line' as punishment (Curate, 1960s). Outside college, a student was regarded as 'a priest in training', subject to the informal supervision of parish clergy and others in the parish who would report 'inappropriate behaviour' to the bishop or the college authorities: 'You were aware that there was always somebody watching you.' It was 'ridiculous' and 'just part of the game' for students (Retired priest, 1950s). One priest recalled his seminary days as 'almost living like a hermit' because of the silences he had to observe during lengthy retreats, solemn night silence, and during meal times (Retired priest, 1960s).

Students who violated college rules were sometimes asked to leave or they were 'docked' by not getting Orders[184] with the rest of their class (Retired priest, 1950s). One priest spoke of how he was not called to take his diaconate with his class because he was 'not always as punctual as he might have been' (Parish priest, 1960s). He considered this punishment to have been a 'harsh blow for something petty' but, as was the custom at the time, he was never given an explanation for his punishment: 'If the authorities felt you weren't suitable, you would be told to stay at home at Christmas or the summer, but other students would never know if you were fired or if you decided to leave' (Parish priest, 1960s). Another student was asked to leave when he was found reading a novel written in a foreign language, even though the dean did not understand the language and knew nothing of its content. He was later accepted into a different seminary outside Ireland and subsequently returned to his first seminary as a staff member. Two priests believe that some students were 'fired' from their seminary because of their country accents, which could not be understood in Dublin (Curate, 1960s).

One pre-Vatican II priest felt his 'grooming' for the priesthood had begun in secondary school and later in the seminary, although he felt that he never lost his sense of 'who he was' (Former priest, 1960s). Other priests also experienced a sense of being groomed or brainwashed for the priesthood. One priest felt he was 'brainwashed' in the seminary and that he was a 'different person' when he came out, but only in terms of discipline and his need to help people (Former priest, 1960s). Another pre-Vatican II priest said that the seminary prepared him for priesthood in a 'functional' sense, by, for example, teaching him how to say Mass (Parish priest, 1960s). The seminary was perceived to be a place where students were 'tested out, where you were challenged to see if you were equal to the life in different ways' (Parish priest, 1960s). Students were regularly told they were free to leave at any time: 'You are here of your freewill and the gates are always open' (Parish priest, 1960s). It was a place where students learnt to accept the relatively harsh regime of seminary life and to obey the often 'unreasonable' instructions of their superiors (Parish priest, 1960s). In this sense, and possibly in this sense only,[185] it was regarded as 'good training' for their lives as priests, where they were expected to obey the instructions of their bishop and parish priest without question (Parish priest, 1960s).

There were many rules in the seminary but some of them were regarded by students as 'the greatest load of rubbish' and not to be taken seriously (curate, 1960s). However, other rules were considered to be important, with serious consequences for violations, and therefore, duly obeyed by most students. While two of the older pre-Vatican II priests felt that they had no choice in accepting lives that were often 'unfair' and 'bound by rules' (Parish priest, 1960s), others admitted to breaking some rules in the seminary. One priest spoke of how he had learnt to 'survive' the seminary by keeping his head down and not attracting attention (Parish priest, 1960s). Another priest said that while the seminary may have 'done its best' to control and make students 'conform' to a certain type of priest, it had 'obviously failed' because there were 'lots of different characters' in Maynooth and the priesthood (Parish priest, 1960s). One priest said that it was accepted that students could break the 'odd rule' but that most of the rules that were broken in the seminary were usually relatively minor, such as 'speaking to lay students in UCD, eating biscuits in our rooms, and listening to the radio or reading newspapers' (Retired priest, 1950s). One priest recalled how he and other students used to pay a gardener to buy 'contraband' in the local shops, such as biscuits and sweets, and that they 'tasted all the better for being hidden under a sack in his wheelbarrow' (Parish priest, 1960s).

Some students were more adventurous and one student, who later left the seminary, 'evaded capture' on many occasions when he climbed the college wall to go into town to the cinema (Parish priest, 1960s). Seminary life was not completely negative and most of these priests could recall some positive elements that helped them to 'survive' the system, including the camaraderie of their classmates, some staff and sport. The importance of sport was singled out by a number of respondents as their 'saviour' in the seminary. Indeed, one priest was rebuked by a classmate when he said that playing football was the single most important part of his seminary life.

5.4.3 The Lived Experience of Obedience for Pre-Vatican II Priests

As previously discussed, obedience was considered to be a 'huge virtue' in the pre-Vatican II Church, and this quality was 'ingrained' in most priests (Parish priest, 1960s). For the most part, parish priests obeyed their bishops, curates obeyed their parish priests, and (anecdotally) everyone obeyed their housekeepers! For many of these priests the process of obedience had begun in their secondary school, most of which were minor seminaries and boarding schools, and reinforced in the seminary. One former priest recalled 'with some bitterness' how his education was all about obedience, although he didn't realise it at the time.

> Guilt was beaten into us and it was certainly a hard decision to leave. Looking back on my education, it was all about obedience and nothing else but obedience. Your personality was kind of destroyed. For me, obedience and goodness were identical. Whoever was the most obedient was the best student. I hardly ever broke a rule. I was very docile.
>
> *Former priest, 1960s*

Five of these pre-Vatican II priests regarded 'disobedience' to their bishop to be 'unthinkable' and 'disloyal'. Priests were expected to do whatever their bishop asked and, for the most part, they did so without question. Five of them said they obeyed their bishops out of loyalty, which was 'very important' because without this 'you would have no order in things at all' (Retired priest, 1950s). However, one priest qualified this statement by saying he 'understood' that a priest would always be able to discuss an appointment with his bishop, especially if 'he was being sent to a parish and there was some reason he didn't want to go' (Retired priest, 1950s). However, when asked, he accepted that he had never actually 'discussed' anything of significance with his bishop. Another priest summarised the culture of obedience that prevailed at this time:

> You more or less did what you were told and you would maybe pay for disobedience by the type of appointment you received. It was very much a clerical Church, very autocratic, which we are paying the price for now. People were rightly critical of the vow of silence imposed on the two boys by (Cardinal) Fr Brady but the Church I knew, if you were asked to do something by your bishop, you didn't size it up and say I won't do it.
>
> *Parish priest, 1960s*

In the pre-Vatican II Church, a bishop usually made parish appointments[186] without consultation with the priests concerned. A number of priests told of how they or their curates were transferred by the bishop without any prior notice. Others sometimes heard of their new appointments from other priests before being contacted by the bishop. However, while most respondents were critical of the process, only three pre-Vatican II priests had ever challenged their bishop, and then only following Vatican II when the environment was more open.

One priest who was falsely charged with child sexual abuse, felt he was being 'disappeared' by his bishop when he was asked to move to a different parish (Parish priest, 1960s). However, when the priest refused to move, the bishop appeared to accept his argument and 'backed down, at least for a while'. Another priest refused an appointment but it 'never crossed his mind' that he was being disobedient, and if the bishop had insisted, 'he would have gone' (Parish priest, 1960s). That was the 'first and only time' he had done that in his fifty years as a priest. Questioning a bishop was rare for priests of this era and any form of confrontation was virtually unheard of. The reason for the lack of consultation was, according to one priest, because of 'power', where the bishop wanted to 'make sure that everyone knew he was in charge' (Parish priest, 1960s). One priest summed up the power of bishops over his priests in one word, 'money':

In the old days the bishop had the threat of moving you if you didn't step up to the mark. There were punishing parishes, which were poor. Money determined where fellows were put. That was the big thing hanging over you, whether you would get a poor parish or a rich parish. If you didn't measure up, you got a poor parish. Money was the big factor in punishing fellows, short of silencing them.

Parish priest, 1960s

In those days, the wealthier parishes were in towns, while some priests lived in virtual poverty in some rural parishes. One priest recalled how he earned just over £500 in 1963, which was 'enough to get by' but that this was very low when compared with the salary received by a curate in the adjoining parish: 'His salary was one of the best kept secrets in Dublin at the time but he told me it went into five figures, which was a lot of money in those days' (Parish priest, 1960s).

Following ordination, a young priest was usually appointed to a parish, as a curate or an assistant. While some parish priests (PPs) were 'gentlemen' (Retired priest, 1950s), many were regarded as 'awkward', 'authoritarian', 'horrible' and 'bullies' (Parish priests, 1960s). One priest told of how his PP punished him when he challenged him on a relatively minor matter by ordering him to say an extra Mass in an outlying parish 'at a time when you had to fast from midnight' (Retired priest, 1950s). He was hungry and tired but 'not bowed down'. Some priests were given duties that were considered to be difficult or awkward by the PP. Some priests told of how they had to find their own accommodation in the parish, with very little money or assistance, while their PPs and senior curates lived 'alone and in relative luxury' (Former priest, 1960s). They were made to feel 'bottom of the pile' and to understand who had the power within the parish (Former priest, 1960s).

The 'grooming' of a young priest was considered to be a normal part of the process in becoming a priest, so it was just something 'you had to go through' as a priest (Former priest, 1960s). For example, attendance at meetings for priests in a particular deanery was compulsory at this time and young priests were often 'picked on' to examine their knowledge about theology (Parish priest, 1960s). However, most priests learnt 'how to handle their parish priest and, in two cases at least, their bishop, by not confronting them directly.

I learnt to get things done in Maynooth by not asking for permission, and just getting on and doing it without fear. When I was ordained I didn't want to create trouble for the sake of it, so I wouldn't go looking for fights. Sometimes you will achieve more by doing something quietly. I have known fellows down through the years who were very direct and I always thought they could have got more if they were less direct. I have enjoyed the confidence of bishops and I know how to handle them. You have to absorb their anger first and then he would be a different man altogether and easier to get things done.

Parish priest, 1960s

One priest told how he regularly 'avoided' asking permission for certain things because 'it was easier to get forgiveness than permission' (Parish priest, 1960s). Two priests recalled how they could only leave the parish with the 'express permission' of their parish priests, even if it was only for a few hours, and while they did not always ask permission, they knew they would be rebuked and punished if their parish priest discovered their disobedience (Curate and parish priest, 1960s). Four priests spoke of 'doing their own thing'. Most of the priests gave examples of how they had done something, which their parish priest would probably have disapproved of, and undoubtedly forbidden if he knew about it in advance. However, they felt that once it was done, there was little the parish priest could do about it. For example, one priest organised activities in the parish for young people, and another introduced meditation into a local school. Both priests 'knew' they would not have been given permission from their parish priests if they had asked, so they proceeded without asking, and 'nothing was ever said, at least not at that time' (Parish priests, 1960s).

Most, but not all, priests knew the boundaries of obedience and dissent and they were careful not to anger the bishop or to place themselves in a situation where they could be formally disciplined. However, not everyone stayed within the boundaries. One former priest, for example, refused to read out a letter from his bishop at Mass detailing the instructions contained in *Humanae Vitae* because he disagreed with the 'absurdity' of telling women with large families that they could not 'stop'. When he had finished Mass and left the altar, his parish priest came out and read the letter to the congregation. There had been no prior discussion with his parish priest and he had not been forewarned of his parish priest's actions. Neither priest ever spoke about the 'difference of opinion'. This same priest also angered some of his clerical colleagues when, in another parish, he and his parish priest donated some of the parish dues to poor people in their parish. Some priests and parishioners labelled him as a 'communist' because of his sermons on social justice. Ultimately, he felt that 'he had to go' because no one was 'allowed to challenge Rome or the diocese' (Former priest, 1960s). Generally, however, it would appear that priests of this generation accepted the status quo with minimal confrontation and one priest criticised the priests of his diocese for being too 'passive' (Parish priest, 1960s).

In the pre-Vatican II Church, there was little scope or expectation of priests dissenting from official Church teachings. The 'law was the law' (Retired priest, 1950s) and there were serious consequences if it was not obeyed. However, over the years, most of this group came to accept the spirit of the Second Vatican Council and to adopt a more liberal, pastoral approach to their ministry. For example, most of them said they would be reluctant to condemn people in morally ambiguous situations, such as people in second relationships, gay people or people who used artificial contraceptives. With the exception of two of the older priests who said they would be sympathetic but that they could not in all conscience give Holy Communion to people in an 'irregular' relationship, most of these priests would have no problem doing so.

> How could you refuse someone you knew to be divorced? How would you know they had not been to confession? How would you know if they are intimately involved in sin? There are a whole lot of factors and you can't really judge people. Our Lord didn't condemn people, so how can we?
>
> *Retired priest, 1950s*

Similarly, most of these priests said they would have no difficulty working with married priests even though they know that this is against current Church policy. The group was more divided in relation to women priests 'because it involved messing around with the sacraments' (Parish priest, 1960s). However, most of them said that the issue of women priests should be discussed more and that they would be open to the possibility some time in the future.

In spite of their unorthodox views on some Church policies, all of these pre-Vatican II priests regard themselves as being obedient and loyal priests: 'We are men of the cloth and like, soldiers in an army we regulate our lives accordingly' (Parish priest, 1960s). However, this does not mean they have to accept everything that 'comes out of Rome' (Parish priest, 1960s). For example, two priests do not believe that a priest would be disobedient if he refused to accept the introduction of the new wording for the Mass,[187] which was clearly 'concocted by a civil servant in the curia to get a promotion!' (Parish priest, 1960s).

> At times, you have to hold the party line in public regardless of your own view. An odd time I depart a little but not often. I would get rapped and I might be told to resign if I persisted, I don't know. But I believe I am right about the new wording in the Mass and I might say it someday. I am not a public person in the sense of speaking out and I have never written anything other than a few homilies and I am never outside the Church in my own pulpit but one day, you never know.
>
> *Parish priest, 1960s*

Rules continue to be important for this group of priests and, as illustrated by the following story, they are willing to be obedient even in situations where they feel 'wronged' by the Church. The following is a story of an elderly parish priest in good standing, who was falsely accused of abusing a young boy.

5.4.4 The Story of Fr Paul[188] who was Falsely Accused of Sexually Abusing a Young Boy

Fr Paul was ordained approximately five years before the Second Vatican Council. From the outset, he was 'always comfortable' with his vocation and he had little difficulty in obeying seminary rules, no matter how 'ridiculous' they were. In hindsight, he realised that the seminary tried to 'programme him for life as a priest' but it failed. He believes that his priesthood is integral to his identity; he is 'always' a priest, which he describes as 'just me', whether he is saying Mass or going on holiday. Over the years, his understanding of obedience has changed from virtual subservience to a situation where he 'is not too bothered with the authorities' and where he is content to do his own thing, although he doesn't break many rules.

We are obliged to 'listen carefully' to our bishop but not to do it blindly like many of the priests in this diocese. Most priests are happy to tow the line and keep their heads down and not ruffle the waters. None of us got too caught up with Vatican II and we let them break up our beautiful altars. I really don't pay too much attention as to whether or not I am being disobedient or not.

Over the years he had 'got into trouble once or twice with the bishop' but nothing serious. Overall, he is regarded as a priest of good standing in the diocese and he did what was expected of him in the various parishes in which he worked. However, in May 2008, his life was turned upside down when his bishop turned up at his parish Mass to inform the people that he, Fr Paul, had been asked to step aside because an allegation of child sexual abuse had been made against him. The following is an account of what transpired when he was accused of sexually abusing a young boy, 'contrary to the sixth commandment and the provisions of canon 1395/2'.

Mid 1980s: The alleged sexual assault allegedly took place.

May 2008: Twenty years later, Fr Paul received a letter in the post from a solicitor alleging that he, Fr Paul, had 'done something terrible' in a previous parish. However, the letter did not contain the details of the accusation. Fr Paul recalls that his heart 'was pounding' and he knew instantly that this was one of 'those accusations', and he 'knew' what was going to happen. Two days later, he rang his bishop's house and arranged to meet with the bishop and his child protection team. The following day, the Gardaí arrested him when he presented himself at a designated Garda station, as requested. The following is his memory of his ordeal in the Garda station.

> When you are arrested, your belongings are taken from you, your shoes are taken off you, and your belt is taken, and your mobile phone, everything. Now I know what they mean when they call the cells a slammer. The cell door is like the door of a safe and they bang it behind you, and you are in this place, with a toilet in the corner, which is not very clean, a hole in the ground. The ground is cold and you have a bench to sit on or lie down, whatever you like. There is a slit in the door and they come down every fifteen minutes or so to see if you have done yourself in or whatever. It was absolutely ludicrous to see the head of a

Garda above the glass looking at you. I was left there for half an hour to, as my solicitor told me, soften me up. I was then taken and put into a fixed chair that won't move, facing a video camera, and I was questioned for two and a half hours.

Then they told me what I was supposed to have done and I absolutely denied it. They fingerprinted me and they took my mugshot. The photograph can never be removed from the police station; it is there for the rest of your life. Then they took me back to the cells and gave me a mug of tea. I was then interviewed for a second time. I wasn't allowed to have my solicitor with me for the initial interview. Some of my friends had been ringing me but I was completely incommunicado; no one knew what had happened to me. I could have been killed. When I spoke with the bishop, he asked me to step aside, but I refused since I was totally innocent. I eventually signed the papers and went off to the caves like a leper. I was advised by another bishop, 'a friend', not to refuse because it would become a battle of wills between me and my bishop, and I could not win.

The following weekend, the bishop came out to Fr Paul's parish to 'proclaim from the house-tops' the allegation that had been made and that 'they were standing me aside'. Fr Paul was told in advance of the announcement, and that he could not defend himself or speak in Church. Parishioners greeted the announcement with shock, and some of them came to him afterwards to give him their support. Fr Paul was removed from the exercise of his office and ministry in May 2008.

July 2008: The Director of Public Prosecutions (DPP) dismissed the case against Fr Paul in less than one month, although he was not told this until later when the Gardaí confirmed through his solicitor that the DPP had directed that there would be no prosecution in relation to Fr Paul arising from the allegations of sexual abuse.

August 2008: Approximately one month following the DPP's decision, the Church began its preliminary inquiry. However, they reached no conclusion and their main concern seemed to Fr Paul to get him out of the parish residence. But he was 'not for moving' against the 'might of the institution'. While he accepted that all allegations concerning children should be investigated, he believed that he was treated like a 'leper' or possibly a 'lamb that was thrown to the wolves' to take pressure off the bishops. As soon as the 'denunciation' was made against him, he believes that 'the shutters came down with the authorities' and he was told nothing about his position in the parish. His bishop wanted him to leave the parish 'quietly in the night' but he refused to go because he believes that 'there is too much control in the Church' and he didn't want 'to be pushed about'.

August 2009: One year later, the Congregation for the Doctrine of Faith in Rome informed Fr Paul's bishop to establish a canonical trial to hear and adjudicate on the allegation.

November 2009: Fr Paul eventually moved residence but he remained in a separate house in the parish. He wanted to resume his life and 'enjoy his enforced leisure'. He also went to Mass in the local Church because he knew he was innocent. His view was later vindicated when a number of people told him that 'they knew he hadn't done anything' when they saw him 'around the Church' and because he hadn't 'run away'.

December 2009: Another statement from the diocese was read out at Masses in the parish reminding parishioners of the allegation against Fr Paul and telling them that the canonical process had begun. However, this process was 'slow to get going', partly because of the shortage of canon lawyers. His bishop later told him that they only 'do cases like mine in their spare time'.

December 2010: Approximately one year later, and more than two years since the accusation and the DPP decision that 'no prosecution' be taken in relation to Fr Paul arising from the allegations of sexual abuse, the Church's judicial process effectively started and the various parties were interviewed. The unanimous decision was to 'clear me and to remove all restrictions'. He was told he could go back to work but then told not to, as the diocese wanted to 'sort out' things first.

October 2011: A short notice was read out in the parish that church and state investigations had been completed and that Fr Paul was returning to ministry and that he remains a priest in good standing in the diocese. However, it fell short of stating he was innocent.

Although reluctant to attribute blame or to express anger, Fr Paul eventually admitted that he feels anger towards the Church and his bishop, partly because he was 'left hanging' for more than three years following the DPP decision that there was no case to answer. He is angry because he believes the diocese abandoned him, in spite of his previously good record as a priest. For example, he believes that his name 'fell off' the diocesan mailing list for priests, and his status as parish priest was effectively revoked without any consultation, when he received letters addressed to Fr Paul instead of Right Rev Fr Paul, as had previously been the case. He knows that his reputation has been damaged seriously, possibly irreparably, and that this has not been helped by the long delay in holding the canonical inquiry. He also fears that his reputation may have been tarnished by the failure of the diocese to use the word 'innocent' in the final statement read out in his church, in spite of the lengthy and exhaustive church and state process. It appears to Fr Paul that the diocese is more concerned with protecting itself against future litigation and criticism from organisations that advocate on behalf of sexual abuse victims, than with his rights. He is confused by his treatment by his bishop and the diocese because he believes he has always been a loyal Catholic priest. He regards his treatment by the diocese as a betrayal of this loyalty. However, he remains loyal to the Church and slow to accuse or condemn anyone for his ordeal. Fr Paul has now retired. His last words to me on the matter, 'Dying should be easy after this!'

5.5 Vatican II Priests' Understanding and Experience of Obedience[189]

As previously detailed in chapter two, the religious landscape of the Vatican II Church into which these Vatican II priests entered was a period of significant change and renewal. It was a time of hope and transformation, when the certainties of the pre-Vatican II Church were replaced by a new model of Church that emphasised collegiality, the Church as community, ecumenism and the enhanced participation of lay people. It was also a time when a new servant-leader paradigm of priesthood emerged, which increasingly replaced the prevailing cultic model with its pastoral agenda. However, ultimately, it was a time of disappointment for many Vatican II priests as the perceived liberal agenda of Vatican II was replaced by an increasingly conservative and orthodox Church. Fr Kevin Hegarty expressed this disappointment, as follows:

The glad confident morning of Vatican II has long vanished. For those of us whose lives have been shaped by a belief in the ideals of democracy, free speech and academic dialogue, the institutional Church, in the last quarter of a century, has often been an inhospitable place.

Hegarty, 2006

5.5.1 How Vatican II Priests Recalled the Vatican II Church

Many of the Vatican II priests have a somewhat ambivalent view of the Second Vatican Council. On the one hand, most of these priests regarded Vatican II as an event or revolution that represented a significant improvement on the more legalistic and regimented pre-Vatican II Church. Most of them spoke of being 'initially enthused', 'impressed by the documents of Vatican II', 'encouraged by modern priests', and generally feeling 'energised' in the immediate aftermath of Vatican II (Parish priests, 1970s). They believed that Vatican II promised the emergence of a Church of the people and that the hierarchical framework of the Church would be replaced by more collegial structures.

However, most of them said that their initial enthusiasm has long since been replaced by frustration and an acceptance that little has changed with the Church's hierarchical form of governance during the past fifty years. In their opinion, the Church is still fundamentally hierarchical and the empowerment of lay people has only occurred to 'a very small extent' (Parish priest, 1970s). While most of these priests had set up various groups in their parishes, such as pastoral councils, liturgy groups and financial groups, they acknowledged that these groups have only limited influence and that many of their colleagues still act as 'plant managers' where they control the 'keys of the parish' (Parish priest, 1970s). In their opinion, the Church is still 'very much controlled from the top' (Parish priest, 1970s).

> I feel we lost a great opportunity in Ireland in Vatican II. We didn't really take it and implement it in the spirit in which it was intended. By and large we are still a hierarchical Church, and I think it is an awful pity that structures haven't changed. I would sometimes despair at the institutional Church.
>
> *Parish priest, 1970s*

Most Vatican II priests said they had been 'disappointed' (Parish priest, 1970s), 'saddened' (Parish priest, 1970s) and 'angered' (Parish priest, 1980s) by the 'failed opportunity' (Parish priest, 1980s) of Vatican II. However, their anger is a controlled anger because they have learnt from experience that 'patience wins more battles than confrontation' (Parish priest, 1970s). Vatican II was 'supposed to be a time when the windows of the Church opened to the world and a lot of change would happen, but this didn't happen', according to one priest (Parish priest, 1980s). He, like others, eventually learnt to accept that any form of change or progress in the Catholic Church is very slow and that 'there is not a lot you can do about it'.

> You discover as you go along that the Church moves in centuries and that everything takes a long time. Sometimes things move backward before they move forward. Vatican II moved the Church forward before it was dragged back by John Paul II. As a young priest I was very frustrated with this and I can see the same thing happening with young priests today. However, when you get older, you see things in a different way. It is not that you are throwing in the towel but you see that things move slowly and that there is not a lot you can do about it.
>
> *Parish priest, 1980s*

While they realised that change on the scale envisaged by Vatican II was never going to be easy or immediate, many of the priests became increasingly frustrated at the perceived reversal in the process towards a more conservative Church that occurred during the papacies of John Paul II and Benedict XVI. Five Vatican II priests said they had no wish to return to the restrictions or control of a cultic Church that prevailed before Vatican II, and three priests reacted with anger towards any initiatives that suggested the Church was returning to a conservative model of Church. Two priests admitted being 'frightened' at the way young priests were 'going around in soutanes, white-cuffed, and saying Latin Mass' (Parish priests, 1980s). Like some of their older pre-Vatican II counterparts, three priests said they would have to consider their positions when the new wording of the Mass missal is introduced because, for them, it symbolises the resurgence of a clericalist Church. They believe that the Church is 'turning back in on itself' and if this continues, it will mean that the past fifty years will be seen as a 'failed opportunity' (Parish priests, 1980s).

Vatican II was a fabulous opportunity for the Church to keep pace with the modern world and in the beginning it was brilliant as poor old Paul VI was virtually out of touch with everything. But then John Paul II and Benedict XVI seem to be saying that it was all a big mistake. That is very sad for me. The feeling seems to be that if we go back to what we had before Vatican II, with the rigid liturgies and all the rest, that we will go back to full churches but we won't.

Parish priest, 1980s

However, in spite of their frustration, most priests accepted that some change has occurred in the Irish Church since Vatican II, even if most of this change has taken place in the attitudes of priests rather than in Church structures. For example, one priest said he no longer regarded a priest's vocation to be superior to that of a lay person.

When I was in the seminary, you either became a priest or you took second best and got married, or maybe you would go as a lay missionary that was not quite up to the mark. That was a dreadful way of understanding your vocation.

Parish priest, 1970s

Another priest said that when he was ordained, the priesthood was 'more spiritualised' (Parish priest, 1980s). He thought that he was 'a channel' to God and that his job was to administer the sacraments and lead the people to God. He now realises that his role is more communal and a 'shared responsibility'. When he was ordained, he didn't see the need for a parish council because he was 'trained' for the job and lay people weren't (Parish priest, 1980s). It was his job to 'take care' of the keys in the parish and no one ever objected, at least not to his face. He was in charge and 'everyone knew it'. However, it is only with the passage of time that he has come to see that he was 'part of the control the Church exercised over people' and that his approach had been 'destructive' in forming a parish.

Most of this generation of Vatican II priests said they are content to live with uncertainty and less power if it means that the Church becomes less authoritarian.

When I grew up and went through the seminary and priesthood, one of the big things was that we had left this older Church behind that had all the answers because it didn't serve us well, where the parish priest was lord and master of all he surveyed. Whatever he said, the whole of society had to bow and scrape and put their shoulder to the wheel. You couldn't question anything. The Church had all the answers, whereas the Church I was ordained into had a new way of thinking, where a priest's own personal experience carried some authority and weight. The whole fact of uncertainty and searching, trying to find our own way within a certain structure, within the teaching of the Church, with scripture as our guide, praying with it, reflecting with it; that was all part of the new Church.

Parish priest, 1980s

The response of these Vatican II priests is to accept the situation, and to do the best they can in their own parishes, where they still have some say. One priest who seriously considered leaving the priesthood because 'there was so little progress' since Vatican II, decided to remain in the priesthood but to 'give up on reforming institutional structures' and instead, to 'work within the situation and to do what he could within his own parish' (Parish priest, 1980s). However, even there, he recognises that his freedom to act is curtailed by the clerical culture where other priests might criticise him for doing something outside the norm. Some priests believe that obedience is not as strict following Vatican II, even though they themselves rarely go against Church policies or practices: 'Maybe it was the air of freedom or the greater sense of fraternity between priests, but even though you had a vow of obedience and you had to obey it, there seemed to be a greater freedom in how this was done' (Parish priest, 1980s).

5.5.2 *Vatican II Priests' Views of Seminary Life*
Seminary life was slow to change following Vatican II and it took some years before theology courses and staff reflected the new theology of Vatican II. During the second half of the 1960s and early 1970s, it remained a 'very regimented' environment and the 'whole idea seemed to be that they should kick you around plenty and if you are tough enough, you will survive on the outside' (Parish priest, 1970s). A description of seminary life in the late 1960s by one of the Vatican II priests illustrates how little seminary life had changed since the pre-Vatican Church, with many practices from that era continuing after Vatican II.

Theology was out of date, with little interaction or understanding of what was taught. Some lecturers hadn't changed their notes for years and very few of the staff ever spoke to students by name. You got home for Christmas and summer but there were no breaks in between. It was a very closed system and you never got out unless you were going to the doctor or a very close family member had died. We couldn't get the newspapers and everything was black. We were identified by a number, like being in a concentration camp. There was no human development and students would receive solemn warnings without notice. There were lots of silly rules.

Parish priest, 1970s

However, change did eventually come in the early 1970s, and there was 'a greater openness' about the seminary (Parish priest, 1970s). The content and style of teaching gradually changed in the 1970s, and new lecturers were appointed, following a strike by theology students in Maynooth, together with pressure by some bishops. Unlike their older counterparts, students were allowed out of college for sporting occasions and increasingly for personal reasons. They were also allowed access to newspapers and radio, to buy sweets and biscuits, and the prohibition on visiting students in their rooms was increasingly ignored. Some seminaries opened their doors to lay students, male and female, in the late 1960s.

The Vatican II priests recalled their seminary life as disciplined but not entirely restrictive. Some priests said that they enjoyed a range of college activities, including studies, sport, debating and drama. The spiritual environment and pastoral activities fulfilled others. In hindsight, however, the majority of priests said that their seminary training did not prepare them well for the priesthood or life as an adult. For one priest, ordained more than thirty years ago, it was 'a prison' to which he has never returned, while another regarded the experience as 'stultifying' (Parish priests, 1970s).

The training in Maynooth was a very rugged and impersonal training, with little awareness of human needs. They prepared us for nothing and the theology was very poor and part of a pre-Vatican Church. The dogma was staid and very dead. It was awful stuff really.

Parish priest, 1970s

Four priests felt that the seminary system emphasised conformity over individuality. For them, the seminary 'tried to kill any spark of initiative' in students and to 'impose obedience, authority, discipline, order, and time-keeping' (Parish priests, 1970s/1980s). Individuality continued to be a serious threat to ordination. However, most priests felt they beat the system,[190] in this regard, at least.

> I think that is what Maynooth trained us for: to be rugged, tough individuals who can survive on their own. That is an awful thing; no one can survive alone. That is one of the awful things about Maynooth. They wanted to make everyone the same and if you put your head above the parapet you were nearly shot on sight. But you just learnt to retain your own personality and to keep your head low. We told each other not to let the system get you down, and you could beat the system with the help of your peers.
>
> *Parish priest, 1970s*

While the seminary had 'streamlined them' and possibly 'conditioned' them 'a bit' to act and think like priests in certain situations, a number of priests felt that their time in the seminary had not significantly changed their vocation or their personality: 'The boy will always out, maybe not for some time, but eventually' (Parish priest, 1970s).

> We are a bit conditioned and it is a pity. It is a mindset and approach to life we were taught in the seminary and reinforced afterwards. It seems to me that anyone with new ideas was seen as a threat. I think we were conditioned in Maynooth to keep your head down and don't get caught. Maynooth trained us to be lone rangers, to be rugged tough individuals but I think that is awfully wrong. It is easy to be a lone ranger but nobody is a lone ranger. It is easy to hide behind your black soutane and your black whatever, but society has changed and we need to form relationships with people. Maynooth wanted to make everybody the same and if you put your head above the parapet you were shot on sight. But you learnt to retain your own personality, to retain your own giftedness and you just kept your head low. The whole idea seemed to be that you should kick students around plenty and if they are tough enough they will last outside the seminary.
>
> *Parish priest, 1970s*

In spite of the changes, seminaries remained places of discipline in the 1970s and 1980s, albeit less regimented than in previous decades. In the words of one priest, his seminary was 'kind of like monastic living for kids', an 'endurance test' that was clerical and closed' (Parish priest, 1980s). There were timetables for everything and everything was spiritualised. Most of these priests believed that a student would be ordained if they 'ticked all the right boxes', such as being present for morning prayer, passing exams, and not getting caught (too often) breaking the rules (Parish priest, 1980s).

5.5.3 The Lived Experience of Priestly Obedience in the Vatican II Church
Vatican II did little to challenge the hierarchical nature of the Church, with priests expected to obey their bishop and to accept the teachings of the Catholic Church without question. For the most part, these Vatican II priests are content to obey their bishop provided they also remain true to themselves. Most priests felt that obedience did not impinge on their day-to-day lives, as they are largely 'independent' of their bishop, provided they do not give him 'reason' to interfere in the parish (Parish priest, 1980s). The important thing was to 'keep your head down and to do your own thing' (Parish priest, 1970s). In contrast to the 'extraordinarily dictatorial' relationship of the past, five priests believe they have developed a 'working relationship' with their bishop. However, while some individuals had queried appointments or other matters, and others felt they could if they needed to, very few have done so.

Nevertheless, everyone acknowledged that the relationship with their bishop is an unequal relationship. One priest is convinced that mandatory celibacy persisted because it is 'easier' to control priests (Parish priest, 1980s). Some Vatican II priests felt they 'didn't have a voice' (Parish priest, 1980s) because they feared being punished by their bishop or being 'dismissed' by Church authorities if they complained about their bishop (Parish priest, 1980s).

> The whole hierarchical Church is a very difficult mechanism and it is very difficult to speak out. Where do you go? You go to your bishop because he is the one you are accountable to but to whom is he accountable? You go to the Nuncio or the Congregations in Rome but you can easily be dismissed. You are such a small player in a global organisation.
>
> *Parish priest, 1980s*

Most Vatican II priests are aware of 'awful stories' where priests had been punished for getting on the wrong side of their bishop (Parish priest, 1970s). A number of priests gave examples of how priests they knew had been punished by their bishop in 'subtle ways'. One priest told of how a 'hot-headed' priest was appointed PP to a parish 'before his time' and while this could be seen as a promotion, it was quite the opposite, as the parish to which he was sent was a place no one would ever want to be appointed (Parish priest, 1980s). For the most part, it would appear that most bishops continue to make appointments and other decisions with minimal consultation with their priests.

A number of Vatican II priests told of how their bishop had 'asked' them to undertake a specific ministry, which, at the time, they didn't wish to do. However, they felt they could not refuse 'God's work' and they had to 'just get on with it' (Parish priest, 1980s). Other priests told of how they had been appointed as newly ordained priests to situations that were difficult and 'something of a test' for them (Parish priest, 1980s). One priest who had 'never been in the countryside in his life' was appointed to an isolated rural parish as a newly ordained priest where his parish priest was known to be 'an alcoholic and a bully' (Former priest, 1980s). Another young priest was 'thrown' into a parish where the parish priest was an alcoholic and had 'let the parish go' (Former priest, 1980s). The advice from more experienced priests was generally to do what was requested and 'await a transfer' to a better parish in due course, even if it took up to ten years (Parish priest, 1970s). When a dispute arose, it was regarded as best for the priests to settle the argument themselves. If the bishop became involved, he tended to support the parish priest.

While most of these Vatican II priests had served with parish priests who were 'gentlemen' (Parish priest, 1980s), most had also encountered parish priests who were bullies. In some parishes, the curates were not allowed to do anything, while, in other parishes, they were restricted by the parish priest in what they could do. One Vatican II priest, for example, only learnt what was happening in his parish by reading the weekly newsletter compiled by the parish priest. Another told of how he was 'given no space whatsoever by his parish priest who was a controller' (Parish priest, 1980s) even though he was a senior curate. Another priest was appointed to a parish where his parish priest insisted on doing all the weddings and baptisms. Whether this was to do with money or simple control was not clear to this priest.

> There is a great tradition of bullying in the Church and the old guys are great at bullying. They would shout everyone down at meetings and intimidate everyone around them. Imagine being with a parish priest who said you could not do weddings or funeral Masses and that he would do everything.
>
> *Parish priest, 1970s*

Curates who were more popular with parishioners than their parish priests were liable to 'shunning' by their parish priests (Parish priest, 1980s). One priest who was subject to this type of behaviour said he would advise any young priest to 'make sure he had a good relationship with his parish priest and not to do anything unless he wants you to do it' (Parish priest, 1980s). However, this same priest did many things 'independently' from his parish priest and in practice, he said that he did what he wanted in the parish. He, like most of his peers, had learnt to 'do their own thing' and to 'keep their head down' while in the seminary. Other priests spoke of approaching their parish priest in an 'indirect' way that 'gave him the impression he was in charge' (Parish priest, 1980s). The danger of directly confronting authority was also mentioned in relation to a bishop.

> Some guys in the diocese have difficulties with the bishop if they come at something head on, particularly if it is a big issue. The bishop may back off but he won't forget. They may not have much vision but they do have long memories. There are many different ways to skin a cat and there are ways of dealing with a bishop.
>
> *Parish priest, 1970s*

Obedience is regarded as an important aspect of their priesthood, although not necessarily subservience. For example, none of these Vatican II priests have ever refused the sacraments to anyone they suspected to be outside of the Church. While they regard rules and regulations to be an important part of any organisation, they believe that they cannot know the state of a person's soul. Like many of their older counterparts, their approach to people is pastoral rather than dogmatic, where 'you have to see the person first' (Parish priest, 1980s). In contrast to the certainty of the pre-Vatican II Church, they believe that many teachings and practices of the Church are not always straight-forward and that they need to be contextualised for different situations and individuals. Four priests said they were 'disappointed' or 'angry' at the way the Church treated people who were divorced or homo-sexual. Their response was to 'interpret' these Church teachings, discretely and compassionately. One priest said that he would 'leave it to the people' in an irregular relationship to tell him if they were sexually active or living as 'brother and sister' under the same roof (Parish priest, 1980s). If they turned up at the altar, he would give them Holy Communion, but if they lied, it would be 'inviting God's condemnation on them'.

Most Vatican II priests are open to the possibility of married priests, women priests, and gay priests. The opposition of the Church towards these groups has 'distanced' some priests from the Church, leading some of them to question their priesthood.

> The Church has done a lot of stuff that has distanced me from it – no discussion of women priests, no concentration on justice – and it wouldn't take much to push me out. If they put in a conservative bishop who told me to wear black clothes and who was anti-women, and lacking in compassion, my tolerance level would be very low.
>
> *Parish priest, 1970s*

One priest who disagreed vehemently with the new wording in the Mass missal felt he would have to stop saying Mass in public if he is 'forced' to say the new wording, because it represented a 'step too far' towards a more archaic Church (Parish priest, 1980s). Like some of his older counterparts, he believes that someone has to 'stand up and say no' because he is 'scared' that the freedoms of Vatican II will be eradicated unless people object. However, he is unsure if he will have the courage to be 'disobedient' by taking such a position, as he regards himself as a 'party man', and he would not wish to do anything to 'embarrass' his bishop or diocese.

In general, this group of Vatican II priests believes that diocesan priests are reluctant to 'speak out' against Church policies and practices with which they disagreed for a variety of reasons (Parish priest, 1970s). One priest felt that his generation of Vatican II priests are 'a bit conditioned' into a clerical mindset in the seminary that regards new ideas and individuality as a threat to the status quo (Parish priest, 1970s). In his opinion, diocesan priesthood does not attract 'free thinkers' and the institutional Church 'doesn't encourage it'. Two priests said they get sufficient opportunities to 'say things' at diocesan level and that 'there is no need to stir up things' outside of these structures (Parish priests, 1970s). Three priests said that they are so busy, that they 'just don't have the energy' to complain (Parish priests, 1970s/1980s). Two priests said that the 'mentality' of a diocesan priest is to be content if he can 'look after' his own patch, with minimal interference from outside the parish (Parish priest, 1980s). One priest felt there is 'little scope' in challenging the Vatican or their bishop, as nothing ever changes. Finally, a number of priests said that while they would not be afraid to challenge their bishop if 'difficult decisions had to be made', this would be exceptional as they 'don't like upsetting anyone' (Parish priests, 1970s/1980s).

The story of Fr Henry illustrates how one Vatican II priest remained obedient and true to his vocation in a situation he found to be 'intolerable'.

5.5.4 The Story of Fr Henry, who was Falsely Accused of Sexual Abuse[191]

Fr Henry is a senior and widely respected Vatican II priest who was falsely accused of sexual abuse. Although the State and the Church declared that there was no case to answer in less than five months, this was not before he went through a 'really horrendous experience' where his priesthood and public ministry were threatened. Immediately the allegation was made, and before he was told anything about it, he was asked to step aside by his bishop. Fr Henry felt his bishop had treated him 'disrespectfully' when he refused to give him details of the accusation or to enter into any form of dialogue. All he knew was that there was an accusation and while they might have said something about it, he was in shock and could not take in what they were saying. Later, when he had asked for a copy of the accusation, he was told that someone had stolen it. This was the beginning of his 'bizarre' story.

He felt he was 'disenfranchised' by his bishop who came out to his parish to announce the allegation to his parishioners. He was not given any time to think about what was happening. Neither was he allowed to speak to the people in his parish to explain that the accusation had nothing to do with him.

I said to the bishop that I absolutely know that you must act on this but just let me have some time to discover what exactly is being said, where it is coming from. If you are coming to my church, I want to be the one who will speak because I want my voice and my face to own this accusation, to own what is happening in my life, to face the people. He said you can't do that. I asked if we could agree a script to be read out and we could stand beside each other so that the people would know we were standing together in addressing these very real issues. He said no and told me that I could never enter this church again. I wrote a statement and stood at the church door and handed it out to the people as they left Mass. They were very confused. I was told to leave my home and live with my family. I was never asked if I had any money or offered a solicitor. When I asked who would pay my bills, the bishop said, 'I won't anyway.' I was told I could give retreats to nuns provided it was a small group of nuns and I told them my full story. The whole thing fell apart very quickly, almost as soon as it was announced, but the process had to take place.

The civil process was completed in four months and I was found to have no case to answer. The canonical process followed, but it was delayed while they appraised themselves of what the elements of a canonical process entailed. I was really angry at this, to think that after four months, knowing that they had to have a canonical process, they hadn't appraised themselves of the procedures. I was subsequently allowed back to my parish after five months. It was awful. I wasn't naive about the institution and its foibles but I had no idea that the Church could extend such callousness to any priest, even if they were guilty. I was just shocked at the way the Church dropped me. I am absolutely supportive of the procedures that are there because people were not listened to in the past but there should also be a real semblance of truth before a priest is asked to step aside and publicly denounced. My particular accusation was so flimsy. Others would naturally ask, am I next?

The experience has brought me closer to the gospel message. It has also brought me into a new awareness of my cherishing of the priesthood. In a moment when it was almost taken away, I realised it is my essence, the very definition of what I am and that I cherish it. I never feared that I would not be back in priesthood during my 'time off' but I did go through terrible, terrible sorrow and wept profoundly. This was a profound pain that I had never before experienced. I remember saying at the time that I wished I had cancer instead of this because cancer has dignity. I am sorry for thinking that now but I did at the time. I was destroyed really. It had huge implications for my family too.

When the bishop told me the case was over and that there was nothing in it, I think he expected me to thank him. He was trying to say that he couldn't see what all the fuss was about but I just said nothing. The statement that was read out when I was asked to step aside was four lines, so I gave him a statement which I had prepared and which I felt was appropriate. He said that he didn't think the lawyers would allow him to use the word 'innocent'. That was the last conversation I had with him. The statement read out at Mass was powerful and quite fulsome but you are left with a residue of pain and grief. It is not the whole story of my priesthood. It is only one chapter but there is no lower you can go.

In summary, the Vatican II generation of priests have grown up in a rejuvenated Church but also one where there have been few changes to its hierarchical structures. Similar to previous generations of priests, they are typically compliant to their superiors and reluctant to engage in behaviour that could be perceived as disloyal. However, their obedience is largely pragmatic in pastoral issues and they are content to voice their dissatisfaction privately through surveys and their representative associations, but not directly to their bishop. This generation of diocesan priests are largely obedient but not necessarily subservient; they are company men, 'with attitude'.

5.6 Post-Vatican II Priests' Understanding and Experience of Obedience[192]

The post-Vatican II Church is a very different Church to the triumphalist Church of the 1950s and early 1960s, and the resurgent Church that followed the Second Vatican Council. It is increasingly secularist, with less people attending Mass or willing to accept Church authority. It is also a Church that has become increasingly polarised between liberal and conservative interests. Following a period of approximately twenty years, the traditional conservatism of the Catholic Church re-emerged in the post-Vatican II era, a period that coincided with the papacies of John Paul II (1978–2005) and Benedict XVI (2005–13). The importance of rules and regulations was given a boost in the publication of the new *Code of Canon Law* in 1983 and the *Catechism of the Catholic Church* in 1994. This generation of post-Vatican II priests have largely experienced a Church in decline and the emergence of a new paradigm of priesthood, one that values orthodoxy, hierarchy, and the distinctive nature of priesthood.

5.6.1 How Post-Vatican II Priests Perceive the Post-Vatican II Church

Whereas the Vatican II generation are frustrated by the lack of perceived progress in the Church following Vatican II, a new generation of priests, ordained during the past twenty years or so, appear to have been energised by a return to tradition and relative certainty. The revolution of Vatican II had come and gone by the time most of these priests entered the seminary, with the result that most of them said that Vatican II *per se* had no significance for their lives as priests. However, further to the inspiration and writings of John Paul II and Benedict XVI, most of them believe that Vatican II 'went too far' and 'lost' its sense of perspective (Curate, 2000s). Accordingly, most of them have adopted a more conservative theology that is at odds with many Vatican II priests: 'When Benedict was elected, a lot of the older priests were in despair, whereas a lot of the younger priests were saying, "Thank God"' (Curate, 2000s). Unlike many of their older counterparts, they find comfort in a Church that moves slowly and in line with orthodox tradition.

> At the end of the day, this is the Church. It moves slowly and it has a theology, not a manifesto. It can be very frustrating sometimes and unfortunately it is terribly undemocratic but that is the nature of it.
>
> *Curate, 1990s*

They claim not to be against change, provided it happens in accordance with the traditions of the Church. They have 'grown up' with disclosures concerning clerical sexual abuse (Curate, 2000s), and most of them said that they and many of their peers have been 'disillusioned' by the 'wave after wave' of scandal in the Church, which they thought 'would never end' (Curates, 1990s/2000s). However, while some older priests 'took it to heart' and were 'fearful' and 'embarrassed' to meet people (Curate, 2000s), most of this cohort believes that these scandals have nothing to do with them and that they have nothing to feel guilty about. They believe that their job is 'to help turn things around' (Curate, 2000s).

> It would get you down when some priest did something or a bishop said something, but then you remember that your ministry is rooted in Christ and that it doesn't depend on anyone, no matter what mistakes they have made'.
>
> *Curate, 2000s*

Most of them said they were 'angry' and 'disappointed' at the way their bishops mishandled the sexual abuse situation:

> Most guys would believe the bishops were way off in the way they covered up the abuse and how they handled the fallout from it. There is no question that this has been very annoying but at the end of the day, they are fallible.
>
> *Curate, 1990s*

Conversely, one of the post-Vatican II priests held more extreme views of the 'failures' of bishops, which he believes reflects 'demonic evil' at work in the world, an evil that can only be overcome by 'prayer and authentic discipleship' (Curates, 2000s).

> It has given me a deeper perspective on the reality of evil in the world and particularly how evil has worked its way through men, some of whom are priests. It also shows how evil has compromised leadership. I am obedient to my bishop. I love my bishop and I pray for him. He is a very good man but I also know that our Church leaders are weak and that they need prayer. It has not destroyed my faith and when I look back at the way clerics were treated in the past, they had almost God-like status given to them and that was very unhealthy for them and also for the people.
>
> *Curate, 2000s*

Most of the other research participants believe the problem is grounded in the weaknesses of bishops who are 'only human with a difficult job to do' (Curate, 1990s). However, in spite of their criticism of bishops and the Vatican, the post-Vatican II priests are unquestionably loyal to their leaders. They believe that everyone has a job to do, including priests, and that it is important they don't give in to 'defeatism' (Curate, 2000s).

5.6.2 Post-Vatican II Priests' Views of Seminary Life
The seminary continued to change during the 1980s and 1990s, with less emphasis on rules, although they are still institutions where discipline is imposed on students. For many of these post-Vatican II priests, the experience was 'formative' and 'interesting at times' but not an experience they would wish to repeat: 'It was grand at the time but I would never go back' (Curate, 2000s). A more liberal atmosphere, with

fewer restrictions on socialising, has replaced the culture of fear that prevailed in the pre-Vatican II Church. Students are encouraged to mix with lay students, male and female, and they can go to the cinema, pubs and even nightclubs without fear of punishment. The emphasis has changed from control to personal discernment with a sense of discipline, where students are increasingly encouraged to take responsibility for their lives. However, in spite of greater freedom and the introduction of new courses on personal development and pastoral studies, most seminaries continue to have regular timetables that are almost monastic in the rhythm of the day. Times are set aside for prayer, study, recreation, spiritual activities and meals. Punctuality and obedience continue to be valued in seminaries, and students have to comply with core rules if they wish to receive Orders and eventually, ordination.

There are substantially less students in seminaries nowadays, and one post-Vatican II priest recalled how he and the other first years had only taken up one tenth of the college chapel for their introductory Mass, a chapel that was filled to overflowing during the visit of John Paul II in 1979:[193] 'The rest of the chapel was in virtual darkness and it was a very bleak experience' (Curate, 2000s). Three post-Vatican II priests admitted to lacking the basics of Catholicism when they entered the seminary that previous generations of seminaries would have taken for granted. For example, one priest had never said the angelus or the rosary before coming to the seminary because his parents had never said these prayers at home. Another priest was embarrassed when he told a spiritual director that he had never prayed to Jesus and that he didn't really know much about the saints or how the Church worked. A third priest recalled, with some embarrassment, how he had brought a large statue of Our Lady with him into the seminary because he was told by people he knew at home that it was expected. Most of the remainder were imbued with Catholicism from their homes and local parishes.

Ironically, given students' historical dislike of the control exerted by seminaries over students, the college authorities were perceived by some post-Vatican II priests to have been too liberal. Some of these students felt victimised by college authorities for 'standing up for their faith'. In one college, for example, the authorities allegedly had to lock the oratory at night to prevent some students from prostrating themselves before the altar and praying all night. One post-Vatican II priest was critical of the formation he received in the seminary because he felt that it lacked an authentic faith basis.

> I had reservations about the formation system, which I felt lacked a certain rigour and weightiness. Some of the reading stuff we were given and some of the people who came in to talk to us were not really the best calibre people to be talking to seminarians … Some people had difficulties with Church teachings in certain areas and some were going through a crisis of faith. Some fellows who were very much into the rosary or Eucharistic adoration got the feeling that these things were not appreciated as much as they should have been. One weakness of the seminary is that it did not facilitate students who were searching for holiness.
>
> *Curate, 2000s*

The fundamentalism that characterised some post-Vatican II students was not, however, universal (chapter six).

As was the case with some of their older counterparts, two priests felt that the real character of seminaries was hidden beneath the surface. One priest said that students learnt to 'play the system' and to 'do anything to get ordained because it was so important to them' (Former priest, 2000s). In one seminary, students were excluded from local pubs but this rule was 'universally ignored by students' (Former priest, 2000s).

> This was pure nonsense. It sort of brought about the attitude that you were doing things behind their back but it was ok once you weren't caught. We weren't supposed to be in the pubs but we were and they knew. It was just so hypocritical and immature. You also had the nonsense of guys coming back to the college late and hopping the wall so that they wouldn't have to sign in at the gate.
>
> *Former priest, 2000s*

In hindsight, most of these post-Vatican II priests were critical of the seminary system because they felt that it did not prepare them for life as a priest, although most accepted that no seminary could ever teach what priests or any other profession 'in the real world' requires: 'You have to learn on the job' (Curate, 1990s). While it may teach philosophy and theology, 'it does not prepare you for the mind-numbing meetings and the number of funerals' (Curate, 1990s). Some felt that the 'monastic lifestyle' was very different to the lives they would eventually live as secular priests and therefore, it was inappropriate (Curate, 1990s).

5.6.3 The Lived Experience of Priestly Obedience for Post-Vatican II Priests

Obedience is highly regarded by post-Vatican II priests and it is part of what gives their priesthood meaning. A number of them said that they had taken a 'solemn promise' to their bishop and that 'order' was important in the Church. Thus, their understanding of obedience is fundamentally ideological and quite different to the pragmatic under-standing of previous generations. These post-Vatican II priests fully realise that, as young curates, they 'occupy the bottom of the ladder' (Curate, 2000s) and that they are subject to the authority of the Vatican, their bishop, and senior priests. It is something that some of them are willing to accept and even embrace, while others are frustrated by their lack of responsibility: 'When you are in the seminary, you think of all that you will do in the parish but then you discover that there is little that you can or are allowed to do.' Even when their voice is heard, 'nothing changes' (Curate, 1990s).

Their experience of obedience is quite similar to that of their older counterparts. Post-Vatican II priests are appointed to parishes by their bishop and, with some exceptions, most bishops do not consult with them before they make their decisions. One priest spoke of the 'trauma' on hearing that his friend was being transferred to another parish without notice (Curate, 2000s). Another remembers 'crying' when he was appointed to a difficult parish (Curate, 1990s). While two priests had asked their bishops to move them from a parish because of bullying by their parish priests, few priests feel they could make such a request or challenge their bishop in any way, because they 'probably got hit hard early on' and that is what they still expect (Curate, 1990s).

> In my experience bishops have very poor people-management skills and guys get hurt when wrong decisions are made because the proper conversation never happens. Even if you get a parish you don't want, you could say to the bishop that you will be back in six or seven years for another parish. There is almost always a plan B, which the bishop would be willing to consider if he is asked.
>
> *Curate, 1990s*

Two of these younger priests said that some of their peers had not learnt that the direct approach rarely works with bishops. Rather than confronting them head-on, especially in public, they believe that it is much more effective to 'work with the bishop and give him some room for manoeuvre' (Curate, 1990s). When a priest challenges his bishop in front of others, there is 'only ever going to be one casualty and it is not going to be the bishop' (Curate, 1990s). While the priest may not be formally sanctioned, 'like the communists, it is noted' (1990s). Most priests agreed that diocesan priests were reluctant to speak out because of 'fear' and 'a learnt discretion'. One priest was told by an older colleague to 'write nothing until you are a parish priest'; once 'you have your own Church, you can basically do what you want' (Curate, 1990s). Another post-Vatican II priest believed that while obedience is important for 'order', he would have 'no problem' criticising the bishop 'if it were necessary and prudent'. However, he added, 'Why should I create trouble for the sake of it?' (Curate, 1990s).

The power of parish priests has diminished somewhat in recent years due to the decline in vocations, resulting in fewer curates and more parish priests working alone in a parish. Nevertheless, a number of priests told of how they had not been able to do things in the their parish because their parish priest did not allow them. One young priest spoke of how he had been 'kept down' by his parish priest for more than twelve years and that he found him to be 'intolerable' and unwilling to listen (Curate, 1990s). Another curate spoke of how his parish priest 'had gone ballistic at a meeting and tore shreds off him afterwards' when he had contradicted him (Curate, 1990s). It is a 'cycle of abuse' that continues to be replicated from generation to generation.

> You have to sink or swim when you come out of the seminary and often you end up with a priest who might bully you because he was bullied himself as a young priest. So unfortunately you have to take care of yourself because other priests are too busy with their own work.
>
> *Curate, 1990s*

The abuse can also come from other priests in their diocese when they 'shun' you for having different views or alternative lifestyles (Curate, 2000s). One priest, for example, spoke of how he and 'other outsiders' club together when confronted with priests who 'are afraid to stand up for what they believe'. However, for the most part, he believes that priests treat each other with respect, if not always warmth (Curate, 2000s).

This generation of post-Vatican II priests are more orthodox and traditional in their views and practices than many of their older counterparts. Most of them said they are 'theologically conservative' and many of them would not be comfortable with the notion of women priests. They also believe it is important to inform people of the 'truth' concerning sin, contraception, and immoral behaviour 'if they are asked' (Curate, 2000s). However, with one exception, they did not usually take the initiative in telling people how to behave, and most of them hold relatively liberal views that are contrary to a strict interpretation of Church norms and law. For example, most post-Vatican II priests believe celibacy should be optional for priests, although not necessarily for themselves, and that homosexuality should not be grounds for excluding people from the priesthood. Furthermore, most of them have never (and would never) considered refusing Holy Communion to a person at the altar, even if they knew the person was, for example, divorced and in a second marriage. However, they do not publicise their views and, if asked, they would 'have no choice' but to 'say things how they are'. Three of the five post-Vatican II priests would prefer to adopt a pastoral approach when confronted by most controversial issues.

Thus, while most of these priests believe themselves to be 'theologically conservative', they perceive themselves to be 'pastorally pragmatic' (Curate, 1990s). For example, when asked to bless a second marriage one priest said he would offer a blessing for the couple's home instead of 'doing something in a formal visible way' (Curate, 1990s). This approach also allows him to 'be fair to what marriage is about'. Two priests acknowledged that 'there is a lot of grey' in the Church and that priests have to minister to the 'grey' (Curates, 1990s). However, this does not mean that 'everything has to be thrown out'. Rather, 'someone has to stand up for marriage and someone has to stand up for people in second relationships'.

> Making a big fuss on the altar would not do anyone any good. At the same time, I wouldn't be afraid to name certain things if people asked me honest questions in confession. I would say that it is up to them to make up their own minds, but this is what the Church teaches. There is an objective truth and this is it.
>
> *Curate, 2000s*

One priest said that he has to be able to minister to a world of 'grey'. In his view, if the Church follows everything 'to the law', it will end up with very few people or priests.

> Many of the people involved in our parish meetings were gay or in second relationships. If you follow the letter of the law, they should have been cast out and yet these are the people who keep things ticking over. It used to amaze me that women continued to come and help, given the attitude of the Church to them.
>
> *Former priest, 2000s*

Another priest, a canon lawyer who trained in Rome, felt that the problem lay in the interpretation of Church law and that Rome 'understood' that 'rules had to be interpreted' for different parts of the world, even if this was contrary to the official stance taken by the Vatican.

> The attitudes of Italians are quite different to Irish attitudes and Northern European attitudes. Our attitude seems to be that if you make a law it is very black and white, and this is what you have to do. All Italian laws are very clear but nobody obeys them and there is never a problem. They see exceptions everywhere.
>
> *Former priest, 2000s*

Conversely, one post-Vatican II priest was adamant that priests need to stand up for the Church in 'telling the truth' to people (Curate, 2000s). He regards himself and other priests like him to be 'prophets in the wilderness' that cannot shirk their responsibilities to tell people that they are committing sin when they use contraception, engage in homosexual sex, or get divorced, and that they should not receive Holy Communion until they have been to confession. He is the only priest in my research to admit he had refused people Holy Communion because 'he knew' they were in 'bad faith' with God.

In summary, the post-Vatican II priests are ideologically obedient and theologically conservative, and they embrace their solemn promise of obedience. Conversely, most of them are pastorally pragmatic and willing to address the needs of people rather than automatically imposing Church law. Thus their relatively tolerant response to obedience is similar in many ways to their older counterparts. They are loyal and reluctant to question their bishop or confront their superiors within the Church hierarchy.

However, they are not always subservient and they have learnt to circumvent rules and 'do their own thing' from time to time.

5.7 CONCLUDING COMMENT

The research participants' stories suggest that Irish diocesan priests are typically 'men of the cloth' who are loyal to their bishops and the Vatican, and who value order and obedience in their clerical lives. Their loyalty is fostered by a number of interlocking factors, some positive and others negative, including their commitment to priesthood, as encapsulated by their sense of vocation and the promise of obedience to their bishop taken during their ordination ceremony; their relative subordinate position within the Church hierarchy; their strict formation in the seminary; the imperative of a clerical culture; the threat of sanctions by their superiors, and a belief that any confrontation on their part would have no significant effect on the outcome. It may also be the case, as suggested by one priest, that diocesan priesthood does not attract free thinkers, or, as suggested by others, that priests are generally content to take care of their own parishes. Like other groups, they know that if they challenge their superiors, it is likely that they will 'find themselves in a battle they are most certainly doomed to lose' (Saunders, 1983, p. 64).

Conversely, the evidence presented in this chapter also suggests that Irish diocesan priests are not necessarily always subservient, and that many of them 'do their own thing' routinely in their day-to-day lives, albeit within parameters consistent with the conditions of their priesthood. While only a minority have challenged instructions given by superiors, most of the research participants have learnt to act relatively independently by keeping their heads down and avoiding confrontation with their superiors. Furthermore, it is clear that most of the research participants can think for themselves, as suggested by their disagreement with some Church teachings and practices. For example, most of the research participants disagree with mandatory celibacy, even though this is the official position of the Church. Some of them also ignore the law of celibacy in their own lives. Others are clearly uncomfortable with the Church's stance on homosexuality and women priests. Furthermore, most of the research participants indicated that they are pastorally pragmatic in how they deal with parishioners and only one priest has ever refused a person Holy Communion. This sense of pastoral pragmatism transcends the three generations of priests, including most of the younger and more orthodox cohort of priests.

The relationship between priests and Church leadership is, like many things in the Catholic Church not particularly straightforward, but readily understood by those involved. I believe that the relationship between priests and Church leadership is mutually beneficial, albeit unequal. On the one hand, priests are clearly subject to the authority of their superiors because of the hierarchical nature of the Church. However, they are allowed some discretion in their behaviour because of the symbiotic relationship that exists between them and their superiors. Further to the writings of French theorist Pierre Bourdieu[194] and others (Bourdieu, 1991; Saunders, 1983), I would argue that the relationship between priests and Church leadership is underpinned by two core principles. First, priests are expected to be loyal to Church leadership, especially in public, but I believe that they are also allowed to be disobedient in certain circumstances, provided their actions are discreet and they do not threaten the position of the Church. For example, a priest who disagrees with the Church's position on homosexuality or women priests only becomes a problem for Church leadership if he voices his dissenting views in public. Similarly, a priest in a sexual relationship is only a problem if his actions cause a scandal. For example, one of the research participants in my study who is in a long-term same-sex relationship is enabled to remain in the priesthood because he keeps his views on homosexuality private and his homosexual behaviour secret, although he believes that his bishop 'probably knows'.

Conversely, the institutional Church allows this 'disloyalty' because of the benefits it receives from having a resource (priests) that is both authoritative and empathetic, moral custodian and spiritual guide, and above all, loyal. This enables the institutional Church to be relatively unyielding in the laws and 'truth' it promulgates. Thus, for example, the Vatican's long-standing opposition to homosexuality or divorce is mitigated to some extent by the more pragmatic and pastoral stance by many of its priests. A priest can, for example, suggest a house blessing or a couple blessing as an alternative to a wedding. He can also give

Holy Communion to a couple in this situation without necessarily breaching Church law.

It is not an equal relationship but it 'works' because both parties accept the 'rules of the game' controlled by the institutional Church. A core principle underpinning the symbiotic relationship between the Church and its priests is the acceptance by both parties that the dominant position of the Catholic Church must be maintained against all threats. The Church has the capacity to reassert its authority if it is unduly challenged by an individual priest or group of priests. Individual priests can be silenced, while others can be 'reminded' of their duties as priests. In the past, 'problem priests' were protected by their superiors and routinely transferred away from the source of the problem, often without regard for the other people involved. Nowadays, some commentators believe that priests accused of abusing children have been abandoned by the bishops in order to protect the image of the Church and to restore its credibility in Irish society.

In summary, this chapter has demonstrated that the research partici-pants are loyal but sometimes disobedient in the way they think or act for themselves. They are constrained but not necessarily controlled by Church structures. They are allowed liberties in how they conduct themselves, provided they tow the party line in public and they don't 'flaunt' the rules of the game. Consequently, they do not generally express their dissent in public because they understand and accept the rules of the game in the religious field, which indicates that their relatively privileged position in the Church and Irish society is subject to the dominance of the institutional Church. Above all, they want to be priests of the Catholic Church and only the Church can permit this to happen and continue happening. Those who can accept these conditions stay, even in times of personal difficulty, while others who cannot cope with these structures tend to leave or become very marginalised men. Some of the research participants had challenged the Church but none were victorious. For example, one of the priests who was falsely accused of abusing a young boy, initially refused to leave his parish residence or to retire. Ultimately, he did both because he was just a 'foot soldier' in the Church's army, a man who was obliged to follow orders.

Chapter Six

The Life Cycle of Irish Diocesan Priesthood

In sum, views of the essence of priesthood have undergone two shifts. The first occurred around the time of Vatican II – from the older model of priest as administrator of the sacraments and teacher of the faith, to a new model of priest as spiritual and social leader of the community. This change was accompanied by the council's new theology of the church as the 'people of God'. The young priests in 1970 were strongly in favor of the new model. The second shift, which began in the early 1980s, continues today and seems to be reversing the first, though not everyone agrees on this point. The question remains open: Is the current attitude shift a return to older forms, or is it something altogether new?

Hoge and Wenger, 2003, p. 59

6.1 INTRODUCTION

The primary aim of this chapter is to explore the research participants' understanding of their priesthood and to investigate if, and how, their understanding has changed during the course of their priesthood. Further to the discussion on evolving models of priesthood in chapter three, I will argue that three different models of priesthood have existed in the Irish Church during the past fifty years, and that at any one time, one model has been on the ascendant, with the other models on the descent. This is the life cycle of diocesan priesthood in modern Ireland. The outcome of the current paradigm struggle is not yet known and further change may be anticipated as liberal and conservative interests strive for position in the Church. The literature suggests that each of these models is comprised of different generations of priests who 'came of age during different periods of time' and who were 'influenced by the prevailing culture of the times' (Gautier et al., 2012, p. 4). This has resulted in the emergence of generations of priests with common experiences and identities that are ideologically different to the other generations of priests (Bacik, 1999; Hoge and Wenger, 2003; Gautier et al., 2012). However, the evidence presented in chapters four and five suggests that Irish diocesan priests share many cultural and practical characteristics of priesthood that transcend the diversity of the different generations. Accordingly, I will argue that the current life cycle of Irish diocesan priesthood is characterised both by ideological differences, together with a common pragmatic approach to ministry, and an underlying commitment to priesthood.

Further to the work of US sociologists Hoge and Wenger (2003), this chapter will map out the research participants' understanding of priesthood, under six headings: vocation, ontological status of the priest, attitudes towards the Church magisterium, liturgy and devotions, theological perspective, and attitudes towards celibacy. As was the case in previous chapters, the data will be presented separately for the three generations of priests: pre-Vatican II, Vatican II, and post-Vatican II priests.

THE RESEARCH FINDINGS: THE LIFE CYCLE OF IRISH DIOCESAN PRIESTHOOD

6.2 HOW PRE-VATICAN II PRIESTS[195] UNDERSTAND THEIR PRIESTHOOD

6.2.1 Pre-Vatican II Priests' Views of their Vocation to the Priesthood

A strong sense of vocation – a call from God – is central to the decision that led the pre-Vatican II priests to become priests. Other motivating factors included, 'the salvation of one's soul' (Retired priest, 1950s), 'doing good, like a doctor' (Curate, 1960s), 'treating people in a Christian way with kindness' (Parish priest, 1960s), and 'I just wanted to be a priest' (Parish priest, 1960s). Initially, five pre-Vatican II priests had considered being a missionary to 'convert the masses' of people in the foreign missions.

> I felt it would be safer as a priest, for the salvation of my soul, particularly a missionary priest. It was something I felt was well worth doing and I would be making a valuable contribution.
>
> *Retired priest, 1950s*

> I felt it was the best thing I could do really. In the long run, God was first and to serve God was the best.
>
> *Semi-retired priest, 1960s*

Four pre-Vatican II priests said their response to God's call was a process, which emerged over time, rather than a 'flash of light'. It wasn't a 'once-off event that just happened' like St Paul falling off his horse on the road to Damascus (Retired priest, 1950s). Rather, they felt that their vocations 'matured' with 'age and experience' (Retired priest, 1950s). While all of these priests were successful in being ordained, others they knew did not reach that stage. One pre-Vatican II priest told of how his brother had entered the seminary 'full of hope and energy' only to leave it a 'broken and dispirited man' a few years later (Curate, 1960s). However, while he and his family were very upset at the time, it did not stop him from entering the seminary some years later. He felt that God had called him and 'I am not my brother' (Curate, semi-retired, 1960s).

Most of the pre-Vatican II priests said they had first considered a vocation to the priesthood during their final year in secondary school. They had all attended a minor seminary or diocesan college where it was 'natural' and 'expected' that a number of boys would 'go for the priesthood'.[196] One priest said, for example, that around twenty of the thirty boys in his Leaving Certificate year went on to a seminary. While he said that this number was higher than average for the 1950s, with most respondents recalling between five and ten boys who 'went for the priesthood' in their year, it is indicative of the popularity of priesthood as a 'career' at a time when the Catholic Church was in a 'pretty strong position' and other employment opportunities were scarce. None of these pre-Vatican II priests could recall being pressurised to become priests, but all of them said that they had been 'encouraged' by family members and friends, and, in most cases, a priest they knew who had impressed them in their parish or school. Most of them also had uncles or cousins who were priests.

> My parents were very religious people and my mother had two brothers who were priests in the US. I suppose religion was very important in our parish and the whole country at that time.
>
> *Parish priest, 1960s*

> Every second house in the parish had at least one priest. It was normal and one of the first things you thought about when you were in secondary school. It was a natural thing for me to do.
>
> *Former priest, 1960s*

Most of the research participants recalled receiving visits from missionaries looking for vocations, while some school principals invited students to declare for 'church or state' in their final year. However, while the pressure was 'subtle', it was nevertheless quite effective. Five of the ten pre-Vatican II priests had initially been most attracted to the 'foreign missions' in order 'to save the world and the conversion of heathens', but all of them ultimately decided to 'go for the home mission' (Irish diocese) following discussions with priests in their school or parish.[197]

Most of these pre-Vatican II priests regarded priesthood as a 'choice' amongst a number of possible careers, such as doctor or farmer (Retired priest, 1950s). However, most of them also felt that their career options were quite restricted in the 1950s, as very few of the alternative career options appealed to them. One priest said that he wouldn't have known what to do if he hadn't been a priest because there was 'an awful lot of emigration from the country in the 1950s' (Retired priest, 1950s). Another priest considered life as a farmer but 'it just seemed such a hard life to sustain' (Parish priest, 1960s). Consequentially, most of this group of priests decided 'to give it a go and see what would happen' (Parish priest, 1960s).

Some of them chose to be priests even though they knew the life would be difficult. One priest, who thought he had a vocation to the priesthood but not a celibate priest, felt 'obliged' to accept celibacy as part of his vocation to the priesthood (Parish priest, 1960s). Others were similarly personally affected by the demands of living a celibate life. For the most part, however, these pre-Vatican II priests did not give much time considering the implications of being a priest at the time of their ordinations. One priest said he had 'not really thought it through' (Parish priest, 1960s) and another said 'it was the thing to do' (Retired priest, 1950s). For example, while they knew that 'celibacy was a condition of priesthood' they did not 'dwell on it' at the time (Parish priest, 1960s). Conversely, two priests 'knew' from the age of seven or eight that they wanted to be priests. One could see himself saying Mass 'from an early age', while the second was 'captivated' as a Mass server (Parish priest, 1960s).

6.2.2 Pre-Vatican II Priests' Views of the Ontological Status of a Priest

While they usually took their position in Irish society for granted, and most of them did not dwell very much on their clerical status, in hindsight, these pre-Vatican II priests believe that their priesthood set them apart from their parishioners by virtue of their vocation, ministry, position in the community, education, and celibate lifestyle. They wore clerical garb virtually everywhere and they had to 'act with decorum at all times' (Retired priest, 1950s). They were 'men of the cloth' and 'representatives of the Church' (Parish priest, 1960s).

> There was a time when I was a man of the cloth. I was visibly a priest at all times and places. One time, four of us went on holidays and we would go to a convent to say Mass and the four of us would put on our clerical gear and take it off when we came out. That was the way it was. You wouldn't dream of getting out of the black suit. You were in the army and you wore the boots and the regulated lifestyle until such time that you became yourself.
>
> *Parish priest, 1960s*

Four pre-Vatican II priests said that they believed that a vocation to the priesthood was generally regarded to be superior, although none of them felt superior. Three priests said that they 'knew' they were different because of the way they were treated by the people in their parish and at home. Only a priest could say Mass or administer the sacraments. He had the 'keys' to the church and parish halls, and most priests were automatically appointed as the chairman of the local GAA clubs. These were things that were generally taken for granted by these priests and part of their clerical culture (Papesh, 2004).[198] This was a culture which some priests subsequently came to regard as 'oppressive' (D'Arcy, 2006, p. 289), while others saw it as supportive (Olden, 2008). As one priest said, 'There is no getting away from it, we had the power.' It was only later in life, following Vatican II and the maturity of years, that some of these priests came to perceive priesthood in a different way that focused more on service than 'apartness'.

Most of these Vatican II priests defined their priesthood as being 'who they were' as people (Parish priest, 1960s). They had been priests for a long time and priesthood defined their lives. One priest perceived himself to be a priest 'always and forever, like Melchizedek of old' (Semi-retired priest, 1960s), regardless of the work he does or the circumstances in which he finds himself.

There is no gap between my priesthood and my work. It is just me. It is my life. I am semi-retired now but I don't feel any different to when I was more active. You do different things but I am the same person. I freely picked this vocation and He called me. A priest can't be just the things he does. It must be the indelible mark you get at priesthood.

Semi-retired priest, 1960s

None of the pre-Vatican II priests felt their priesthood was affected by falling Mass attendance or the clerical sexual abuse disclosures. They blamed the bishops for 'trying to avoid scandals at all costs' and for their being 'tarred with the one brush' (Parish priest, 1960s). One priest said that the Church had 'gone through worse and it would survive this too' (Parish priest, 1960s). As priests, they had to 'continue doing what God had called them to do' (Semi-retired priest, 1960s).

For the most part, they were not particularly concerned with the alleged conservatism of young priests, although they disagreed with the conservative shift in attitude 'if it is true' (Retired priest, 1960s). One priest, who had 'heard that some young priests were going back to a time when priests were more interested in the sacristy' thought this might be a 'passing phase' and that no priest should ever 'be afraid to profess his beliefs' (Retired priest, 1950s). Furthermore, any difference of opinion between the different generations of priests is perceived to be primarily theological, with little evidence of personal tensions between older and younger priests. Overall, they have a good degree of respect for their younger colleagues. One older priest criticised some of his own peers for not 'moving on from being sacristy priests' (Semi-retired priest, 1960s). He believes that while the sacraments are important, so too is the need for priests to work with people. Overall, this cohort of pre-Vatican II priests are sceptical that a new model of priesthood is emerging, partly because there are relatively few young priests in the Church, and partly because they imagine 'things will settle down' as the younger priests got older (Retired priests, 1950s). The two former pre-Vatican II priests have been laicised and no longer regard themselves as priests. In one case, his identity as a Catholic priest had 'reached the tipping point' when, amongst other things, he was asked to preach against the use of artificial contraception (Former priest, 1960s), while the other decided to leave 'when I fell in love' (Former priest, 1960s). Their circumstances had changed and so too did their identity as priests.

6.2.3 Pre-Vatican II Priests' Attitudes Towards the Church Magisterium[199]

As previously discussed, in chapter five, all of these priests believe that it is important to obey their bishop and that they are loyal to the institutional Church. Obedience is regarded as a 'virtue' and the culture of the pre-Vatican II Church 'programmed' these priests to obey their superiors (Parish priest, 1960s). However, legalism was so pervasive in the Church at that time that little attention was given to their promise of obedience to the bishop during the rite of ordination: 'I can't recall obedience being emphasised that much. You were told you had to take a promise of obedience when you got ordained but I don't think it was anything stronger than that' (Retired priest, 1950s). To disobey an instruction from a superior would be tantamount to going against societal and Church norms, and to risk the imposition of sanctions.

> [Everything was] very rigid but the whole system was governed by canon law, which in pre-Vatican II days loomed very large. Everybody was bound by it. I found it very restricting. You nearly lived more for the law than life. You didn't break away from the rules and as a result you missed out on life to some extent.
>
> *Retired priest, 1950s*

The Church was strictly hierarchical and these priests rarely challenged their superiors, at least not directly. Some of them also learnt to bypass Church authority on occasion by keeping their heads down and doing their own thing. Thus, while these priests accepted the hierarchy of the Church and its strict regime of rules, they did not always 'value' it. Following Vatican II, most of these priests reacted against the extreme legalism of the Church and adopted a more liberal approach to their priesthood.

6.2.4 Pre-Vatican II Priests' Views on Liturgy and Devotions

In the pre-Vatican II Church, liturgies and devotions were frequent and regulated by rubrics. Most ceremonies were conducted in Latin and often behind railings that separated the priest from the people. While some of their colleagues were regarded as being too scrupulous, fearing that they would commit a mortal sin if they didn't follow all the rules exactly as they were laid out in the rubrics, most of these priests were satisfied to 'do their best' to follow the rules. In the words of one priest, 'the rules were the rules, so that is what you had to do in those days'

(Parish priest, 1960s). Two priests said they didn't always say their breviary and they felt guilty as a result. One former priest told of how he had been travelling all day but he had been awoken by his sister, as requested by him, to finish his breviary before midnight. He was exhausted but he did what was required. One priest said that he had never considered experimenting with different liturgies or changing the wording of devotions, mainly because it never occurred to him, but also because the people were so familiar with the liturgies that they would probably report him to the bishop if he tried to change anything.

The liturgies of the pre-Vatican Church were remembered with fondness and longing by five of the older priests, although each of them also welcomed the end of legalism. One priest recalled how, on Christmas Eve, 'you had around seven hours of confession and you would be cross-eyed coming out of the box' (Parish priest, 1960s). Another said it was a 'good time' to be a priest and 'there was a great buzz giving out communion in a big church, four or five of us marching out' (Former priest, 1960s). Two priests said they 'still had a hankering after Latin in the Mass' (Semi-retired priests, 1960s). It was a time of certainties and everyone 'knew where they stood' (Retired priest, 1950s). One former priest said that he had 'glorified being on the pedestal' as a priest and that he 'missed the certainties' of the pre-Vatican II Church.

> The Devotions were unbelievable, the Novenas were thronged with people. Priests had enormous swades of people to get through for communion, so that they had to cleave their way through like a great harvester going through a harvest field. It was non-stop for confession and the same for communion. The priests had to do everything. There was an altar rail and the priest behind it and the laity shuffling their way up to get the Bread of Life. That was the Church.
>
> *Parish priest, 1960s*

6.2.5 Pre-Vatican II Priests' Views of Theology
Their theology was underpinned by strict legalism that varied little over the years. With the exception of three former academics, these priests were not too familiar with Church theology when they were ordained and two of them said they had 'learnt all they knew from the *Penny Catechism*' (Semi-retired priest, 1960s). They were taught theology in Latin and most of them recalled their lectures to be boring and unchanging from year to

year. For the most part, they said that their job was to inform people what the Church taught and to forgive them when they sinned. Accordingly, they accepted its precepts without any fuss or discussion. One exception to this was the rule forbidding attendance at funerals of Protestant friends. One priest regarded this practice to be wrong but nevertheless, a rule he had to obey.

6.2.6 Pre-Vatican II Priests' Attitudes Towards Celibacy

As previously discussed in chapter four, all of these priests accept that celibacy is an essential part of their priesthood, something they had to accept if they were to become priests. However, with one exception, they also disagreed with the imposition of mandatory celibacy. Some felt it was a Church discipline that had been imposed on priests to keep them under control, while others said it was introduced for practical rather than theological reasons. None of these priests would object to working with a celibate homosexual priest, although two of them had not 'seriously' considered the matter and one former priest would feel a 'bit awkward' (Parish priest, 1960s). The general view was that, provided the priest was celibate 'like the rest of us' there would not be a problem.

6.2.7 Pre-Vatican II Priests' Views on Vatican II

Significant changes occurred in the lives of these pre-Vatican II priests following Vatican II. Five of the younger pre-Vatican II priests embraced the council, with most of the remainder 'welcoming' the end of legalism, but they were also somewhat concerned about the loss of certainty that had characterised their Church and priesthood before Vatican II. The big change for all of these priests was that 'legalism was gone from the Church' (Retired priest, 1950s) and they were no longer controlled by canon lawyers and 'pernickety' Church rules (Semi-retired priests, 1960s). However, Vatican II did not change the Church overnight and neither did it change the lives of these priests straight away. The oldest priest in this group said, for example, that 'nothing too much changed following Vatican II' and that he felt he was 'doing much the same thing afterwards, apart from saying Mass in English and some nuns stopped wearing the habit' (Retired priest, 1950s). Another said that the biggest change following Vatican II was that he had to shave and make himself presentable for Mass because now he had to face the people. Another said that apart from noting that there were sixteen documents in Vatican II and 'only reading tiny snitches of them at Mass' (Semi-retired priest, 1960s), change was slow to happen because his Archbishop, John Charles McQuaid was against it.

> I don't remember much about Vatican II at all. John Charles wasn't allowing much to happen and then only inch-by-inch. The vernacular wasn't allowed for a long time and then he allowed the 'I confess' in English. There was nothing allowed until he said it. The biggest change was a few years following Vatican II when they started putting the Mass into English.
>
> *Semi-retired priest, 1960s*

Three of the older pre-Vatican II priests were critical of Vatican II for moving too fast and trying to change too much. They continue to value order, obedience, and Church traditions, and they are nostalgic for the full churches and certainty of the pre-Vatican II Church. They believe that the Church has 'lost the plot' following Vatican II, leading to a 'lack of balance' in the Church (Retired priest, 1950s). Consequentially, they approve of the conservative shift that was introduced during the papacies of John Paul II and Benedict XVI. However, they are also less subservient and more pastorally minded than they would have been in a pre-Vatican II Church. None of them would, for example, ever refuse Holy Communion to people in second relationships, although three priests said they would insist on speaking with the couple first to 'make sure' they understood the Church's position.

The younger pre-Vatican II priests found the mid-1960s to be 'a most exciting time with great hope and enthusiasm for the future' (Parish priest, 1960s). The opening of Vatican II coincided with the launch of television in Ireland, making the experience even more 'exhilarating' (Parish priest, 1960s). They had no sense of the change that would come with Vatican II when they entered the seminary in the late 1950s and early 1960s: 'The Church was very conservative and regulated at that time' (Parish priest, 1960s). Consequentially, the new theology and the young theologians gave one priest 'great life' and 'fire in his belly' to share this 'vision of faith' (Parish priest, 1960s). Over the course of a number of decades, the identities of these five younger priests were effectively transformed. They came to see their priesthood primarily in terms of service in addition to sacramental duties.

Priests are called to be servants and Christian. The sacramental Church is part of who we are but it can't be the sole focus.

Parish priest, 1960s

Priesthood is a combination of service and sacraments and I believe the strongest quality is serving the people, looking after them, especially when they are sick, bereaved or dying. The priest is there to serve the people but one would never think that looking at the structures that exist in the Church.

Parish priest, 1960s

Many of the restrictions on their lifestyles disappeared following Vatican II. Ireland and the Irish Church became more open and less restrictive. In the cases of four priests, their new vision of priesthood was informed by travel to other countries for study and ministry, together with a 'great interest' in reading and talking to people from different faiths (Parish priest, 1960s). Their world had 'opened and expanded' with Vatican II and there was 'no turning back' (Parish priest, 1960s). However, it took some years before they were able to 'release' themselves from the 'legacy of clericalism', which they feel many of their colleagues have not yet managed (Parish priest, 1960s). When they were ordained, the younger pre-Vatican II priests had accepted that celibacy was an inherent part of priesthood, but now they believe that celibacy should be optional. Three of them thought that optional celibacy would be introduced following Vatican II. They also came to disagree with the Church's stance on women priests, pre-marital sex, contraception, and mortal sin. In brief, their priesthood has become more pastoral and liberal.

It is all very well insisting on the ideal but it is not that rare for a child to be born before marriage nowadays, but that is probably the best the couple can do. You have to encourage people and hope they will work it out by themselves. Who can tell what is in their hearts or if they have been to confession. Judge not and you shall not be judged.

Parish priest, 1960s

The transition between cultic and servant-leader priest was not easy and some of them remain 'divided' in their loyalties to the old and the new.

Our generation is divided. There are two Joes[200] in me, one that has lived for years in a very conservative Church and is bound by it, and the other that is seeking to be more free and independent, and to say what needs to be done. There are a lot of people like me in my generation. They recognise that we should be greater but we are tied down by the baggage we carry. My regret is that I didn't speak my mind more often and yet here I am in my seventies and I am more liberated than I ever was. We are getting old and there is not that much time left to give a stronger push for the Church.

Parish priest, 1960s

While they learnt to question Church authority on some issues, they have difficulties with other issues, particularly divorce and people living together in second relationships. Marriage is a sacrament and, as one priest said, 'you don't want to go messing with the sacraments' (Parish priest, 1960s). Conversely, he would have no problem in believing that a group of people could legitimately celebrate the Eucharist without a priest present if they did so in the name of Jesus.

Obedience and loyalty are important virtues for this group and they would be very reluctant to speak out in public against their bishop or Rome, especially in matters of doctrine. Conversely, they are not always willing to accept change without question. Most of them, for example, questioned the wisdom of introducing new wording for the Mass, which one priest said would 'just make you despair'. Three of them were angry that Rome should consider the introduction of archaic language in the Mass as being more important than the crisis in the Church and priesthood, suggesting that it was reminiscent of 'tidying deckchairs when the Titanic was sinking' (Parish priest, 1960s). They are unhappy with the Missal changes because it 'confirmed what they suspected', that the Church is returning to a more conservative stance. However, it remains to be seen if they will follow through on their threats to 'say something' when the changes are introduced: 'I am never outside the Church in my pulpit but I might when they introduce the new wording of the Mass – it is crazy' (Parish priest, 1960s).

In summary, the pre-Vatican II priests initially regarded their priesthood in cultic terms, as this was the prevailing model of priest-hood when they were in the seminary. Following their ordinations, they were 'set apart' from the people by their superior vocation, celibate lifestyle, ministry and clerical garb, and they were placed on a pedestal by their parishioners and society. They were the centre of their communities and perceived to be men of substance and power, but they were also subject to the constraints imposed by a hierarchical and structured Church. Obedience was regarded as a virtue and their lives were largely governed by canon law and the norms of a strictly hierarchical Church. Their liturgies were regulated by detailed rubrics, and their theology was static and underpinned by legalism. They accepted the discipline of mandatory celibacy as part of priesthood, although not necessarily a discipline they all approved of. In brief, they were obedient, theologically conservative, ontologically distinctive, dutiful and institutionalised. Over time, as the Church and priesthood became more liberal, so too did many of these men. The younger priests in this cohort embraced the spirit of Vatican II and the emerging servant-leader model of priesthood. However, their transition remains incomplete and some of them are still struggling and bound by the baggage of a conservative pre-Vatican II Church.

6.3 HOW VATICAN II PRIESTS UNDERSTAND THEIR PRIESTHOOD[201]
6.3.1 *Vatican II Priests' Views of their Vocation to the Priesthood*
The late 1960s and early 1970s was a time when ordinations peaked in the Irish Church, and Irish seminaries attracted relatively large numbers of students. Priesthood continued to be a respected career for many Irish men, although there were many more opportunities than was the case in the 1950s. Most of the Vatican II research participants said they had considered another career, such as medicine, teaching or banking, before 'finally opting' for priesthood (Parish priest, 1970s). While none of them felt pressurised into this choice, all of them said that family, friends and local priests supported them once they decided to 'try it out' (Parish priest, 1970s). One priest said that his father had made only one remark when he told him he was interested in becoming a priest: 'If you don't like it, come home' (Former priest, 1980s). He felt that this short comment was 'just the right thing to say' and he knew his father was behind him.

At least half of these priests had an uncle or cousin who was a priest. In hindsight, one priest described the support he received from his family and community as 'psychological channelling' (Parish priest, 1970s). The majority of priests also said that they had found support for their decision in prayer. Like their older counterparts who had grown up in a Catholic country, priesthood was 'natural' for these priests (Parish priest, 1980s). One priest said he had 'kind of fallen into priesthood' (Parish priest, 1970s). Others suggested the same had happened to them.

> I don't think there was ever one moment when I said I had a vocation. My whole background had such a lot of prayer. My mom and dad were both great people for prayer and in the 1970s there was a lot of prayer in the community. My entering the seminary was kind of normal. It was in the atmosphere, in the ground, and in one sense, I fell into it rather than deciding anything.
>
> *Parish priest, 1970s*

Most of this Vatican II group were 'full of idealism' when they decided to become priests and six of them had initially considered a missionary vocation. While five of them did eventually work for a number of years on the missions, they did so as diocesan priests when they were persuaded to become diocesan priests following a 'talk' with a priest or bishop. Their reasons for considering the priesthood were similar to those mentioned by the pre-Vatican II priests. All of them felt 'a call from God'. Other motivating factors included, 'I felt blessed by God for the gift of priesthood' (Parish priest, 1970s), a desire to do 'good' and 'wanting to help people' (Parish priest, 1970s), a 'call' from God (multiple respondents), it was an 'attractive thing to do at the time' (Parish priest, 1980s), to 'convert the world' (Parish priest, 1980s), and to live a life that was 'holy' (Parish priest, 1980s). Some priests had quite specific reasons for considering the priesthood but over time their sense of vocation had changed. For example, one priest was initially prompted to consider the priesthood when he met a priest who worked in the same town as his favourite football club. While he did not go to this diocese in the UK, he still remembers how the thought of combining priesthood and a love of football was 'just perfect' (Parish priest, 1970s). He subsequently decided to study for an Irish diocese and to play golf instead of premiership football!

Most of this generation of priests said that their prayer lives and a belief in Jesus Christ were at the heart of their vocations and that this was constant throughout their lives. It was a life they could believe in and one that would make a difference. Two priests said they were led to believe that the vocation of a priest was 'somehow better' and 'on a higher plane' to other Christian vocations (Parish priests, 1980s). Conversely, the others did not feel this way, stating that Vatican II taught them that 'there was only one Christian vocation' and priesthood was one 'specific form' of this vocation (Parish priest, 1970s). Two Vatican II priests regarded their vocation to be a 'vocation within a vocation', insofar as their vocation to the priesthood was prompted by their love of Our Lady and their involvement in the Legion of Mary.

> I have always seen my vocation to the priesthood as a calling within a calling. Both are specific vocations. If I look back on my life, I was reared in a good Catholic family and I had a good Catholic education but it wasn't enough. It was at that crucial time that Our Lady intervened through her Legion of Mary; she took my hand and led me to faith in God, faith in Jesus, to the apostolate and to the priesthood.
>
> *Parish priest, 1980s*

Both of these priests were quite conservative when they entered the seminary and they largely adopted the cultic model of priesthood. They loved ritual, accepted Church teachings and governance without question, and both of them regarded celibacy to be an essential part of priesthood. One of them initially found it difficult to communicate with women or to trust lay people in his parish. Over time, however, one of these priest's identities shifted and he is now very much in the mode of a servant-leader priest. He explained that he is 'not sure' why he changed but that it was partly because of 'theological difficulties, celibacy issues, and the way the bishops handled the abuse situation' (Parish priest, 1980s). He recalls that he was 'very conservative and that he had a tendency to spiritualise everything, but no longer.

> I thought my role was to administer the sacraments but now I see myself as the centre of a community. I began to have doubts; how the hell can you believe in a wandering preacher 2,000 years ago and how can he say he is God. My biggest problem is anger with clericalism and the way the Church is run. My response was to do my own thing.
>
> *Parish priest, 1980s*

Five of these Vatican II priests felt that they had a vocation but not necessarily to a celibate priesthood. One priest who is in a long-term gay relationship believes that God called him to the priesthood, knowing he was gay. He 'never believed in celibacy' and he does not believe that God would have wanted him to be celibate. He sees his vocation as 'a vision to try and bring the Church, kicking and screaming if necessary, where it will be a small community of caring and dedicated people, where everyone, gay and straight, are welcome' (Parish priest, 1980s). Another priest who had 'difficulties with the whole concept, that to celebrate the Eucharist you had to be a celibate male', nevertheless accepted this 'sacrifice' as a condition of his priesthood' (Parish priest, 1980s). Many other priests in this cohort felt the same way towards celibacy (see chapter four).

Most Vatican II priests said they felt called by God and that they just had to 'try it out', no matter how unsure they were. One priest described the feeling like 'a toothache', while another said the main reason he went to Maynooth was to 'get the monkey off his shoulders'.

> If I had a plan for my life at sixteen I would have invented a cure for cancer but I also felt that God too may have had a plan for me and while he might have got it wrong I would have to correct him. I discovered that God was suggesting to my spirit that I would lead my life through serving him in the priesthood. I fundamentally disagreed with his shortness of vision, so to help him out I went to Maynooth, but not to be a priest. I went to get the monkey off my shoulders. I went to get that settled so that I would be free to live my life and not feel guilty that God had been disappointed in me or that I had manipulated God in any way. I got ordained but it was a long process. I discovered the ability to say no, so that I could more freely say yes. It was an evolution. I definitely did get a sense of being chosen and that has never left me.
>
> *Parish priest, 1970s*

6.3.2 Vatican II Priests' Views of the Ontological Status of a Priest

These Vatican II servant-leader priests believe that priesthood is primarily about service, and establishing relationships with people within the context of the Church. They believe that their role is to show compassion to people where they are 'broken' by life. Most of them welcomed the transition in priesthood that had occurred following Vatican II; from a cultic, sacramental priesthood to one where they are essentially servants of the people. Their role is to help people in their spiritual search, a *'saggart a rún*,[202] if you will' (Parish priest, 1970s). The sacraments continue to be important for them, and some priests said that saying Mass was the most important part of their day, but not in isolation from their service to people. They do not distinguish between their priestly identity and the rest of their lives. Their professional identity as priests defines their personal and religious identities. One priest said, 'It is who I am' (Parish priest, 1970s), while another said that his identity was 'very much tied up with my whole being' (Parish priest, 1980s). A number of priests said that their identities are 'rooted' in their parishes: 'You become part of the community in which you live and you belong to the people of your parish' (Parish priest, 1970s).

Their pastoral identity is reinforced at diocesan level. One bishop, for example, often refers to a priest by the name of his parish rather than the priest's own name. Consequently, some of his priests do the same and everybody knows to whom they are referring. However, while their ministry is important in framing their vocation, it does not determine their sense of priesthood. Most of this group said they feel their priesthood is more 'authentic' in a pastoral situation; however, they all came to realise that it doesn't matter where they minister, that their identity as priests is 'an awareness that they are doing God's work, where you are representing the person of Christ to people' (Parish priest, 1980s). For example, one priest who had originally decided against entering a religious order because he did not wish to teach, subsequently spent most of his life teaching in the diocesan college. He was initially very disappointed but eventually he came to see it as ironic and he, like others in a similar situation, came to accept that 'this is where Jesus wants me to be as a priest'.

Three Vatican II priests disapprove of what they perceive as the conservatism of some younger priests and their tendency to become sacristy priests. They believe that this is the wrong direction for priesthood and the wrong direction for the Church. One priest was critical of his curate for not wanting to get involved in 'ordinary' parish duties, such as visiting schools or taking care of the parish hall. Another felt that his curate was trying to 'push' traditional prayers in the parish, and another was made to feel a little uneasy when he encountered a prospective seminarian who was 'more clerical than any priest ought to be'.

Priests are by and large conservative and younger priests are even more conservative. They are very conservative in their thinking, very black and white, and they are dressed up to the nines, and there is smoke everywhere at Mass. My own curate has more vestments than God. I find they can also be uncaring and dismissive. They are not good at visiting the sick or that kind of stuff. They mark out what they will do within their own square, which is generally what I call 'sacristy priests'. They are good at that but not if they are asked to go to a GAA or rugby club function.

Parish priest, 1970s

One priest was highly critical of the younger priest who took over from him when he was appointed to a new parish, for 'dismantling' the parish council and 'taking back control' of the parish (Parish priest, 1980s). Another priest criticised his curate for his intolerance towards people's difficulties and his 'hang-ups' with people who were in second relationships or who drank too much (Parish priest, 1970s). Two other priests had difficulties with younger priests who wanted to say the Latin Mass and who were caught up in 'the ritual and ceremony of the Church' (Parish priests, 1970s/1980s). Ultimately, many of the Vatican II priests are critical of their younger counterparts, not because of their actions or ideological stance, but because they fear a return to a Church they hoped had been 'left behind' before Vatican II.

However, for the most part, this cohort of Vatican II priests is unsure if a new paradigm of priesthood is emerging, since they know that not all young priests are conservative. Some of them said that they themselves had been 'overzealous' at times when they were younger but that they had 'grown out of it' over time. Two priests put the difference down to an age gap between curates and parish priests. Whatever their views or fears of a return to a cultic priesthood, there was little evidence of animosity from this group towards younger priests.

6.3.3 Vatican II Priests' Attitudes Towards Church Magisterium

As previously discussed in chapter five, most Vatican II priests are loyal to but not necessarily subservient to their superiors. They believe that Vatican II was a 'missed opportunity' for the Irish Church and that 'unfortunately' the Church is still a hierarchical Church, 'with structures that haven't changed' (Parish priest, 1980s). They believe that lay people have not been empowered because the Church 'likes control too much' and they 'ran the show the way they wanted' (Parish priest, 1980s). While the Vatican II document, *Dogmatic Constitution on the Church (Lumen Gentium)* had focused on how the laity would be involved in the Church, 'this had not happened to any real extent and the Church remained very much controlled from the top' (Parish priest, 1980s).

> We lost a great opportunity in Ireland for Vatican II. We didn't implement it in the spirit it was intended. By and large we are still a hierarchical Church and structures haven't changed.
>
> *Parish priest, 1970s*

> The sense of Church that was promoted over the years, to pay up, pray up and shut up, is still a good description of how the Church operates. I am really disappointed with the failure of Vatican II, it just hasn't happened. The past forty years is a failed opportunity in the Church because the Church went back in on itself.
>
> *Parish Priest, 1980s*

The Vatican II priests are generally loyal to Church teaching, insofar as most of them said they would always give the official Church position on issues if they were asked. However, they have also a very strong pastoral sense, where they believe that there are few absolutes in the lives of their parishioners. They are against rules for the sake of rules. According to one priest, 'life is not all squares and absolutes; there are lots of circles and tangents too' (Parish priest, 1970s). In the past, people lived in a 'black and white world' where they were told what to believe and how to live (Parish priest, 1970s). They do not believe this is the case any longer and instead they would advocate a more human, pastoral approach to moral problems. When they sometimes break the letter of the law in favour of its spirit, they usually do so discreetly in the tradition of many priests who came before them. One priest recalled how his father wondered if he should attend the funeral of his Protestant neighbour at a time when this was forbidden by the Church. His parish priest told him to go to the funeral and say his prayers for his friend but 'not to broadcast it'. This is how this priest has lived his priesthood since then – 'a measure of generosity and friendship whilst bringing people with me as far as I can' (Parish priest, 1970s).

Another priest said that he and many of this counterparts had been taught to view matters flexibly, with 'broad mental reservations', where he would 'couch things in such a way that people would get the import of what he meant without having to actually say the words' (Parish priest, 1970s). None of the research participants in this cohort has ever refused Holy Communion to a person, even in situations where they knew or suspected a person was not in 'full union' with the Church.

> If you walk up to me for the Eucharist I cannot judge your soul at that moment and I would not even try to. If I can help you and you come to me privately I will tell you what the Church teaches but I am not going to refuse anyone Holy Communion. While I understand that any club or organisation, like a golf club, has to have rules, that doesn't mean it is applied black and white wherever you go. I have never had any real problems with Church teachings.
>
> *Parish priest, 1970s*

They believe that they cannot tell if the person is in a 'state of grace' or not, and 'neither should we be able to'. Furthermore, they believe the Church should be more open to people who are divorced and in second relationships, and to people in homosexual relationships.[203] They have boundaries in what they will and won't do as priests. Like some of their counterparts ordained before the Second Vatican Council, the sacramental nature of marriage is problematic for priests when dealing with 'irregular relationships'; however, 'it is nothing that can't be resolved with compassion' (Parish priest, 1980s). Contraception is a non-issue for these priests and none of them would ever preach on it. This does not mean, however, that they disagree with *Humanae Vitae*, and one priest said it was a 'wonderful document' (Parish priest, 1980s) that is a 'guide for people to make up their own minds, but nothing more than a guide'.

> You don't categorise a person as a problem and only see a problem. I believe the Church has to be open and I believe on the pastoral level it is open to people who are gay, to people who have abortions, to people who use contraception, but it must always set the ideal. The tragedy is that the ideal sometimes becomes an end in itself instead of an aspiration. The Church must love people because we are all sinners.
>
> *Parish priest, 1980s*

6.3.4 Vatican II Priests' Views of Liturgy and Devotions

Liturgies and devotions are important to these priests and most of them enjoy liturgies, especially when they are creative. One former priest, for example, recalls feeling 'really enriched and nourished' when there was 'exposition and celebration of the Eucharist, and experimental liturgies around the cross' (Former priest, 1980s). On another occasion, he held a special service for his parishioners, which 'used incense, gave Holy Communion under both kinds, and which had a great core liturgy'. He felt that it was the 'liturgical highlight' of his ministry. Others said that they tried to be creative and it helped when liturgy groups assisted them. Two priests just felt tired and did 'what was required'. Another two priests said that the sacraments were 'meeting places' that enabled the priest to communicate Christ's love and message to the people in their parish.

> The paraphernalia of the sacraments is all right but it is only the machinery to meet people, whether it is their joys at baptism or marriage, or their sorrows at funerals, or sickness, it is people and community and belonging that matters. That is what keeps me going. You get a lot of life from the people and they get life from you.
>
> *Parish priest, 1970s*

One priest, who loved the 'mystery of the Mass' contrasted the solemnity that surrounded the High Mass when he was an altar server with the more personal liturgies of his own parish: 'There was a great clerical caste and when someone important died in your parish, they would hold a High Mass in Latin and in black robes, with incense everywhere' (Parish priest, 1980s). His preference is for the more personal liturgies.

6.3.5 Vatican II Priests' Views of Theology

Theology changed significantly when this group were in the seminary. This was a time when 'the Latin tomes and elderly lecturers were gradually replaced by new ideas and energetic theologians' (Parish priest, 1970s). Theirs was a more flexible theology that allowed for theological differences; ecumenism, liberation theology, and an assumption of vocational equality. One priest who was ordained in the 1980s said that the theology he 'came out of' was liberation theology, which said, let's look at the issues in the Church and see what we can do. There were a lot of things we had not addressed before, like morality and the sexual teaching of the Church, the place of women in the Church, the need to de-ritualise and de-clutter liturgies, and the reorganisation of the governing system of the Church.

Parish priest, 1980s

In response to criticism from diverse sources in recent years, a number of priests accepted that their theology is quite 'relativistic' and 'almost Protestant' but that is 'not a problem' (Parish priests, 1980s). For example, one priest, in reference to a comment by a journalist that the Association of Priests in Ireland was comprised of liberal Protestants, said that 'maybe a bit of Protestantism would do us good' (Parish priest, 1980s).

This is a generation of priests who want to make the world more just and the Church more Christian. Most of them disagree with the Church's position on contraceptives, homosexuality, and women priests. However, not all priests of this generation are quite so liberal, and two priests disagreed with women priests. Others were conflicted in how to deal with people in second relationships because marriage is a sacrament, but they did not agree with treating people in second relationships as 'second-class citizens' (Parish priests, 1980s).

As was the case with some pre-Vatican II priests, four Vatican II priests took particular exception to the proposed introduction of what they perceived as archaic language into the new translation of the Roman Missal. They are angry at this development because they believe it represents a return to a more conservative Church that 'seems to be saying that Vatican II was a terrible mistake' (Parish priests, 1970s/ 1980s). Three of them said they would have to consider their public ministries if and when these changes are made:

> One of the things that is niggling me, which will make me uncomfortable, is the publication of the new Roman Missal. If we are forced to use this archaic language, I will feel very uncomfortable with that and I will have to say to myself, if I can't do this and do it with some sense of belief, comfort, feeling it is part of who I am as a priest, then I will have to just turn and do something else. At the moment, the only thing I feel uncomfortable with as a priest is the certainty. If all this certainty is being pushed upon us and we are told this is the style of priest you have to be if you want to be part of the Church, that will make me so rebellious I will have to have a good chat with myself and do something different.
>
> *Parish priest, 1980s*

One Vatican II priest said that he would consider becoming a minister in the Church of Ireland if he was 'made to do things he did not wish to do' (Parish priest, 1980s), such as saying a Latin Mass, or possibly the imposition of new wording in the Mass. He realises that this would be a radical change in his priestly identity but also one that would allow him to stay in ministry and give time to his prayer life.[204]

6.3.6 Vatican II Priests' Views Towards Celibacy

As previously noted in chapter four, mandatory celibacy is problematic for this generation of priests. With one exception, they disagree with mandatory celibacy and they do not believe that it is an inherent part of priesthood. Their attitude towards celibacy is very similar to the older generation of priests, who, for the most part, reject mandatory celibacy and regard it as having more to do with control than theology. In summary, the Vatican II research participants were formed as priests when a servant-leader model of priesthood prevailed in the Catholic Church. Accordingly, they have experienced the highs and lows of priesthood, where they were initially enthused and liberated by the spirit and organisational changes promised by Vatican II, only to be frustrated by a perceived lack of progress in the implementation of these changes and a conservative shift in the Church. They fear that their vision of the Church and the priesthood is being replaced by a conservative shift that coincided with the papacies of John Paul II and Benedict XVI. In contrast to their cultic counterparts, their approach is more pastoral than sacramental, and more flexible than regimented, although they are reluctant to contravene the sacraments by, for example, blessing a second relationship. While they are loyal to the Church and committed to their priesthood, they believe that the Church should be less hierarchical and more inclusive. They would prefer to have optional celibacy and more tolerance towards people on the margins of the Church. They are reluctant to judge people and none of them would refuse Holy Communion to anyone who approached them at the altar. In spite of their opposition to some Church teachings and practices, they have remained true to their personal beliefs and the demands of priesthood by keeping their opposition hidden and adopting a pragmatic approach to their ministry.

6.4 How Post-Vatican II Priests Understand their Priesthood

6.4.1 Post-Vatican II Priests' Views of their Vocation to the Priesthood

The nine post-Vatican II priests were all ordained in the past two decades, during the papacy of John Paul II. This was a time of decline for the Church on many fronts and vocations to the priesthood dropped sharply. However, while there was less support for the Church in Irish society, this cohort of post-Vatican II priests was supported by their families, friends and people they knew at home when they announced they were going into the seminary. Their reasons for wanting to be priests were similar to those of previous generations. Most attributed their vocation to 'a call from God'. One priest said he felt 'completely humbled by God' to have been given the 'gift of priesthood' through prayer to Our Lady (Curate, 2000s). Other motivating factors included, 'wanting to help people' (Curate, 1990s), 'a question of faith' (Curate, 1990s), 'a sense of duty and obligation' (Curate, 2000s) and 'a desire to give' themselves to God (Curate, 2000s).

> I suppose the whole idea of being a priest was something I felt was an expression of my faith and a feeling that I had a role to share that faith. I am not the answer to the Church's problems but I know this is my vocation and what I should be doing with my life. I am comfortable with it and it is who I am.
>
> *Curate, 2000s*

A number of post-Vatican II priests said that they had been inspired by the theology and general conservative outlook of Pope John Paul II and Benedict XVI. Four priests feel that their vocations are connected to the Church and that it is more than a personal vocational journey that depended on their making a specific choice. Consequently, they see their vocations as different to that of lay people. Theirs is a sacramental priesthood, whose identity is rooted in Christ. One priest, for example, said that he felt his vocation was 'in some way connected to the Church, with the people in the parish, and his bishop' (Curate, 2000s). Others said something similar and suggested that if the Church were to change significantly, then so too would their vocations. One priest, for example, said that while he could accept changes in Church discipline to allow married priests, he could not cope with women priests because it involved a sacrament. This is a view that is also shared by some priests in the other cohorts.

If they ordained women I would leave. I would be very uncomfortable
if the Church changed its mind on things that are absolute.

Curate, 2000s

Five priests mentioned a piece of scripture that had inspired them to
become priests, while some said they had been inspired by the lives of
saints and priests who were 'heroes' (Curate, 2000s). One priest spoke
of how his vocation had developed with his spirituality and interior life.
Three priests said their vocation had come to fruition following a
pilgrimage to a Marian shrine (Lourdes and Medjugorje). One priest,
who had not previously been particularly religious, recalled how an
impromptu pilgrimage to Medjugorje had resulted in a mystical
experience[205] or locution[206] in which he 'definitely got an awareness that
he was being called to the priesthood' (Curate, 2000s).

> For some reason, there was just this desire to go to Medjugorje. Towards
> the end of the first week I had what you might call a bit of an experience
> of God. In that experience I definitely got an awareness that He was
> calling me to the priesthood. It was not seeing any visions at all. It was
> an interior experience or what theologians would call a locution that was
> based on a voice, that was very gentle and authoritative, calling me to
> the priesthood. Again I would emphasise its gentleness and warmth, a
> sense of truth behind it. The second locution was based on an interior
> image where I saw a beautiful area of light and I was being called out of
> darkness to this beautiful area of light, with this voice – 'think about the
> priesthood, think about the priesthood'. This thing happened one night
> when I was trying to fall asleep but I am aware it was not a dream.
>
> *Curate, 2000s*

He, like many of the other priests in this study, said that he fought
the urge to be a priest, because he wanted to get married and have a
family, and because he was unsure if he truly had a vocation.

Two post-Vatican II priests had been uncertain about their vocation
and they had entered the seminary to 'get rid of a nagging doubt'
(Curates, 1990s). Another two priests said that they had 'no sense' of
Church when they went into the seminary but decided to give the
priesthood 'a try' because of a 'feeling' they had been called by God:
'Every year I went back to Maynooth to get it out of my system and I
nearly hoped and prayed that someone in Maynooth would say I wasn't
suitable. The discernment process was agony really and I laboured over

it' (Curate, 1990s). Conversely, five post-Vatican II priests said they had 'always known' from an early age that they were going to be priests and that it was something they had always 'felt comfortable with'.

> My vocation story goes back as far as I can remember. I always wanted to be a priest, even before I went to school. I pretended to say Mass and when I was an altar server, and I loved dressing up in the soutane and surplice. It was very exciting being involved, especially during the big feasts of Christmas and Easter.
>
> *Curate, 2000s*

One former priest, who is gay, felt his vocation was defined and ultimately destroyed by his sexual orientation. He believes he has a vocation to the priesthood but because he could not live a life of celibacy, he felt he had to leave the priesthood. This was all the more difficult for him to accept, because he personally knew a bishop and some priests who were closet gays and publicly hypocritical in their opposition to gay priests. When he told his bishop why he was leaving, he got a 'very strong vibe from him' and he was given 'a hug and a kiss, which no bishop should give anybody'. He, like two other former priests in this cohort, believes that they had a vocation to the priesthood, but 'no longer'. Their experience in the priesthood, and particularly its leaving, have led them to feel distant from the Church, with the result that they no longer attend Mass regularly.

One former post-Vatican II priest chose to become a minister in the Church of Ireland because it more closely reflected his identity as a minister and Christian. He felt that he was 'always quite liberal' in his theology and he could not countenance the fact that the Catholic Church seemed to 'place belief in the Blessed Trinity on the same level as contraception'. While he had questions before his ordination to the Catholic priesthood, he 'felt very strongly that he was called to the priesthood'. Ultimately, he became disillusioned and demoralised with the 'hypocrisy' of some priests and his lack of acceptance of some Church teachings. He is now 'extremely happy' in his ministry, where his priesthood is regarded as a job rather than a sacrament. In hindsight, he believes that he was called to priesthood 'but not exclusively to the Catholic priesthood'.

6.4.2 Post-Vatican II Priests' Views of the Ontological Status of Priesthood
Orthodoxy is, perhaps, the principal defining characteristic of this generation of post-Vatican II priests. They value orthodoxy in a wide range of areas in the Church, especially dogma and liturgy. They love and are committed to the Catholic Church and they have a strong respect for their bishops and the pope. Most of them said that they had been inspired by the theology and writings of Pope John Paul II, which they believe represents a legitimate reinterpretation of Church teachings following the 'imbalance' that was created by Vatican II (Curate, 2000s). However, they are not against everything that happened following Vatican II. For example, they are happy to say the 'new Mass' and some of them 'hope for a time when the Church will be more democratic' (Curate, 2000s).

One of the criticisms levelled against this generation of priests is that they are sacristy priests who are primarily interested in administering the sacraments to the detriment of pastoral activities. The present study suggests this is the case for some younger priests but not all of them. Three priests said that service and sacraments are both important dimensions of priesthood. One priest described his priesthood as 'a service thing' (Curate, 1990s), while another priest believes that 'ultimately priesthood is about service, service through sacraments' (Curate, 2000s). He feels that 'every sacrament is evangelical' and he uses baptism, weddings and funerals as 'an opportunity to minister to people in some way' (Curate, 2000s). However, his service is done within a 'faith dimension', which is different to the 'call of a social worker' (Curate, 2000s). One post-Vatican II priest thought the alleged conservatism of younger priests was exaggerated:

> I think there are definitely some young priests who are conservative but not as much as some older priests might think. Some lads are very much into the sacramental Mass and stuff but most of us think revising the Missal is silly and there are not many of us floating around in soutanes or saying Mass in Latin. One priest I know is very trendy like that but it is only skin deep and not the core of his being. It is like being into Gothic art or Chopin and I don't think he imposes his views on people. Sometimes he will float around in a soutane, but maybe he will wear a pair of shorts and flip-flops the next day.
>
> *Curate, 1990s*

Two post-Vatican II priests admitted that they were primarily attracted to the sacramental side of priesthood when deciding to become priests. For them, priesthood has a 'sacramental focus' (Curate, 2000s) and the celebration of the sacraments is very important.

For the most part, they do not see a new type of priest emerging in the Irish Church and neither do they feel cut off from their older colleagues. They feel they are just 'defending the Church they are in now' and they are likely to be 'just like the priest who came before them when they get older' (Curate, 1990s). They believe that change is a natural part of any organisation and their role is to help ensure 'we don't lose the important bits' (Curate, 1990s). One priest thought that most young priests are 'just going through a phase' (Curate, 2000s), while another said this trend was no different to the 'fear' of change in previous generations of priests who had not wanted anything to change (Curate, 1990s). One post-Vatican II priest thought that too much 'fuss' was being made about the tendency for young priests to wear ostentatious clerical garb. However, he also acknowledges that priesthood is 'moving towards sacristy priests' and that some of his peers have been drawn into the priesthood because it offers them certainty 'in a world that is so uncertain' and that they will 'cling to this certainty for dear life' (Curate, 1990s). One priest admitted being a little worried when he recalled conversations with classmates in the seminary about the 'number of tassels on a stole and stuff like that' (Curate, 1990s). Another spoke of how 'his heart sank' at ordinations when he saw the priest and Mass servers 'caught up' in how they should hold their hands (Curate, 1990s). However, the biggest source of tension between these priests and their older counterparts has more to do with practical issues than theological divisions. A number of them complained that they or their counterparts were not allowed to do what they wanted by their parish priest or bishop. One parish priest was judged to be 'intolerable' and unwilling to listen, while a bishop was described as a 'man without a vision' (Curate, 2000s).

6.4.3 Post-Vatican II Priests' Attitudes Towards the Church Magisterium
As previously discussed in chapter five, this cohort of priests is committed to the Church and they value the hierarchical nature of the Church. This does not mean that they believe their superiors to be

without fault or that they are against change. One priest, for example, hopes that the Church will become more the 'Diarmuid Martin Church' where 'there is a stronger sense of lay collaboration, of lay people working in parishes, and lay people ministering informally to lay people' (Curate, 2000s). However, he also acknowledges that the Church is different from other organisations, insofar as it doesn't have a 'manifesto' and that it moves 'frustratingly' slowly. One priest criticised his bishop for 'refusing to listen' to his priests, while most were highly critical of the way the bishops handled the clerical abuse cases (Curate, 2000s). Ultimately, they have a very high regard for authority and they do not see the value of criticising Church leadership. However, while they are obedient, they also recognise that there are different ways of 'getting things done' in the Church. Like many other priests, they are pastorally pragmatic in how they deal with their superiors and their parishioners.

6.4.4 Post-Vatican II Priests' Views of Liturgy and Devotions

This post-Vatican II group of priests 'love' liturgies, old and new. They spoke of 'loving the Mass' and being 'true' to the traditions of the Church (Curate, 2000s). They do not see the Latin Mass as regressive or reactionary. Rather, it is part of the 'integration and synthesis' process in the contemporary Church (Curate, 2000s). They are priests of the Vatican II Church who also believe that some elements of the pre-Vatican II Church should be restored.

> I am more conservative than other priests but I am not an extremist. Most younger priests are quite clear about where we stand but not in a reactionary way. We operate out of a genuine spirit of Christian love. The celebration of the sacraments is very important to me and it is very, very important that the sacrament is celebrated in an integral way as it is laid down. That is the way it works. I believe in what the Church teaches. I would have no issue with the Tridentine liturgy and if people wanted me to celebrate it, I would. I know some priests would see that as the ultimate symbol of something that is wrong in the Church. I certainly wouldn't. I am a priest of the era of the Second Vatican Council. I grew up in this Church and it is a Church I want to be part of. I can't imagine the Church going back to what was there before Vatican II but I still would have no problem celebrating Mass in Latin.
>
> *Curate, 2000s*

They like using incense when 'appropriate' and they generally believe that sacraments are central to the life of the Church.

6.4.5 Post-Vatican II Priests' Views of Theology

Four post-Vatican II priests described themselves as 'theologically conservative and pastorally pragmatic' (Curates, 1990s). They have little personal difficulty in accepting Church teachings, but they regard themselves as 'pastorally pragmatic'. For example, most of them would not condemn a person in public if they could avoid it, and neither would they feel comfortable in preaching on controversial issues from the altar. They believe that the world of morality is a 'grey area' and one that requires compassion, even if they feel somewhat uncomfortable 'questioning' 2,000 years of Church tradition.

> In theology, we were taught there is an internal forum and an external forum. In other words, what you say to someone in the confessional isn't necessarily what you are going to say in the pulpit. In the public forum I am not going to say something that is directly contrary to Church teaching; that just wouldn't be me. I am not going to preach about contraception or divorce; I am just not going to go there. If you are dealing pastorally with a couple in a second relationship or a young lad who is gay or a mother who had an abortion, I will deal pastorally and sensitively with them. You are dealing with people and a more pragmatic approach is required.
>
> *Curate, 1990s*

Furthermore, with one exception, this cohort of post-Vatican II priests would never refuse anyone Holy Communion at Mass, unless it was a potential source of scandal in the parish. However, that being said, they are committed to the Church and its teachings, and if possible, they will inform the person of the Church's position on an issue in the hope that they might 'do the right thing' themselves. They are not always comfortable in adopting a pastoral approach, but it may be the best option in a 'grey world' (Curate, 1990s). Three priests said, for example, that the use of contraceptives is 'wrong' because it is an 'objective truth' of the Catholic Church. Accordingly, they will inform people of this truth if they are asked. However, ultimately, people have to make up their own minds on this and other Church teachings. One priest said there is a 'lot of grey in the world and the Church has to be able to minister to the grey' (Curate, 1990s). Thus, while priests must preach the ideal, they also have to find some way of ministering to people in second unions, gay relationships, or same sex unions. A number of them reminded me that mortal sin exists but only when three conditions are met – grave matter, full knowledge, and full consent. None of them would be comfortable in giving a blessing to a second relationship because it is a sacrament, and most would find 'another way', such as blessing the couple's house.

While most of these priests veered towards conservative orthodoxy, one priest was highly orthodox and conservative in all aspects of his priestly life. He perceives himself to be in a 'grey zone' where he has to fight for the faith and stand up against the sinfulness of the world and the Church. He believes that a priest is 'defined' by the stance he takes towards controversial Church teachings and that a priest must be willing to withstand the pressures from liberal groups, including other priests, not to take the 'easy option'. He is also in full agreement with the interpretation of Vatican II by John Paul II and Benedict XVI. He is 'deeply committed to, and loves, the Tridentine Mass', although he also recognises that the Tridentine Mass is just one form of the rite. He loves the 'solemnity, the ritual, the mystery, and the depth of the liturgical tradition that reaches back over 1,500 or 1,600 years'.

> I am not a priest who is alone. I am part of a small number of priests who are dedicated to authentic reform. The important thing for us as priests is to follow the orthodox faith in the Church. There is a holiness in the Church but there is also a sinful side as well. Priests have a huge responsibility in preaching. We can all teach on the necessity for forgiveness when you come to the controversial teachings of the Church, particularly moral teachings in relation to contraception, homosexuality, divorce and remarriage, and being in a state of grace to receive communion. But if you are going to be a Catholic priest, you have to preach the truth in love, even against opposition from other priests. There is a huge disunity within the priesthood and some priests are afraid to say something that might be reported in the media. I believe I have a responsibility to tell the truth to my people, whether they like it or not.
>
> Curate, 2000s

He is the only priest in this study to admit refusing Holy Communion to people 'he knew' were not in a state of grace because of their public behaviour. This priest does not see his behaviour to be in any way judgemental.

6.4.6 Post-Vatican II Priests' Attitudes Towards Celibacy

As previously noted in chapter four, all of the priests in this cohort have freely chosen celibacy as an inherent part of their priesthood, and something they feel defines their priesthood. While they are tolerant towards priests who breach this rule, they believe that every priest should try their best to be celibate. Similarly, none of these priests would have any difficulty working with a homosexual priest, provided he is celibate. Two of the former priests in this cohort left the priesthood because of difficulties with celibacy.

In summary, the post-Vatican II priests are quite different in their ideology and motivation to both of the previous generations of priests. While they share many of the characteristics of the pre-Vatican II cultic priests, the legalistic context of the Church has changed and they are motivated by a love of the Church rather than rules. They embrace the orthodoxy, conservatism and certainty of the contemporary Church. They love the Mass and other liturgies, including the Latin Mass, so much so in some cases that they are referred to as 'smoke and lace' priests. However, while all of them are attracted to the sacramental dimension of priesthood, some of them perceive their priesthood to be a combination of service and sacramental duties. They see themselves as defenders of the Catholic faith and a means by which orthodoxy can be restored into the Church. They value strict hierarchy and established rules, and they believe that celibacy is a central part of their priesthood. Above all, they value orthodoxy and they do not see themselves as reactionaries. They consider themselves to be theologically conservative but pastorally pragmatic.

6.5 CONCLUDING COMMENT

The primary aim of this chapter was to explore how the research participants understand their priesthood, and to establish how, and if, their understanding of priesthood has changed since ordination. The literature suggested that distinct generations of priests exist in the Catholic Church with diverse values, beliefs and understandings of priesthood (Bacik, 1999; Hoge and Wenger, 2003; Gautier et al., 2012). The literature review also suggested that diocesan priests have a strong sense of vocation or professional identity. Overall, my research found evidence to support an evolving life cycle of priesthood within the Irish Church. Specifically, it suggests that three models of priesthood prevailed at different times during the past fifty years amongst the research participants, each of which presents a different understanding of priesthood. A cultic model of priesthood prevailed before Vatican II, followed by a servant-leader model in the years following Vatican II, and a neo-orthodox model that emerged during the papacy of John Paul II (1978–2005). Although they are distinct models, the division between the three models was blurred over time, resulting in priests adopting some characteristics of more than one model. For example, a number of pre-Vatican II priests who had originally understood priesthood in cultic terms later came to value most aspects of the servant-leader model.

The research indicated that most of the younger research participants are theologically and ideologically more conservative than their older counterparts. In this regard, their views reflect the conservative shift in the Church associated with the papacies of Pope John Paul II and Benedict XVI. The renewed focus on the sacramental dimension of priesthood and traditional Church practices appeals to many of these younger priests because it gives them greater certainty and direction in their lives. It will be interesting to see how this group of neo-orthodox priests, and indeed all priests will react to the less conservative agenda of Pope Francis (Francis, 2013).

Conversely, my research also found an underlying culture of priestly practice in Ireland, which most priests share. This is where most priests are pastorally pragmatic in their dealings with parishioners, and flexible in how they relate to their superiors. Most of the research participants also had a strong sense of priestly identity, where they feel called by God to a career that is more than a job or a religious belief system, and where their professional priestly identity consumes their personal identity. Regardless of age and background, they are first and foremost, priests of the Catholic Church.

Chapter Seven

Change and Continuity in the Lives of Irish Diocesan Priests, 1960–2010

7.1 INTRODUCTION

By any standards, diocesan priesthood is a highly distinctive lifestyle and career, and the personal stories told by the priests and former priests in this book are both complex and intriguing. The public face of priesthood is familiar to most Irish people. It entails a vocation, a life of Christian service, a celibate lifestyle, a distinctive garb, and a workload that combines sacramental and spiritual duties with relatively mundane administrative tasks. A priest is expected to be present at weddings and funerals, baptisms and Masses, school meetings and numerous parish events. In this regard, he rarely disappoints. Conversely, a priest's private life is something of an enigma, and very few people would claim to know much about the private lived experience of Irish diocesan priests. In many ways, we see what priests wish us to see and no more. Accordingly, the openness and frankness of the thirty-three individuals who participated in this research is highly significant and I believe that it provides important insights into our understanding of Irish diocesan priests as 'humans, believing Christians' (United States Conference of Catholic Bishops, 2001).

The main aim of this study was to document and explore the lived experience of thirty-three Irish diocesan priests and former priests, in order to gain some insights into the reality of diocesan priesthood in contemporary Ireland, and to investigate how, if at all, diocesan priesthood has changed in Ireland during the past fifty years. It sought to do this by interrogating the stories of twenty-four diocesan priests and nine former diocesan priests, and by placing their individual stories within the broader context of Irish society and the Catholic Church, during the fifty-year period, 1960–2010. The main findings from the research are reiterated overleaf.

7.2 THE CELIBACY CONTINUUM

The lived experience of the thirty-three research participants suggests that celibacy is typically understood and experienced by Irish diocesan priests along a continuum, ranging from total acceptance to rejection, with most priests somewhere in the middle of this spectrum. There is also evidence to suggest that the celibacy continuum varies across clerical generations, with younger priests most likely to embrace the ideal and practice of celibacy. Conversely, the older priests ordained in the two decades surrounding Vatican II are most critical of the mandatory nature of celibacy, and many of them continue to experience difficulties living a celibate lifestyle. While some older priests could see a value in celibacy for priesthood, they feel that it should be an optional rather than a non-negotiable part of priesthood. Furthermore, while some priests believe that celibacy can have ideological and practical benefits for ministry, such as giving priests greater freedom to be more available to their parishioners, they suggest that these benefits can be overstated, and that the value of celibacy is often overshadowed by the many difficulties caused by a celibate lifestyle.

For most priests, celibacy is a sacrifice that is required if they wish to be priests and celebrate the Eucharist. However, unlike the Church's traditionally intolerant view of sexual behaviour outside of marriage, these priests are relatively understanding when they or their fellow priests fail to live up to the ideals of celibacy, provided it does not lead to scandal. They believe that celibacy is just another part of being a priest, no more or less important than other aspects. While most of them believe they have a vocation to the priesthood, it is not necessarily a vocation to a celibate priesthood. Conversely, the younger post-Vatican II priests believe that celibacy is central to the priesthood and that it is embodied into their lives as priests. They perceive celibacy to be a privilege and a challenge, which they have freely chosen. Thus, while celibacy is difficult at times for some of the younger group, it is not perceived to be a sacrifice or a significant loss in their lives. They believe that it helps define their identity as priests in a positive way for themselves and others.

Few priests, young or old, said they had considered the implications of celibacy at the time of their ordination because of their desire to become priests, and many of them thought that any 'difficulties' would eventually pass. However, they subsequently discovered that while their sexual desire lessened over time, their need for intimacy had not, and, if anything, it had increased. Most of the thirty-three research participants said they found celibacy difficult, leading some of them to leave the priesthood, while others suffered from loneliness.

The research also discovered that homosexuality is a reality in Irish diocesan priesthood. However, for too many, it remains a hidden and shameful reality, with students and priests fearful of disclosing their sexual orientation to anyone, sometimes even themselves. This suggests that while celibacy is difficult for most priests, there is an added level of complexity when a priest is gay, due to the traditional secrecy surrounding homosexuality and the Church's public negative stance towards gay seminarians and priests.

The continued existence of mandatory celibacy in the Catholic Church is somewhat of a puzzle given the opposition from many different interests in the Irish Church, including the majority of priests and people (*The Irish Catholic*, 2004; *The Irish Times*, 2012). For some priests and commentators, it is associated with loneliness and an increasingly demoralised priesthood; its gospel foundations are disputed; and it is perceived to pose a threat to the Eucharist and priesthood (Schoenherr and Young, 1993; Standún, 1993). In addition to its ideological underpinning and witness value, some commentators believe that celibacy continues to be mandatory because of its benefits to the institutional Church, whereby priests are more easily controlled (Anderson, 2005). This is also the opinion of some of the research participants across the three generations of priests, who believe that celibacy makes it easier for bishops to control priests, while others referred to the potential financial and property-related difficulties of having a married clergy.

I believe that celibacy continues to be mandatory in the Catholic Church because the Church and its priests accept it as a condition of priesthood. One group of priests endorses mandatory celibacy because they see it as a gift from God, an inherent part of priesthood, and a distinctive part of a priest's countercultural lifestyle. For this group, to change the discipline of celibacy would be to change the nature of priesthood and they are opposed to this move. Conversely, another group of priests believes that celibacy should be optional because not everyone is given the gift of celibacy. This has resulted in a decline in vocations and many priests being forced to leave the priesthood. The Vatican has consistently ruled out any change in this discipline. Accordingly, those who oppose mandatory celibacy are reluctant to speak out against it, because they anticipate a negative reaction and possible sanctions from their superiors. They also know that priests do not need to be totally celibate because their peers and their leaders are quite tolerant towards indiscretions in this area of their lives, provided they don't 'flaunt' the rules of the game and cause public scandal.

7.3 CLERICAL OBEDIENCE

Irish diocesan priests are typically obedient and loyal men. They learn to obey rules and respect authority in the seminary, and their loyalty as priests is subsequently reinforced by a number of factors, including their personal commitment to priesthood, their subordinate position within the Church hierarchy, the influence of a clerical culture, and the threat of diverse sanctions that may be imposed on priests who publicly challenge Church norms or teachings. Most of the research participants indicated that they felt constrained by Church rules. This was especially the case with the pre-Vatican II priests who were formed in a Church that was highly legalistic and hierarchical, and where obedience was considered to be a virtue. They spoke of the 'pernickety rules' in the seminary, where guilt was ingrained and where they were groomed to be obedient priests. They also spoke of the 'regimented' nature of their lives as priests, where rules and rubrics dictated much of their lives. A number of them also referred to the 'dictatorial' way they were treated by some parish priests. Most of them regarded disobedience as 'unthinkable' and they obeyed their bishop, usually without question or consultation. The 'law was the law' and there were serious consequences if it was not obeyed.

The Catholic Church and priesthood changed following Vatican II. It was a time of organisational change and liturgical renewal, where the certainties and legalism of the pre-Vatican II Church were gradually replaced by more liberal and collegial values, and a servant-leader model replaced the long-standing cultic model of priesthood. However, while the Church and the priesthood became less legalistic and seminary training less restrictive, the experiences of the research participants suggest that diocesan priests are still expected to obey Church leadership without question. Obedience continues to be regarded as a virtue or, at least, a requirement of priesthood. Most of the research participants are aware of priests who have been punished by a bishop, and many of them gave personal accounts of being bullied by a parish priest. For the most part, their training and experience has taught them not to expect change or to cause any trouble, and to concentrate on looking after their own parishes. This is also the case with the younger priests, most of whom regard obedience to be a virtue and an important part of their priesthood. Their promise of obedience to their bishop is a solemn occasion for them, which they believe gives meaning to their priesthood. Yet, in spite of their ideological commitment to obedience, their experience of obedience is quite similar to that of their older counterparts, and some of them said they are frustrated by the lack of consultation and domineering attitude of their superiors. Typically, they are appointed to their parishes by a bishop, usually without consultation, and they are expected to obey their parish priests.

My research suggests that while Irish diocesan priests are constrained in many ways by a highly structured and strictly hierarchical Church, they also have the capacity to think and act relatively independently in certain circumstances. For example, some of the research participants disagree with the Church's official stance on homosexuality, women priests, and mandatory celibacy, and most of them said they have difficulties with some aspect of Church teaching on morality, such as the laws forbidding the use of artificial contraceptives. Furthermore, a number of the Vatican II priests are very upset by what they perceive to be a conservative shift in the Church and priesthood, leading some of them to consider withdrawing from public ministry when the revised wording of the Mass missal is introduced. The younger priests are also willing to stand up for what they believe, even if their relatively conservative views mean they face opposition from their older colleagues rather than the Vatican.

There is also evidence to suggest that most of the research participants exercise a degree of agency in their pragmatic approach to pastoral activities. Thus, while most of them are unwilling to 'mess with the sacraments', very few of the research participants would consider refusing Holy Communion to anyone who approached them at the altar who they knew, for example, to be in a second relationship. Unless they are directly challenged, they will try to find a pastoral response to most situations. Similarly, most of them are reluctant to publicise their views on controversial issues where they disagree with the Church's official position. They understand that there are boundaries which they should not cross if they wish to remain in their ministry. For example, one gay priest said that while he preaches as often as he dares about homosexuality within the context of diversity and Christian values, he could not risk being more direct in his comments. He, like most of his colleagues, has learnt to reconcile his personal views with those of the Church in a way that allows him to remain true to his own values and remain a priest of good standing in the Church.

The cognitive dissonance that characterises the lives of many 'new Catholics' described in chapter two is also evident amongst Irish diocesan priests. Most of the research participants have a shared way of understanding priestly practice that is sufficiently pragmatic to enable them to be true to their core values ('This is what I think as a priest') and to hold contradictory values, whilst remaining loyal to the Church. A number of them said that they had learnt to circumvent Church authority by keeping their heads down and not confronting their superiors. Others said that it was possible to maintain a good relationship with their bishop and parish priest by doing their own thing and not giving their superiors any reasons to interfere in their ministry. They are loyal priests but not necessarily, or always, subservient. They are company men, 'with attitude'.

As previously mentioned, I believe that the pragmatic pastoral practice of priests allows the institutional Church to be simultaneously empathetic and strong. On the one hand, the human side of the Church is reflected in the actions of individual priests when they act in a pastoral way. On the other hand, the institutional Church is enabled to protect the 'truth' of the Church by being unyielding in the laws and truth it promulgates. The relationship between priests and their superiors is typically mutually beneficial, and difficulties only occur when a priest is too public about his dissent or the institutional Church acts in a way that is perceived to be too harsh, thereby provoking a response from the opposing group. For example, the bishops have been criticised by some commentators for summarily abandoning priests who have been accused of child sexual abuse, while individual priests have been sanctioned for unduly criticising Church policy or practice.

In summary, my research suggests that diocesan priests can be simultaneously loyal and disobedient; severely constrained but not controlled by Church structures. They can exercise agency in certain aspects of their priesthood but usually only within the parameters allowed by the institutional Church. Accordingly, they do not usually express their dissent in public because they understand and accept the rules of the game, where they accept their subordinate position in the Church hierarchy. To do otherwise would be to threaten their priesthood and their relatively privileged position in Irish society. Above all, they want to be priests of the Catholic Church and only the Church can permit this to happen and continue happening.

7.4 EVOLVING IDENTITIES OF DIOCESAN PRIESTHOOD

Overall, my research found evidence of three distinct cohorts of priests amongst the research participants, each of which prevailed at different times during the past fifty years and each of which presents a different understanding of priesthood (see chapter three). A cultic model of priesthood prevailed before Vatican II, followed by a servant-leader model in the years following Vatican II, and a neo-orthodox model that emerged during the papacy of John Paul II (1978–2005). At the present time, it would appear that the neo-orthodox model is on the ascent, with the servant-leader model descending, albeit still in a strong position within the Irish Church. However, the division between the different models is somewhat blurred, resulting in movement from one paradigm to another. This is the natural and inevitable life cycle of priesthood in the Irish Church.

These findings are largely consistent with the research by Hoge and Wenger (Hoge and Wenger, 2003) in their study of US priests, which found that the essence of priesthood had shifted twice since Vatican II, resulting in the emergence of two generations of priests. It is also consistent with the work of various theorists, such as Bourdieu (Maton, 2008), and Mannheim (Mannheim, 1952), who suggest that different political generations evolve over time that reflect the prevailing cultural and historical context within which they came of age. The 1960s was, for example, a time of significant socio-economic and cultural change for Irish society and the Catholic Church. Accordingly, it is not surprising that a new model of priesthood should have emerged at this time. Similarly, a significant conservative shift occurred in the Church and the priesthood in the 1980s during the papacy of John Paul II, leading to the emergence of a neo-orthodox model of priesthood. It remains to be seen if and how the papacy of Pope Francis will lead to a new direction in the prevailing paradigm of priesthood if he continues to emphasise the pastoral care of the Catholic Church and to reach out to marginalised groups within the Church (Francis, 2013).

In addition to inter-generational differences, my research also found evidence of similarities across the different cohorts of priests. In the first instance, priests from the three cohorts had similar motivations for wanting to be priests; with most of them believing that they are called by God to work as priests in the Catholic Church. They also share a common commitment to the priesthood that is sufficiently strong to withstand personal difficulties and societal challenges to the profession of priesthood. The greatest similarity between the research participants is to be found in the underlying culture of clerical practice that transcends the different generations of priests. Regardless of their ideological positions or personal circumstances, most of the research participants were prepared to be pastorally pragmatic when dealing with their parishioners. While most of them were reluctant to 'mess with the sacraments', they were quite prepared to advise people in ways that did not always correspond with official Church practices or teachings. A number of the research participants said that morality is a grey area and one that requires compassion, even if they sometimes feel somewhat uncomfortable questioning 2,000 years of Church tradition. Some of the main inter-generational differences and similarities are summarised in Table 7.1, overleaf.

Table 7.1 Evolving Models of Priesthood: Irish Diocesan Priesthood

Identity Indicators	Pre-Vatican II Cultic Priesthood	Vatican II Servant-Leader Priesthood	Post-Vatican II Orthodox Priesthood
Ontological status of the priest	A man set apart. Focus on sacramental duties, and teaching of faith.	Pastoral leader. Focus on service and sacraments.	A man set apart. Importance of sacramental aspect of priesthood.
Attitudes towards the Church magisterium	Loyal but not subservient. Accepts Church hierarchy as part of legalistic culture.	Loyal but not subservient. Favours less strict hierarchy and questions Church moral teachings.	Loyal but not subservient. Values Church authority and hierarchy, and embraces sense of duty.
Liturgy and devotions	Follows established rules and rubrics.	Favours creativity.	Loves liturgy, old and new.
Theological perspective	Orthodox, conservative, unchanging.	Allows for theological differences, uncertainty and questioning.	Defender and restorer of orthodoxy.
Attitudes towards celibacy	Optional for priesthood.	Optional for priesthood.	Inherent to priesthood.
Attitudes towards women priests	Unsure but willing to discuss.	A possibility that many favour.	Against.
Priestly practice	Pragmatic and pastoral approach. Reluctant to 'mess with the sacraments'.	Pragmatic and pastoral approach. Reluctant to 'mess with the sacraments'.	Pragmatic and pastoral approach. Orthodoxy paramount.

Based on model in Hoge and Wenger, 2003, p. 144.

In summary, the research suggests that Irish diocesan priesthood has evolved during the past fifty years, leading to the emergence of different models of priesthood. While there are clear areas of difference between the three cohorts of priests, there is also an underlying culture practice of priesthood that unites Irish diocesan priests.

7.5 A Crisis in Diocesan Priesthood?

The social world of Irish diocesan priesthood has shifted significantly during the past fifty years. This has led some commentators to suggest that Irish priests are experiencing a crisis in different areas of their lives: ministry, morale, intimacy, leadership, and identity. It is suggested that this clerical malaise is increasingly widespread and associated with changes in Ireland's socio-religious landscape and a conservative shift in the Church and priesthood. In brief, it is suggested that Irish diocesan priests are increasingly ageing, overworked, lonely, marginalised, lacking effective leadership, confused about their identities as priests, and generally living lives that are less privileged than many of them would have experienced in the past (Fitzgibbon, 2010). Furthermore, it is argued that many priests ordained around the time of Vatican II have become disillusioned with the prevailing conservative models of priesthood and the Church. Thus, Vatican II priests tend to be most disappointed at the slow rate of progress in the Church since Vatican II, and most disillusioned with the conservative shift in priesthood and the Church during the papacies of John Paul II and Benedict XVI. I believe that all of these assertions are true but not for all Irish diocesan priests. Younger priests, for example, are most satisfied with the conservative shift and the restoration of orthodoxy to the Church and priesthood.

The stories of the thirty-three research participants confirm the inconclusive nature of the evidence that currently exists on this sensitive and controversial topic. My evidence suggests that priesthood is in crisis for some priests but not all. While some of the research participants had experienced a crisis in their lives, prompting nine of them to leave the priesthood, most of the research participants had successfully managed to address any problems they encountered in their priestly lives. When asked if they felt their priesthood was in crisis, most of the priests said they are 'managing fine for the moment', although they admitted to sometimes feeling lonely, demoralised, overworked and uncertain about their vocation and priesthood. They also felt that some other priests may be adversely affected by the amount of work they were obliged to do, and that some priests were lonely and marginalised. If there is a crisis in priesthood, they felt that it would be the result of continued falling vocations, rather than any other area of priesthood. Overall, I did not sense that any of the priests were in crisis.

7.6 CONCLUDING COMMENT

The stories of the thirty-three research participants indicate that a priest's life can be both challenging and rewarding. Overall, I was left with the impression that their deep, personal commitment to priesthood has energised and sustained most of them in times of personal difficulties and societal challenges to their priesthood. They believe that they have been called by God to be a priest in the Catholic Church, and while a number of them said that they had been 'rocked' by the child sexual abuse cases and the way the bishops mishandled the situation, they remain priests because their commitment to the priesthood is so strong. Above all, they want to be priests and they are willing to accept most restrictions placed on their lives by celibacy, obedience, and their commitment to Christian service in a clerical 'grey zone', with few of the certainties of the pre-Vatican II Church. They believe they have been called by God to be priests and, for most of them, it is probably the best job in the world.

Statistical and Age Profile of Irish Diocesan Priests

STATISTICAL PROFILE OF IRISH DIOCESAN PRIESTS[207]

In 2006, there were approximately three thousand active diocesan priests in Ireland, representing a steady decline in the number of priests since 1980. However, as will be evident from the following chart, the numerical and statistical decline for diocesan clergy was less than other sectors of the Irish Church (Council for Research and Development, 2007).

Figure A1 Total Church Personnel in Ireland, 1901–2006

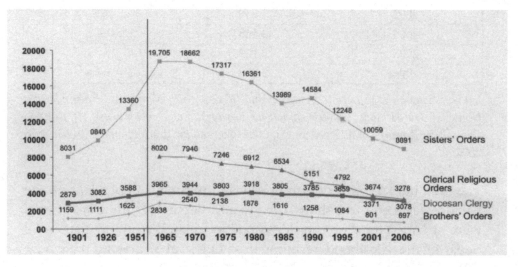

The downward decline for diocesan priests has been consistent since 1965 with 887 less diocesan clergy (-22%) in 2006 than in 1965. Most of the numerical decline has taken place since 1990, when the number of diocesan clergy declined by 707 or 80% of the total decline since 1965. The number of clerical students also fell quite dramatically during the 1990s (Table A.1, overleaf).

Table A.1 Numbers of Irish Diocesan Clergy and Clerical Students 1901–2006

Year	Number of Irish Diocesan Clergy	Clerical Students
1901	2,879	n/a
1951	3,588	n/a
1965	3,965	n/a
1970	3,944	670
1975	3,803	n/a
1980	3,998	n/a
1985	3,805	n/a
1990	3,785	556
1995	3,659	332
2000	3,403	150
2001	3,371	120
2002	3,289	88
2003	3,238	78
2004	3,168	90
2005	3,129	n/a
2006	3,078	n/a

Sources: Lennon et al., 1971; MacGréil and Inglis, 1977; Weafer and Breslin, 1983; Hanley, 1995; Hanley, 2000b; Council for Research and Development, 1971–2004; Council for Research and Development, 2005; Council for Research and Development, 2007.

The total number of diocesan priests at any time is dependent on the balance between ordinations, deaths, and departures. In 2005, 11 men were ordained for diocesan priesthood in Ireland, while 38 died and 8 departed the priesthood, resulting in a net loss of 35 priests (Table A.2).

Table A.2 Statistical Profile of Irish Diocesan Clergy 1966–2005

Year	Number of Irish Diocessan Clergy	Ordinations for Irish Dioceses	Deaths of ordained priests	Departures of ordained priests	Net Balance (Ordinations – Deaths & departures)
1966	3,958	82	88	1	-7
1970	3,944	67	55	6	+6
1975	3,803	52	83	20	-51
1980	3,998	78	78	8	-8
1985	3,805	86	80	2	+4
1990	3,785	73	70	10	-7
1995	3,659	59	82	19	-42
2000	3,403	24	75	27	-78
2005	3,129	11	38	8	-35

Sources: Lennon et al., 1971; MacGréil and Inglis, 1977; Weafer and Breslin, 1983; Hanley, 1995; Hanley, 2000b; Council for Research and Development, 1971–2004; Council for Research and Development, 2005.

The decline in numbers of diocesan clergy is directly related to the sharp deterioration in the number of ordinations and entrants to seminaries. For example, the average number of ordinations in the first half of the 1960s was 91, compared with only 18 in the first half of the 2000s (Table A.3).

Table A.3 Ordinations to Irish Dioceses 1951–2005

	Total Ordinations	Average per Annum
1951–1955	396	79
1956–1960	451	90
1961–1965	457	91
1966–1970	381	76
1971–1975	364	73
1976–1980	350	70
1981–1985[208]	418	84
1986–1990	373	75
1991–1995	309	62
1996–2000	176	35
2001–2005	88	18

Source: Lennon et al., 1971; Hanley, 1995; Hanley, 2000b; Council for Research and Development, 2005.

The number of entrants to diocesan seminaries has also fallen sharply since the 1960s, with 291 entrants to diocesan seminaries in 1967, compared with only 27 entrants in 2005. Furthermore, a substantial number of clerical students left the seminary over the past 40 years. Thus, while 1,750 men entered a diocesan seminary between 1971 and 1980, almost half this number (n=842) left the seminary (Figure A2/Table A.4).

Figure A2 Vocations in Ireland, 1965–2005

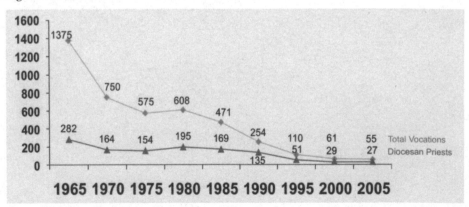

Source: Council for Research and Development.

Table A.4 Entrants and Departures of Clerical Students 1965–2005

Year	Entrants 'Vocations'	Departures
1965	282	n/a
1966	254	n/a
1967	291	n/a
1968	219	n/a
1969	221	n/a
1970	164	n/a
1971	179	169
1972	184	102
1973	157	101
1974	144	95
1975	154	50
1976	181	54
1977	206	72
1978	175	69
1979	175	71
1980	195	59
1981	176	34
1982	187	25
1983	154	95
1984	154	40
1985	169	57
1986	170	63
1987	168	76
1988	155	76
1989	139	93
1990	135	51
1991	120	81
1992	101	88
1993	93	31
1994	98	94
1995	51	67
1996	52	59
1997	53	43
1998	45	40
1999	46	41
2000	29	24
2001	32	27
2002	20	28
2003	19	7
2004	28	11
2005	27	8

Sources: Lennon et al., 1971; Weafer and Breslin, 1983; Hanley, 1995; Hanley, 2000b; Council for Research and Development, 2005.

AGE PROFILE OF DIOCESAN PRIESTS

While the age profile of diocesan clergy is younger than their religious counterparts, it is nevertheless ageing (Council for Research and Development, 2005). In 1970, just over 1 in 10 priests were aged between 20 and 29 years. In 2005, the figure had fallen to just 1%. Conversely, the proportion of priests in the older age categories has progressed steadily since 1970 (Table A.5). In 2005, seven in ten Irish diocesan priests were aged over 50 years of age, and it is estimated that approximately 50% of Irish Catholic priests are over 65 years of age.

Table A.5 Age Structure of Irish Diocesan Clergy, 1970–2005

Age Group	1970	1981	1990	2001	2005
	%	%	%	%	%
24–29 years	11	9	9	3	1
30–39 years	22	18	18	15	12
40–49 years	20	21	18	18	20
50–59 years	22	20	21	21	21
60–69 years	16	19	17	21	22
70–79 years	8	11	13	16	17
80+ years	3	2	4	6	9
Total	100	100	100	100	100

Sources: Weafer and Breslin, 1983; Hanley, 1995; Council for Research and Development, 2005.

In 1970, diocesan clergy had higher proportions in the two youngest age groups (24–29 and 30–39 years), when compared with their counterparts in the total male population. However, by 1981, this trend was reversed for these age groups, and conversely, most age groups above 40 years had higher proportions of priests by comparison with the proportion of total males (Weafer and Breslin, 1983). The ageing of diocesan priests relative to the Irish male population has continued into the 2000s (O'Mahony, 2007). In 2011, just over three quarters (75%) of priests in Ireland were aged between 45 and 74 years of age, compared with just less than seven in ten (69%) in 2007 (O'Mahony, 2011). The age of entrants to the diocesan priesthood is also older than was the case in the 1970s and 1980s, with most entrants older than 20 years but younger than 35 years (Council for Research and Development, 2005).

Bibliography

ADAMS, K. M., 'Clergy Sex Abuse: A Commentary on Celibacy', *Sexual Addiction & Compulsivity*, 10, 91–2, 2003.

AGNEW, P., 'Magazine exposes "double life" of Vatican's gay priests', *The Irish Times*, 2010.

AGNEW, P., 'Dissident priest "very surprised" by decision', *The Irish Times*, 27 September 2013.

ANDERSEN, K., 'Irish Secularization and Religious Identities: Evidence of an Emerging New Catholic Habitus', *Social Compass*, 57, 15–39, 2010.

ANDERSON, J., *Priests in Love: Roman Catholic Clergy and Their Intimate Friendships*, London, Continuum, 2005.

ANDERSON, J., 'The Contest of Moralities: Negotiating Compulsory Celibacy and Sexual Intimacy in the Roman Catholic Priesthood', *The Australian Journal of Anthropology*, 18, 1–17, 2007.

ANONYMOUS, 'A Catholic Perspective on Gay Priestly Ministry from the Closet', *Journal of Gay & lesbian Social Services*, 6, 39–53, 2008.

ARCHBISHOP MICHAEL NEARY, Homily of Archbishop Michael Neary for the Annual Pilgrimage to Croagh Patrick 2003. http://www.catholic bishops.ie/media-centre/press-release-archive/5-2003/56-34-2003: Press Release issued by the Catholic Communications Office on behalf of the Archdiocese of Tuam. Accessed 14 June 2012.

ASSOCIATION OF CATHOLIC PRIESTS, Contemporary Catholic Perspectives, Dublin: The Association of Catholic Priests/Amárach Research, 2012.

ASSOCIATION OF IRISH PRIESTS, Priests Leaving the Active Ministry. Dublin, 1972.

AUER, A., 'The Meaning of Celibacy', *The Furrow*, 18, 299–321, 1967.

BACIK, J., 'The Priest as Pastor: Rooted in Christ, the Holy Spirit, and the Church', in DIETRICH, D. J. (ed.), *Priests for the 21st Century*, New York: The Crossroad Publishing Company, 2006.

BACIK, J.J., 'The Practice of Priesthood: Working Through Today's Tensions', in SMITH, K.S. (ed.), *Priesthood in the Modern World*, Franklin, Wisconsin: Sheed & Ward, 1999.

BANVILLE, J., 'Memory and Forgetting: The Ireland of de Valera and O Faolain', in KEOGH, D., O'SHEA, F. & QUINLAN, C. (eds), *The Lost Decade: Ireland in the 1950s*, Cork: Mercier Press, 2004.

BARTLEY, B. & KITCHEN, R. (eds), *Understanding Contemporary Ireland*, Dublin: Pluto Press, 2007.

BENEDICT XVI, *Address of His Holiness Pope Benedict XVI: Meeting with the Parish Priests and the Clergy of Rome* [Online]. Vatican: Vatican. Available: http://www.vatican.va/holy_father/benedict_xvi/speeches/2013/febr uary/documents/hf_ben-xvi_spe_20130214_clero-roma_en.html [Accessed 11 March 2013].

BERGER, P., *The Social Reality of Religion*, Harmondsworth, Penguin, 1973.

BIEVER, B.F., *Religion, Culture, and Values. A Cross-National Analysis of Motivational Factors in Native Irish and American Irish Catholicism*, Ayer Co Pub, 1976.

BIRCH, P., 'Priesthood of the Laity', *The Furrow*, 34, 80–9, 1979.

BLEICHNER, H.P., *View form the Altar: Reflections on the Rapidly Changing Catholic Priesthood*, New York, Crossroad, 2004.

BOHAN, H., *Community and the Soul of Ireland: The Need for Values-based Change*, Dublin, The Liffey Press, 2002.

BOHAN, H., *Swimming Upstream: Finding Positives in a Negative Ireland*, Dublin, The Columba Press, 2013.

BOHR, D., *The Diocesan Priest: Consecrated and Sent*, Collegeville, Minnesota, Liturgical Press, 2009.

BORDISSO, L.A., *Sex, Celibacy & Priesthood: A Bishop's Provocative Inquisition*, Bloomington, iUniverse, 2011.

BOURDIEU, P., 'Genesis and Structure of the Religious Field', *Comparative Social Research*, 13, 1–44, 1991.

BRADY, C., *Up With The Times*, Dublin, Gill & Macmillan, 2005.

BRADY, P., 'My Priesthood', *The Furrow,* 31, 706–16, 1980.

BRADY, R., 'Priesthood at Risk – Courage to Be', *The Furrow,* 41, 9–16, 1989.

BRADY, R., 'The Confession of a Country Curate', *The Furrow*, 42, 415–26, 1991.

BREEN, M., 'Part Two: Statistical Analysis and Tables', in LANE, D. A. (ed.), *Reading the Signs of the Times: A Survey of Priests in Dublin*, Dublin: Veritas, 1997.

BREEN, R., HANNAN, D. F., ROTTMAN, D. B. & WHELAN, C. T., *Understanding Contemporary Ireland: State, Class and Development in the Republic of Ireland*, Dublin, Gill and Macmillan, 1990.

BRENNAN, T. J., 'A Tale of Two Comings Out: Priest and Gay on a Catholic Campus', *Modern Language Studies*, 34, 66–75, 2004.

BRESLIN, A., Vocations in 1980. A Profile of the Entrants. Maynooth: Council for Research & Development, Irish Bishops' Conference, 1981.

BRESLIN, A. & WEAFER, J. A., A Survey of Senior Students' Attitudes Towards Religion, Morality, Education. Maynooth: Council for Research & Development, Irish Bishops' Conference, 1982.

BRESLIN, A. & WEAFER, J. A., Religious Beliefs, Practice and Moral Attitudes: A Comparison of Two Irish Surveys 1974–1984. Maynooth: Council for Research & Development, Irish Bishops' Conference, 1985.

BRESLIN, A. & WEAFER, J. A., Vocations to the Priesthood and Religious Life. Attitudes of Students and Parents in the Diocese of Killaloe. Maynooth: Council for Research & Development, Irish Bishops' Conference, 1986.

BRODY, H., *Inishkillane: Change and Decline in the West of Ireland*, Harmondsworth, Penguin, 1973.

BROPHY, P. J., 'The Christian Life – IV: Holiness in the Priesthood', *The Furrow*, 11, 226–40, 1960.

BROWNE, N., *Against the Tide*, London, Gill and MacMillan, 1986.

BRUNETTE-HILL, S. & FINKE, R., 'A Time for Every Purpose: Updating and Extending Blizzard's Survey on Clergy Time Allocation', *Review of Religious Research*, 41, 47–63, 1999.

CALLANAN, T. A., 'The Role of Clergy in a Society in a Dynamic State, with Particular Reference to the Mid-West Region – the View of a Planner (in collaboration with Rev. Fr H. Bohan)', *Social Studies: Irish Journal of Sociology*, 1, 551–64, 1972.

CAPPS, D., 'John Henry Newman: A Study of Vocational Identity', *Scientific Study of Religion*, 9, 33–51, 1970.

CARDINAL MONTINI, *The Priest*, Dublin, Helicon, 1965.

CAREY, R. G., 'Correlates of Satisfaction in the Priesthood', *Administrative Science Quarterly*, 17, 185–95, 1972.

CASTLE, T., 'A Married Priest', *The Furrow*, 60, 146–50, 2009.

CENTRAL STATISTICS OFFICE, This is Ireland. Highlights from Census 2011, Part 1. Dublin: Government of Ireland, 2012.

COGHLAN, N., 'So does religion have a future?', *Studies: An Irish Quarterly Review*, 99, 395–405, 2010.

COLLINS, M. L. & KAVANAGH, C., 'For Richer, For Poorer: The Changing Distribution of Household Income in Ireland, 1973–94', in HEALY, S. & REYNOLDS, B. (eds), *Social Policy in Ireland. principles Practice and Problems*, Dublin: Oak Tree Press, 1998.

COLLINS, P., 'Maturing as a Priest', *The Furrow*, 41, 605–24, 1990.

COMBAT POVERTY AGENCY, First Annual Report, Dublin: Combat Poverty Agency, 1987.

CONGREGATION FOR THE CLERGY, *The Priest, Pastor and Leader of the Parish Community*, Vatican City, Catholic Truth Society, 2002.

CONNER, P. M., *Celibate Love*, London, Sheed and Ward, 1979.

CONNOLLY, L. & O'TOOLE, T., *Documenting Irish Feminisms: The Second Wave*, Dublin, The Woodfield Press, 2005.

CONNOLLY, P. R., 'The Church in Ireland since Vatican II', *The Furrow*, 30, 755–66, 1979.

CONSIDINE, M. & DUKELOW, F., *Irish Social Policy: A Critical Introduction*, Dublin, Gill & Macmillan, 2009.

CONWAY, B., 'Foreigners, Faith and Fatherland: The Historical Origins, Development and Present Status of Irish Sociology', *Sociological Origins*, 5, 5–36, 2006.

CONWAY, E. (ed.), *Priesthood Today: Ministry in a Changing Church*, Dublin: Veritas, 2013.

COOGAN, T. P., *Disillusioned Decades. Ireland 1966–87*, Dublin, Gill and Macmillan, 1987.

COOLAHAN, J., *Irish Education: Its History and Structure*, Dublin, Institute of Public Administration, 1981.

COONEY, J., *John Charles McQuaid: Ruler of Catholic Ireland*, Dublin, The O'Brien Press, 1999.

COONEY, J., 'Anglican Dean Quits Catholic Church "over celibacy rules"', *The Irish Independent*, Dublin, 2008.

CORBETT, T., 'The Image of the Priest', *The Furrow*, 30, 450–6, 1979.

CORNWELL, J., *The Pope in Winter: The Dark Face of John Paul II's Papacy*, London, Penguin Books, 2004.

COSTELLO, T., *Forming a Priestly Identity. Anthropology of Priestly Formation in the Documents of the VIII Synod of Bishops and the Apostolic Exhortation Pastores dabo vobis*, Rome, Editrice Pontificia Universita Gregoriana, 2002.

COULTER, C., 'The End of Irish History? An Introduction to the Book', in COULTER, C. & COLEMAN, S. (eds), *The End of Irish History? Critical Reflections on the Celtic Tiger*, Manchester: Manchester University Press, 2003.

COUNCIL FOR RESEARCH AND DEVELOPMENT, Vocations in Ireland. Maynooth: Council for Research and Development, Irish Bishops' Conference, 1971–2004.

COUNCIL FOR RESEARCH AND DEVELOPMENT, A Survey of Religious Practice, Attitudes and Beliefs, 1973–1974. Volumes 1 to 4. Dublin: Council for Research and Development, Irish Bishops' Conference, 1975.

COUNCIL FOR RESEARCH AND DEVELOPMENT, Ten Years of Research and Development, 1971–1980. Maynooth: Council for Research & Development, Irish Bishops' Conference, 1981.

COUNCIL FOR RESEARCH AND DEVELOPMENT, Religious Confidence Survey, Republic of Ireland. Maynooth: Irish Marketing Surveys/Council for Research and Development, Irish Bishops' Conference, 1997.

COUNCIL FOR RESEARCH AND DEVELOPMENT, CRD Fact Sheet Series 2006. Maynooth: Council for Research and Development, Irish Bishops' Conference, 2007.

COUNCIL FOR RESEARCH AND DEVELOPMENT, Vocations in Ireland. Maynooth: Council for Research and Development. A Commission of the Irish Bishops' Conference, 1971–2004.

COUNCIL FOR RESEARCH AND DEVELOPMENT, Vocations and Church Personnel 2005. Maynooth: Council for Research and Development, 2005.

COZZENS, D.B., *Freeing Celibacy*, Collegeville, Minnesota, Liturgical Press, 2006.

COZZENS, D.B., *The Changing Face of the Priesthood: A Reflection on the Priest's Crisis of Soul*, Collegeville, Minnesota, Liturgical Press, 2000.

CROTTY, R., *Ireland in Crisis: A study in capitalist colonial undevelopment*, Dingle, Brandon Book Publishers, 1986.

CURCIONE, N.R., 'Family Influence on Commitment To The Priesthood: A Study Of Altar Boys', *Sociological Analysis*, 34, 265–80, 1973.

CURRAN, C.E., 'The Risks of Theology: Enda McDonagh and Vatican II', *The Furrow*, 57, 410–23, 2006.

CUTIÉ, A., *Dilemma: A Priest's Struggle with Faith and Love*, New York, Celebra, 2011.

D'ARCY, B., *A Different Journey*, Dublin, Sliabh Ban Productions, 2006.

DALTON, W., 'The 1990 Synod of Bishops: Priestly Formation', *The Furrow*, 41, 92–100, 1990.

DALY, C.B., *Steps On My Pilgrim Journey: Memories and Reflections*, Dublin, Veritas, 1998.

DALY, E., *Mister, Are You A Priest?*, Dublin, Four Courts Press, 2000.

DALY, E., *A Troubled See: Memoirs of a Derry Bishop*, Dublin, Four Courts Press, 2011.

DANNEELS, G., 'Priests of Our Time', *The Furrow*, 44, 331–40, 1993.

DE ROSA, P., *Vicars of Christ: The Dark Side of the Papacy*, London, Bantam Press, 1988.

DENZIN, N.K. & LINCOLN, Y.S., 'Introduction: the Discipline and Practice of Qualitative Research', in DENZIN, N.K. & LINCOLN, Y.S. (eds), *Handbook of Qualitative Research*, 2nd edn, London: Sage Publications, 2000.

DOBBELAERE, K., *Secularization: An Analysis at Three levels*, Oxford, P.I.E. – Peter Lang, 2005.

DOHERTY, J., 'The Priest in the Youth Club Scene', *The Furrow*, 28, 687–93, 1977.

DOHERTY, T., 'The Challenge of Clericalism', *Reality*, June, 10–15, 2013.

DOLAN, M., *Partnership in Lay Spirituality: Religious and Laity Find New Ways*, Dublin, The Columba Press, 2007.

DONADIO, R., 'On Gay Priests, Pope Francis asks, "Who am I to judge?"', *The New York Times*, 29 July 2013.

DONNELLY, J.S., 'A Church in Crisis: The Irish Catholic Church today', *History Ireland*, 8, 12–17, 2000.

DONNELLY, S. & INGLIS, T., 'The Media and the Catholic Church in Ireland: Reporting Clerical Child Sex Abuse', *Journal of Contemporary Religion*, 25, 1–19, 2010.

DORR, D., 'Changing Our Pastoral Priorities', *The Furrow*, 54, 583–92, 2003.

DORR, D., 'Celibacy', *The Furrow*, 55, 138–44, 2004.

DORR, D., 'A Christian Spirituality of Celibacy', in MCDONAGH, E. & MAC-NAMARA, V. (eds), *An Irish Reader In Moral Theology: The Legacy Of The Last Fifty Years. Volume II: Sex, Marriage and The Family*, Dublin: The Columba Press, 2011.

DOYLE, T. P., 'Clericalism: Enabler of Clergy Sexual Abuse', *Pastoral Psychology*, 54, 189–213, 2006.

DRAPER, A., 'I Must be Listening to My Friends', *The Furrow*, 52, 349–53, 2001.

DRUMM, M., 'The Catholic Priesthood in a New Millennium', *The Furrow*, 50, 587–95, 1999.

DRUMMOND, E., 'Attitudes Towards Sexuality: A Pilot Study in Ireland', *Learning Disability Practice*, 9, 28–34, 2006.

DUFFY, E., 'Towards What Kind of Priest?', *The Furrow*, 44, 208–14, 1993.

DUFFY, E., 'Help for Priests', *The Furrow*, 53, 536–47, 2002.

DUFFY, E., 'Of Bishops and Priests', *The Furrow*, 57, 339–47, 2006.

DUFFY, E., 'Clustering Parishes: Practice and Theology', in DUFFY, E. (ed.), *Parishes in Transition*, Dublin: The Columba Press, 2010a.

DUFFY, E., 'Introduction', in DUFFY, E. (ed.), *Parishes in Transition*, Dublin: The Columba Press, 2010b.

DUFFY, E. (ed.), *Parishes in Transition*, Dublin: The Columba Press, 2010c.

DUFFY, E., 'When the Christian Community Gathers on Sunday in the Absence of the Presbyter: What Happens?', *50th International Eucharistic Congress*, Dublin, 2012.

DULLES, A., *Models of the Church*, London, Gill and Macmillan, 1976.

DULLES, A., *The Priestly Office: A Theological Reflection*, New York, Paulist Press, 1997.

DUNN, J., *No Lions in the Hierarchy: An Anthology of Sorts*, Dublin, The Columba Press, 1994.

ETHERINGTON, K., *Becoming a Reflexive Researcher: Using Our Selves in Research*, London, Jessica Kingsley Publishers, 2004.

EUROFOUND, Third European Quality of Life Survey – Quality of life in Europe: Impacts of the crisis. Luxembourg: Publications Office of the European Union, 2012.

F. BRINLEY BRUTON, *Pope Francis' No. 2: Clerical celibacy is open to discussion* [Online], NBCNEWS.com. Available: http://worldnews.nbcnews.com/ _news/2013/09/11/20433950-pope-francis-no-2-clerical-celibacy-is-open-to-discussion [Accessed 13 November 2013].

FAGAN, S., *Has Sin Changed? A Book on Forgiveness*, Wilmington, Delaware, Michael Glazier, 1977.

FAHEY, T., 'Religion and Sexual Culture in Ireland', in EDER, F., HALL, L. & HEKMA, G. (eds), *Sexual Cultures in Europe: National Histories*, Manchester: Manchester University Press, 1999.

FAHEY, T., 'Religion and Prosperity', *Studies: An Irish Quarterly Review*, 90, 39–46, 2001.

FAHEY, T., 'Population', in O'SULLIVAN, S. (ed.), *Contemporary Ireland: A Sociological Map*, Dublin: University College Dublin Press, 2007.

FAHEY, T., HAYES, B. & SINNOTT, R., *Conflict and Consensus: A Study of Values and Attitudes in the Republic of Ireland and Northern Ireland*, Dublin, Institute of Public Administration, 2005.

FALLON, B., *An Age of Innocence: Irish Culture 1930–1960*, Dublin, Gill and Macmillan, 1998.

FERRITER, D., *The Transformation of Ireland 1900–2000*, London, Profile Books, 2004.

FERRITER, D., *Occasions of Sin: Sex & Society in Modern Ireland*, London, Profile Books, 2009.

FITZGERALD, G., *Garret Fitzgerald: An Autobiography*, Dublin, Gill and Macmillan, 1991.

FITZGIBBON, É., 'The Person Within Priesthood', *The Furrow*, 47, 226–8, 1996.

FITZGIBBON, É., 'The Diocesan Priesthood in the 21st Century', in DUFFY, E. (ed.), *Parishes in Transition*, Dublin: The Columba Press, 2010.

FLANAGAN, D., 'The Church: Participation in Decision Making', *Christus Rex*, XXIV, 96–109, 1969.

FLANNERY, A., 'Priest, Architect and Community I', *The Furrow*, 13, 627–35, 1962.

FLANNERY, A. (ed.), *The Basic Sixteen Documents, Vatican Council II: Constitutions, Decrees, Declarations*, Dublin: Dominican Publications, 1996.

FLANNERY, T., 'Celibacy for the Kingdom', *The Furrow*, 46, 623–8, 1995.

FLANNERY, T., *The Death of Religious Life*, Dublin, The Columba Press, 1997.

FLANNERY, T., *From the Inside: A Priest's View of the Catholic Church*, Cork, Mercier Press, 1999.

FLANNERY, T., *A Question of Conscience*, Dublin, Londubh Books, 2013.

FOGARTY, J. C., *The Catholic Priest: His Identity and Values: A Ministerial Profile of the Joliet Presbyterate*, Kansas City, Sheed & Ward, 1988.

FOGARTY, M., RYAN, L. & LEE, J., *Irish Values and Attitudes: The Irish Report of the European Value Systems Study*, Dublin, Dominican Publications, 1984.

FORDE, W., 'The Hours I Keep', *The Furrow*, 38, 693–6, 1987.

FORRISTAL, D., 'Part One: Surveying the Survey', in LANE, D. (ed.), *Reading the Signs of the Times: A Survey of Priests in Dublin*, Dublin: Veritas, 1997.

FOX, M., *The Pope's War: Why Ratzinger's Secret Crusade Has Imperiled the Church And How It Can Be Saved*, New York, Sterling Ethos, 2011.

FRANCIS, *Evangelii Gaudium, 'The Joy of the Gospel'. Apostolic Exhortation on the Proclamation of the Gospel in Today's World*, Dublin, Veritas, 2013.

FREENEY, P., 'The Priest in Local Politics', *The Furrow*, 30, 71–9, 1979.

FULLER, L., *Irish Catholicism since 1950: The Undoing of a Culture*, Dublin, Gill & Macmillan, 2002.

FULLER, L., 'Religion, Politics and Socio-Cultural Change in Twentieth-Century Ireland', *European Legacy*, 10, 41–54, 2005.

GALLAGHER, M. P., *Help My Unbelief*, Dublin, Veritas Publications, 1986.

GALLAGHER, R., 'Morality in a Changing Irish Society', *The Furrow*, 32, 713–24, 1981.

GALLAGHER, R. & HANNON, P., 'Can Gay Men Be Priests?', *The Furrow*, 57, 67–80, 2006.

GALLUP INTERNATIONAL, Millennium Survey. Dublin: Gallup/Irish Marketing Surveys, 1999.

GARVIN, T., *Preventing the Future: Why was Ireland so poor for so long?*, Dublin, Gill & Macmillan, 2005.

GARVIN, T., *News From A New Republic: Ireland in the 1950s*, Dublin, Gill & Macmillan, 2010.

GAUGHAN, J. A., *At the Coalface: Recollections of a city and country priest 1950–2000*, Dublin, The Columba Press, 2000.

GAUTIER, M. L., PERL, P. M. & FICHTER, S. J. (eds), *Same Call, Different Men: The Evolution of the Priesthood Since Vatican II*, Collegeville, Minnesota: Liturgical Press, 2012.

GIORDAN, G. (ed.), *Vocation and Social Context*, Leiden: Brill, 2007.

GOERGEN, D., *The Sexual Celibate*, New York, The Seabury Press, 1974.

GOFFMAN, E., *Asylums: Essays on the Social Situation of Mental Patients and Other Inmates*, London, Pelican, 1968.

GOODE, H., MCGEE, H. & O'BOYLE, C., *Time To Listen: Confronting Child Sexual Abuse by Catholic Clergy in Ireland*, Dublin, The Liffey Press, 2003.

GOVERNMENT OF IRELAND, The National Recovery Plan 2011–2014, Dublin: Stationery Office, 2010.

GREELEY, A., 'Andrew M. Greeley: Sociologist, Author, Novelist' in: UNSWORTH, T. (ed.), *The Last Priests in America: Conversations with Remarkable Men*, New York: Crossroads, 1991.

GREELEY, A., *Priests: A Calling in Crisis*, Chicago, The University of Chicago Press, 2004.

GREELEY, A. & WARD, C., 'How "Secularised" is the Ireland we Live in? Report on a Survey', *Doctrine and Life*, 50, 581–617, 2000.

GREELEY, A. M., *Priests in the United States*, Garden City, New York, Doubleday & Company, 1972.

HAGAN, J. W. (ed.), *The Economy of Ireland: Policy and Performance*, Dublin: Irish Management Institute, 1984.

HANAFIN, W., Radical Chic. In conversation with Ruairí Quinn, Minister for Education. *LIFE, TheSunday Independent*, 18–21, 2012.

HANLEY, A., Trends in Irish Church Personnel, 1990–1994. Maynooth: Council for Research and Development, Irish Bishops' Conference, 1995.

HANLEY, A., Religious Confidence Survey Northern Ireland 1998. Maynooth: Council for Research & Development, Irish Bishops' Conference, 1998.

HANLEY, A., A New Survey on Religious Belief and Practice in Ireland: Summary and Analysis. Maynooth: Council for Research and Development, Irish Bishops' Conference, 2000a.

HANLEY, A., Trends in Irish Church Personnel, 1995–1999. Maynooth: Council for Research and Development, Irish Bishops' Conference, 2000b.

HANNAN, D., *Rural Exodus: A study of the forces influencing the large-scale migration of Irish rural youth*, London, Geoffrey Chapman, 1970.

HARDING, M., *Staring at Lakes: A Memoir of Love, Melancholy and Magical Thinking*, Dublin, Hachette Books Ireland, 2013.

HARDING, M. P., *Priest*, Belfast, The Blackstaff Press Limited, 1986.

HAUGHTON, J., The Historical Background in O'HAGAN, J. W. (ed.), *The Economy of Ireland: Policy & Performance of a European Region*, 8th edn, Dublin, Gill & Macmillan, 2000.

HEALY, J., *No One Shouted STOP. Formerly Death of an Irish Town*, Achill, The House of Healy, 1968.

HEBBLETHWAITE, P., *John XXIII: Pope of the Century*, London, Continuum, 1994.

HEDERMAN, M. P., *Underground Cathedrals*, Dublin, The Columba Press, 2010.

HEGARTY, K., 'Failing Better', *The Furrow*, 57, 474–9, 2006.

HEGARTY, K., 'Time to free church from clammy grip of clericalism', *The Irish Times*, 10 April 2012.

HEPWORTH, M., SIMONDS, L.M. & MARSH, R., '"Catholic priests" conceptualisation of scrupulosity: a grounded theory analysis', *Mental Health, Religion & Culture*, 13, 1–16, 2010.

HOBAN, B., 'Priesthood at Risk – The Celibacy Factor', *The Furrow*, 40, 195–203, 1989.

HOBAN, B., 'Priesthood in Trouble', *The Furrow*, 41, 410–14, 1990.

HOBAN, B., 'What Are We At?', *The Furrow*, 43, 491–6, 1992.

HOBAN, B., 'Elephants in the Living Room', *The Furrow*, 47, 659–67, 1996.

HOBAN, B., 'A Time for Courage', *The Furrow*, 60, 342–54, 2009.

HOBAN, B., 'A New Association of Priests?', *The Furrow*, 61, 483–6, 2010.

HOBAN, B., *Where Do We Go From Here? The Crisis in Irish Catholicism*, Killala, Banley House, 2012.

HOBAN, B., 'Does "isolated and at risk" describe the rural priest today?', *Western People*, 16 April 2013.

HOBAN, B., *Who will break the bread for us?*, Ballina, Banley House, 2013.

HOENKAMP-BISSCHOPS, A. M., Catholic Priests and Their Experience of Celibacy, *Journal of Religion and Health*, 31, 327–36, 1992.

HOGAN, E.M., *The Irish Missionary Movement: A Historical Survey, 1830–1980*, Dublin, Gill and Macmillan, 1990.

HOGAN, F., *A Path to Healing a Nation*, Dublin, The Columba Press, 2013.

HOGAN, L., 'Divide over Vatican II's legacy is wider than ever', *The Irish Times*, 12 October 2012.

HOGE, D.R., *The First Five Years of the Priesthood: A Study of Newly Ordained Catholic Priests*, Minnesota, The Liturgical Press, 2002.

HOGE, D.R. & WENGER, J.E., *Evolving Visions of the Priesthood: Changes from Vatican II to the Turn of the New Century*, Minnesota, The Liturgical Press, 2003.

HOLMES, P.A., 'Sacramental Psychology: Treating Intimacy Failure in Catholic Priests', *Journal of Religion and Health*, 35, 125–40, 1996.

HOOPER, J., *'Pope Francis effect' credited with boosting Italian congregations* [Online], theguardian.com. Available: http://www.theguardian.com/world/2013/nov/10/pope-francis-effect-italy-catholicism [Accessed 10 November 2013].

HORNSBY-SMITH, M.P., 'Social and Religious Transformations in Ireland: A Case of Secularisation?', in GOLDTHORPE, J.H. & WHELAN, C.T. (eds), *The Development of Industrial Society in Ireland*, New York: Oxford University Press, 1992.

HOUTART, F.H., 'Critical Decisions and Institutional Tensions in a Religious Institution: The Case of Vatican II', *Review of Religious Research*, 9, 131–46, 1968.

HUMPHREYS, A., *New Dubliners*, London, Routledge & Keegan Paul, 1966.

HUMPHREYS, J., *God's Entrepreneurs: How Irish Missionaries Tried to Change the World*, Dublin, New Island, 2010.

INGLIS, T., *Religious Ideology of Irish University Students*, M.Soc.Sc., University College Dublin, 1979.

INGLIS, T., 'Sacred and Secular in Catholic Ireland. A review article of Irish Values and Attitudes: The Irish Report of the European Value Systems Study', *Studies*, 74, 38–46, 1985.

INGLIS, T., 'The Separation of Church and State in Ireland', *Social Studies*, 9, 37–48, 1986.

INGLIS, T., *Moral Monopoly: The Catholic Church in Modern Irish Society*, Dublin, Gill and Macmillan, 1987.

INGLIS, T., 'Foucault, Bourdieu and the Field of Irish Sexuality', *Irish Journal of Sociology*, 7, 5–28, 1997.

INGLIS, T., *Moral Monopoly: The Rise and Fall of the Catholic Church in Modern Ireland*, Dublin, University College Dublin Press, 1998.

INGLIS, T., 'Catholic Church, Religious Capital and Symbolic Domination', in BOSS, M. & MAHER, E. (eds), *Engaging Modernity: Readings of Irish Politics, Culture and Literature at the Turn of the Century*, Dublin: Veritas, 2003.

INGLIS, T., 'Religion, identity, state and society', in CLEARY, J. & CONNOLLY, C. (eds), Cambridge: Cambridge University Press, 2005.

INGLIS, T., 'Catholic Identity in Contemporary Ireland: Belief and Belonging to Traditions', *Journal of Contemporary Religion*, 22, 205–20, 2007.

INTERNATIONAL COMMITTEE ON ENGLISH IN THE LITURGY, The Rite of Ordination of Priests, Dublin: Veritas, 1975.

IONA INSTITUTE, 'Attitudes towards the Catholic Church', An Amárach Report for the Iona Institute. Dublin: The Iona Institute, Amárach Research, 2011.

IPSOS MRBI, 'Irish Attitudes and Values Survey', Dublin: Ipsos MRBI, 2012.

IRISH BISHOPS' CONFERENCE, *Programme for the Formation of Priests in Irish Seminaries*, Dublin, Veritas, 2006.

IRISH CATHOLIC, 'The Irish Catholic National Survey of Priests in Ireland 2004: The Future of Priests and Priests of the Future', *The Irish Catholic*, 2004.

IRISH CATHOLIC BISHOPS' ADVISORY COMMITTEE ON CHILD SEXUAL ABUSE BY PRIESTS AND RELIGIOUS, *Child Sexual Abuse: Framework for a Church Response (The 'Green' book)*, Dublin, Veritas Publications, 1996.

IRISH MARKETING SURVEYS, Survey of an Irish Diocese – Archdiocese of Cashel & Emly, Dublin: Irish Marketing Surveys, 1998.

IRISH TIMES, *Catholicism Now*, Dublin, *The Irish Times*/Ipsos MRBI, 2012.

JOHN PAUL II, *Post-Synodal Apostolic Exhortation Pastores Dabo Vobis to the Bishops, Clergy and Faithful on the Formation of Priests in the Circumstances of the Present Day* [Online]. Vatican City: The Vatican. Available: http://www.vatican.va/holy_father/john_paul_ii/apost_exhortations/documents/hf_jp-ii_exh_25031992_pastores-dabo-vobis_en.html [Accessed 15 November 2011].

JOHN PAUL II, *Gift and Mystery: On the Fiftieth Anniversary of My Ordination*, 1997.

KEENAN, M., *Child Sexual Abuse & The Catholic Church: Gender, Power, and Organizational Culture*, New York, Oxford University Press, 2012.

KENNEDY, K. A., GIBLIN, T. & MCHUGH, D. (eds), *The Economic Development of Ireland in the Twentieth Century*, London: Routledge, 1988.

KENNY, E., Speech by Enda Kenny to the Dáil on the revelations of the Cloyne report, *The Irish Times*, 21 July 2011.

KENNY, M., *Goodbye to Catholic Ireland: A social, personal and cultural history from the fall of Parnell to the realm of Mary Robinson*, London, Sinclair-Stevenson, 1997.

KERKHOFS, J. (ed.), *Europe Without Priests?*, London: SCM Press, 1995.

KERR, D. A., *Peel, Priests and Politics: Sir Robert Peel's Administration and the Roman Catholic Church in Ireland, 1841–1846*, Oxford, Clarendon Press, 1982.

KERRIGAN, G., *Another Country: Growing up in '50s ireland*, Dublin, Gill & Macmillan, 1998.

KIRBY, P., *Is Irish Catholicism Dying? Liberating an Imprisoned Church*, Dublin: Mercier, 1984.

KIRBY, P., *Celtic Tiger in Collapse: Explaining the Weaknesses of the Irish Model*, Basingstoke, Palgrave Macmillan, 2010.

KREJSLER, J., 'Professions and their Identities: How to explore professional development among (semi-) professions', *Scandinavian Journal of Educational Research*, 49, 335–57, 2005.

KÜNG, H., *The Catholic Church: A Short History*, London, Weidenfeld and Nicolson, 2001.

LANDSBERG, M., 'Pope Benedict rejects calls to end celibacy rule', *Los Angeles Times*, Los Angeles, 2010.

LANE, D. (ed.), *Reading the Signs of the Times: A Survey of Priests in Dublin*, Dublin: Veritas, 1997.

LANE, D. A., 'Vatican II: The Irish Experience', *The Furrow*, 55, 67–81, 2004.

LAVEN, M., 'Sex and Celibacy in Early Modern Venice', *The Historical Journal*, 44, 865–88, 2001.

LAWLER, S., *Identity: Sociological Perspectives*, Cambridge, Polity Press, 2008.

LAYTE, R., MCGEE, H., QUAIL, A., KUNDLE, R., COUSINS, G., DONNELLY, C., MULCAHY, F. & CONROY, R., The Irish Study of Sexual Health and Relationships. Dublin: Crisis Pregnancy Agency and the Department of Health and Children, 2006.

LENNON, J., School Leavers' Attitudes Towards Vocations. Dublin: Research and Development Unit, Irish Bishops' Conference, 1974.

LENNON, J., RYAN, L., MACGRÉIL, M. & DRAKE, N., A Survey of Catholic Clergy and Religious in Ireland, 1970. Dublin: The Research and Development Unit, Catholic Communications Institute of Ireland, 1971.

LENNON, J., RYAN, L., MACGRÉIL, M. & DRAKE, N., Survey of Catholic Clergy and Religious personnel 1971, *Social Studies*, 1, 137–230, 1972.

LIBRERIA EDITRICE VATICANA, *Catechism of the Catholic Church*, Dublin, Veritas, 1994.

LINDAU, S.T., SCHUMM, P., LAUMANN, E.O., LEVINSON, W., O'MUIRCHEARTAIGH, C. A. & LINDA, J.W., 'A Study of Sexuality and Health among Older Adults in the United States', *The New England Journal of Medicine*, 357, 762–74, 2007.

LYNCH, B., *A Priest on Trial*, London, Bloomsbury, 1993.

LYNCH, J. E., 'Chapter III: The obligations and Rights of Clerics', in BEAL, J. P., CORIDEN, J. A. & GREEN, T. J. (eds), *New Commentary on the Code of Canon Law*, New York: Paulist Press, 2000.

MACGRÉIL, M., Religious Beliefs and Practice of Dublin Adults, *Social Studies*, 3, 1974.

MACGRÉIL, M., *Prejudice and Tolerance in Ireland*, Dublin, College of Industrial Relations, 1977.

MACGRÉIL, M., *Prejudice in Ireland Revisited*, Maynooth, Survey and Research Unit, St Patrick's College, Maynooth, 1996.

MACGRÉIL, M., Irish Seminarians Today. Report on a Survey of the Background and views of Seminarians of St Patrick's College, Maynooth. Maynooth: The Survey and Research Unit, Department of Social Studies, 1997.

MACGRÉIL, M. & INGLIS, T., Irish Priests and Religious 1970–1975. Survey of Catholic Clergy and Religious in Ireland. Dublin: Research and Development Unit, Irish Bishops' Conference, 1977.

MACGRÉIL, M. & RHATIGAN, F., The Challenge of Indifference. A Need for Religious Revival in Ireland. Maynooth: NUI Maynooth, 2009.

MACKEY, J.P., 'Power at the heart of imposing celibacy on diocesan priest-hood', *The Irish Times*, 24 August 2010.

MACNAMARA, A., 'News and Views' (Letters to the Editor), *The Furrow*, 40, 239–41, 1985.

MACNAMARA, V., Morality and Law: Experience and Prospects. *Studies: An Irish Quarterly Review*, 74, 373–92, 1985.

MALONEY, R., 'The Ordination of Women', *The Furrow*, 32, 438–48, 1981.

MANNHEIM, K., *Essays on the Sociology of Knowledge*, London, Routledge & Kegan Paul, 1952.

MANUEL, G.M., 'Religious Celibacy from the Celibate's Point of View', *Journal of Religion and Health*, 28, 279–97, 1989.

MARTIN, D., The Church in the Modern World. *50th International Eucharistic Congress* [Online]. Available: http://www.dublindiocese.ie/content/11062012-church-modern-world [Accessed 5 February 2013].

MASON, J., *Qualitative Researching*, London, Sage Publications, 2002.

MATON, K., Habitus in GRENFELL, M. (ed.), *Pierre Bourdieu: Key Concepts*, Durham: Acumen, 2008.

MATTE, I., 'The Pope's Children, Génération Lyrique: The Decline of Catholic Practices in Ireland's Celtic Tiger and Quebec's Révolution Tranquille', *The Canadian Journal of Irish Studies*, 33, 22–30, 2007.

MAXWELL, E., 'Catholic schools play vital part in pluralist society', *The Irish Times*, 28 January 2014.

MCALEESE, M., Report of the Inter-Departmental Committee to establish the facts of State involvement with the Magdalen laundries. Dublin: Department of Justice and Equality, 2013.

MCALLISTER, I., 'Religious Commitment and Social Attitudes in Ireland', *Review of Religious Research*, 25, 3–20, 1983.

MCBRIEN, R.P., 'Catholic Identity in a Time of Change', *The Furrow*, 55, 455–64, 2004.

MCCALL, D., 'Sex and the Clergy', *Sexual Addiction & Compulsivity: The Journal of Treatment & Prevention*, 9, 89–95, 2002.

MCCARTHY, J., 'New priest body denies rift with ACP', *The Sunday Times*, 2 February 2014.

MCCARTHY, P., *The Unheard Story: Dublin Archdiocese and the Murphy Report*, Dublin, Londubh Books, 2013.

MCCONVILLE, L. & MCCONVILLE, G., 'The Liturgy and Church Architecture: The Principles Illustrated', *The Furrow*, 13, 645–52, 1962.

MCCORMACK, W. H. D., 'Priest, Architect and Community II', *The Furrow*, 13, 636–41, 1962.

MCCULLOUGH, D., Inquiry Into Certain Matters Relating To Maynooth College. Maynooth: Maynooth College, 2005.

MCDEVITT, P. J., 'Sexual and Intimacy Health of Roman Catholic Priests', *Journal of Prevention & Intervention in the Community*, 40, 208–18, 2012.

MCDONAGH, E., 'The Risk of Priesthood', *The Journal*, 51, 592–601, 2000.

MCDONAGH, E., 'The Crisis of Trust', *The Furrow*, 60, 67–70, 2009.

MCGAHERN, J., 'The Church and Its Spire' in DER ZIEL, S. (ed.), *Love of the World Essays*, London: Faber and Faber, 2009.

MCGARRY, P., 'Priest banned from writing', *The Irish Times*, 13 November 2010.

MCGARRY, P., 'Archbishop says Dublin diocese facing crisis', *The Irish Times*, 14 December 2011.

MCGARRY, P., 'McAleese in support of same-sex marriage', *The Irish Times*, 9 October 2012.

MCGARRY, P., 'Archbishop Diarmuid Martin in robust defence of Murphy Commission', *The Irish Times*, 30 October 2013.

MCGARRY, P., '"Singing priest" sentenced for sex abuse', *The Irish Times*, 8 June 2013.

MCGARRY, P. & AGNEW, P., 'Silenced priest told to reflect on situation', *The Irish Times*, 11 April 2012.

MCGOVERN, T. J., *Priestly Identity: A Study in the Theology of Priesthood*, Dublin, Four Courts Press, 2002.

MCGREEVY, R., 'Most people no longer trust Church, Government or banks', *The Irish Times*, 29 April 2010.

MCGUANE, J., 'The Professional Cleric', *The Furrow*, 59, 553–62, 2008.

MCMAHON, B., A Study of Religion Among Dublin Adolescents. Maynooth: Council for Research & Development, Irish Bishops' Conference, 1982.

MCVEIGH, J., *Taking a Stand: Memoir of an Irish Priest*, Cork, Mercier Press, 2008.

MCWILLIAMS, D., *The Pope's Children: Ireland's New Elite*, Dublin, Gill & Macmillan, 2005.

MISHLER, E. G., *Storylines: Craft Artists: Narratives of Identity*, Cambridge, M.A., Harvard University Press, 1999.

MOLONEY, G., 'Successes and failures of Vatican II could help shape better Vatican III', *The Irish Times*, 9 October 2012.

MOLONEY, R., 'Sundays Without Priests', *The Furrow*, 58, 397–401, 2007.

MOORE, C., *Betrayal of Trust: The Father Brendan Smyth Affair and the Catholic Church*, Dublin, Marino books, 1995.

MORAN, G. (ed.), *Radical Irish Priests 1660–1970*, Dublin: Four Courts Press, 1998.

MRBI, Sources of influence on our society. 25th Anniversary Survey. Dublin, 1987.

MRBI/THE IRISH TIMES, MRBI 21st anniversary poll. *The Irish Times*, Dublin, 1983.

MULCAHY, B., Parish Missions, Parish Retreats and Priests' Retreats. Dublin: Research and Development Unit, Irish Bishops' Conference, 1971.

MULCAHY, B., Report of a Survey of Views of Irish Clergy. Dublin: Research and Development Unit, Irish Bishops' Conference, 1974.

MURPHY, A. & DE ROSA, P., *Forbidden Fruit: The True Story of My Secret Love for the Bishop of Galway*, London, Little, Brown and Company, 1993.

MURPHY, A. E., 'The "Celtic Tiger" – An Analysis of Ireland's Economic Growth Performance, *EUI Working Papers*, San Domenico, Italy: European University Institute. Rober Schuman Centre for Advanced Studies, 2000.

MURPHY, D., 'Introduction', in REDMOND, A. (ed.), *That was then, this is now*, Dublin: Stationery Office, 2000.

MURPHY, F., BUCKLEY, H. & JOYCE, L., The Ferns Report, presented by the Ferns Inquiry to the Minister for Health and Children. Dublin: Stationery Office, 2005.

MURPHY, Y., MANGAN, I. & O'NEILL, H., Commission of Investigation. Report into the Catholic Archdiocese of Dublin, submitted to the Minister for Justice, Equality and Law Reform. Dublin: Stationery Office, 2009.

MURPHY, Y., MANGAN, I. & O'NEILL, H., Report into the Catholic Diocese of Cloyne. Dublin: The Department of Justice and Law Reform, 2011.

MURRAY, D., 'The Priest in Context: The Irish Republic', in BOHAN, H. (ed.), *Being a Priest in Ireland Today*, Dublin: Dominican Publications, 1988.

MURRAY, D., 'To Serve the People Faithfully', *The Furrow*, 46, 607–14, 1995.

MURRAY, P., *Life in Paradox: The Story of a Gay Catholic Priest*, Ropley, O Books, 2008.

MYERS, J., '"Senior Priest" Retirement Alternative', *The Furrow*, 52, 471–80, 2001.

NATIONAL BOARD FOR SAFEGUARDING CHILDREN IN THE CATHOLIC CHURCH, Safeguarding Children. Standards and guidance Document for the Catholic Church in Ireland. Dublin: The National Board for Safeguarding Children in the Catholic Church, 2008.

NEWMAN, J., 'Vocations in Ireland 1966', *Christus Rex*, xxi, 1966.

NEWMAN, J., *Ireland Must Choose*, Dublin, Four Courts Press, 1983.

NEWMAN, J., RYAN, L. & WARD, C., 'Attitudes of Young People Towards Vocations', *Social Studies*, 1, 531–50, 1972.

NEWMAN, J., WARD, C. & RYAN, L., Vocations Survey 71. A Survey of Vocations in Ireland, 1971. Dublin: Research and Development Unit. Catholic Communications Institute of Ireland, 1971.

NIC GHIOLLA PHÁDRAIG, M., 'Religion in Ireland: Preliminary Analysis', *Social Studies*, 5, 113–64, 1976.

NIC GHIOLLA PHÁDRAIG, M., 'Lapsing Children: A Sociologist's Comment', *Doctrine and Life*, 32, 485–8, 1982.

NIC GHIOLLA PHÁDRAIG, M., 'Religious Practice and Secularisation', in CLANCY, P., DRUDY, S., LYNCH, K. & O'DOWD, L. (eds), *Ireland: A Sociological Profile*, Dublin: Institute of Public Administration, 1986.

NOLAN, J., Youth Culture and the Faith. Dublin: Irish Episcopal Conference, 1974.

NORRIS, K., *The Cloister Walk*, New York, Riverhead Books, 1996.

O'BRIEN, P., 'A Letter to the Papal Nuncio', *The Furrow*, 46, 13–22, 1995.

O'CALLAGHAN, D., *Putting Hand to the Plough: A Memoir*, Dublin, Veritas, 2007.

O'CARROLL, M., 'Has the Priesthood been Devalued?', *The Furrow*, 38, 449–54, 1987.

O'CONNOR, F., *The Collar: Stories of Irish Priests*, Belfast, The Blackstaff Press Limited, 1993.

O'DOHERTY, C., 'Archbishop Martin: Church in Ireland on brink of collapse', *The Irish Examiner*, 2011.

O'DOHERTY, K., 'Where have all the faithful gone? A survey of religion in the university', *The Furrow*, xx, 575–91, 1969.

O'DONOHUE, J., 'Minding the Threshold – Towards a Theory of Priesthood in Difficult Times', *The Furrow*, 49, 323–35, 1998.

O'DRISCOLL, L., 'Response to Bishop Murray', in BOHAN, H. (ed.), *Being a Priest in Ireland Today*, Dublin: Dominican Publications, 1988.

O'GORMAN, C., *Beyond Belief*, London, Hodder & Stoughton, 2009.

O'HANLON, G., 'At a Crossroads: Irish Catholicism Fifty Years after Vatican II', *Studies: An Irish Quarterly Review*, 101, 2012.

O'MAHONY, E., Report on the Age profile of Diocesan Priests Currently Working in Ireland's Dioceses. Maynooth: Council for Research & Development, Irish Bishops' Conference, 2007.

O'MAHONY, E., Religious Practice and Values in Ireland. A summary of European Values Study 4th wave data. Maynooth: Council for Research & Development, Irish Bishops' Conference, 2010.

O'MAHONY, E., Diocesan Priest Age Profile. Maynooth: Council for Research & Development, Irish Bishops' Conference, 2011.

O'MAHONY, E., Diocesan Priest Age Profile. Maynooth: Irish Bishops' Conference, 2013.

O'MALLEY, J. W., 'Some Basics About Celibacy', *America*, 187, 7–11, 2002.

O'MALLEY, J. W., *What Happened at Vatican II*, London, The Belknap Press of Harvard University Press, 2008.

O'MEARA, D., 'One Priest and His Role', *The Furrow*, 47, 157–60, 1996.

O'MORAIN, P., 'The loneliness at the heart of the priesthood', *The Irish Times Healthplus*, 14, 2010.

O'MORAIN, P., 'Clergy and Sex? Now there's a ridiculous idea', *The Irish Times Healthplus*, 2012.

O'RIORDAN, S., 'The Furrow: 1950–1990', *The Furrow*, 41, 71–80, 1990.

O'TOOLE, F., 'Being a priest could be a lot of fun', *The Irish Times*, Dublin, 2010.

OLDEN, M., 'Tomorrow's Parish', *The Furrow*, 55, 2004.

OLDEN, M. G., 'Priesthood in Changing Times', *The Furrow*, 59, 2008.

PAPESH, M. L., *Clerical Culture: Contradiction and Transformation*, Collegeville, Minnesota, Liturgical Press, 2004.

PARFREY, P., 'Religious Practice and Beliefs of Cork Undergraduates', *Social Studies. Irish Journal of Sociology*, 5, 103–12, 1976.

PARISH, H., *Clerical Celibacy and Clerical Marriage in the West, c.1100–1700*, Farnham, Surrey, Ashgate Publishing Group, 2010.

PAUL VI, *Sacerdotalus Caelibatus*. Encyclical of Pope Paul VI on the celibacy of the priest. Available: http://www.vatican.va/holy_father/paul_vi/encyclicals/documents/hf_p-vi_enc_24061967_sacerdotalis_en.html [Accessed 5 February 2013].

PETERSON, R. W. & SCHOENHERR, R. A., 'Organizational Status Attainment of Religious Professionals', *Social Forces*, 56, 794–822, 1978.

PHILIBERT, P. J., *The Priesthood of the Faithful: Key to a Living Church*, Collegeville, Minnesota, Liturgical Press, 2005.

PLANTE, T. G., 'Homosexual Applicants to the Priesthood: How Many and are they Psychologically Healthy?', *Pastoral Psychology*, 54, 495–8, 2007.

POWER, B., 'Opinions and Attitudes of Irish University Students', *Reality*, 1969.

POWER, R., *The Hungry Grass*, Dublin, Poolbeg, 1969.

PRINCE, S., 'The Global Revolt of 1968 and Northern Ireland', *The Historical Journal*, 49, 2006.

PRO MUNDI VITA, The Vocation Ministry in North America, 1987.

QIRKO, H., The Institutional Maintenance of Celibacy. *Current Anthropology*, 43, 321–9, 2002.

RAFTERY, M. & O'SULLIVAN, E., *Suffer the Little Children: The Inside Story of Ireland's Industrial Schools*, Dublin, New Island, 1999.

RICE, D., *Shattered Vows: Exodus From The Priesthood*, London, Michael Joseph, 1990.

RIEGEL, R., 'Catholic hierarchy burying its head in sand, says top priest', *The Irish Independent*, 5 November 2011.

ROSE, R., *Governing without Consensus: An Irish Perspective*, London, Faber and Faber, 1971.

ROSSETTI, S. J., *The Joy of Priesthood*, Notre Dame, Indiana, Ave Maria Press, 2005.

ROSSETTI, S. J., 'Becoming Priests for the First Time', *The Furrow*, 59, 455–70, 2008.

RTÉ, 'Attitudes to Economic and Religious Issues', Dublin, 1974.

RTÉ, 'Attitudes Towards the Catholic Church', Dublin: RTÉ/MRBI, 1998.

RTÉ, Religious Issues Poll. Dublin: RTÉ *Prime Time*/MRBI, 2003.

RYAN, A., 'Parish Priorities', *The Furrow*, 59, 340–4, 2008.

RYAN, L., The Changing Direction of Irish Seminaries. Dublin: Research and Development Unit of the Catholic Communications Institute of Ireland, 1972.

RYAN, L., 'Church and Politics. The Last Twenty-five Years', *The Furrow*, 30, 3–18, 1979.

RYAN, L., 'Faith Under Survey', *The Furrow*, 34, 3–15, 1983.

RYAN, L., 'Is there a Shortage of Priests?', *The Furrow*, 39, 619–26, 1988.

RYAN, S., 'The Priesthood Today: Outgoing President's Address', in BOHAN, H. (ed.), *Being a Priest in Ireland Today*, Dublin: Dominican Publications, 1988.

SAMMON, S. D., *An Undivided Heart: Making Sense of Celibate Chastity*, New York, Alba House, 1993.

SAUNDERS, P., *Urban Politics: A Sociological Interpretation*, London, Hutchinson, 1983.

SCHNEIDER, L. & ZURCHER, L., 'Toward Understanding the Catholic Crisis: Observations on Dissident Priests in Texas', *Scientific Study of Religion*, 9, 197–207, 1970.

SCHOENHERR, R. & YOUNG, L., *Full Pews. Empty Altars: Demographics of the Priest Shortage in United States Catholic Dioceses*, Madison, Wisconsin, The University of Wisconsin Press, 1993.

SCHOENHERR, R. A., *Goodbye Father: The Celibate Male Priesthood and the Future of the Catholic Church*, New York, Oxford University Press, 2002.

SCHOENHERR, R. A. & GREELEY, A. M., 'Role Commitment Processes and the American Catholic Priesthood', *American Sociological Review*, 39, 407–26, 1974.

SCHOENHERR, R. A. & YOUNG, L. A., 'Quitting the Clergy: Resignations in the Roman Catholic Priesthood', *Journal for the Scientific Study of Religion*, 29, 463–81, 1990.

SHARE, P., TOVEY, H. & CORCORAN, M. P., *A Sociology of Ireland*, Dublin, Gill and Macmillan, 2007.

SIPE, A. W. R., *Sex, Priests, and Power: Anatomy Of A Crisis*, New York, Brunner/ Mazel Publishers, 1995.

SIPE, A. W. R., 'The crisis of sexual abuse and the celibate/sexual agenda of the Catholic Church', in PLANTE, T. G. (ed.), *Sin Against the Innocents: Sexual Abuse by Priests and the Role of the Catholic Church*, London: Praeger, 2004.

SIPE, A. W. R., 'Celibacy Today. Mystery, Myth and Miasma', *Crosscurrents*, 57, 545–62, 2007.

SKINNER, D., TAGG, C. & HOLLOWAY, J., 'Managers and Research. The Pros and Cons of Qualitative Approaches', *Management Learning*, 31, 163–79, 2000.

SMITH, M., 'Profound and positive change took root despite all the obstacles and doubt', *The Irish Times*, 11 October 2012.

SMYTH, J., 'Archbishop Martin criticised for failure to support priests', *The Irish Times*, 28 January 2010.

SOCIAL RESEARCH ASSOCIATION, Ethical Guidelines. Available: http:// the-sra.org.uk/sra_resources/research-ethics/ethics-guidelines [Accessed 5 February 2013], 2003.

SOCIOLOGICAL ASSOCIATION OF IRELAND, Ethical Guidelines. Available: http://www.sociology.ie/docstore/dls/pages_list/3_sai_ethical_guidel ines.pdf [Accessed 5 February 2013], 2004.

STANDÚN, P., 'Priestly Options in a Retrenching Church', *The Furrow*, 44, 84–7, 1993.

STARK, R. & FINKE, R., 'Catholic Religious Vocations: Decline and Revival', *Review of Religious Research*, 42, 125–45, 2000.

STICKLER, A. M., 'The Evolution Of The Discipline Of Celibacy In The Western Church From The End Of The Patristic Era To The Council of Trent', in CHARUE, A. M., CHAUCHARD, P., CROUZEL, H., GRUCHON, G., BOVIS, A. D., FOLLIET, J., GUITTON, J., HACKER, P., HODL, L., HOFFNER, C. J., JEDIN, H., KOSNETTER, J., LEGRAND, L., LELOIR, L., MARINI, M., MASSAUT, J. P., NEDONCELLE, M., RAMBALDI, G., STICKLER, A. M., STEENBERGHEN, F. V. & COPPENS, J. (eds), *Priesthood and Celibacy*, Milano-Roma: Editrice Ancora, 1972.

SUNDAY TIMES, Opinion Poll. Dublin: *The Sunday Times*/Behaviour & Attitudes, 2013.

SUNDAY TRIBUNE, Public Opinion Poll. Dublin: *The Sunday Tribune*/Millward Brown, 2005.

SWEENEY, E., *Down, Down Deeper and Down: Ireland in the 1970s and 1980s*, Dublin, Gill & Macmillan, 2010.

SWEENEY, F., Commissions of Investigation and Procedural Fairness. A Review from a legal perspective of the Commissions of investigation Act 2004 and of the Report into the Catholic Archdiocese of Dublin (the 'Murphy Report') forwarded to the Minister on 21 July 2009 and released on 26 November 2009. Dublin: Association of Catholic Priests, 2013.

SWENSON, D., 'Religious Differences between Married and Celibate Clergy: Does Celibacy Make a Difference?', *Sociology of Religion*, 59, 37–43, 1998.

TAYLOR, A. & GOSNEY, M., 'Sexuality in older age: essential considerations for healthcare professionals', *Age and Ageing*, 40, 538–43, 2011.

THE IRISH CATHOLIC, National Survey of Priests in Ireland 2004: The Future of Priests and Priests of the Future, *The Irish Catholic*, 28 October 2004.

THE MURPHY REPORT, Commission of Investigation. Report into the Catholic Archdiocese of Dublin, Dublin, 2009.

THOMSON, P., 'Field' in GRENFELL, M. (ed.), *Pierre Bourdieu: Key Concepts*, Durham: Acumen, 2008.

TIERNEY, M., 'The Challenge of a Changing Priesthood', *The Furrow*, 37, 41–6, 1986.

TIERNEY, M., *No Second Chance: Reflections of a Dublin Priest*, Dublin, The Columba Press, 2010.

TOBIN, F., *The Best of Decades: Ireland in the Nineteen Sixties*, Dublin, Gill and Macmillan, 1984.

TUATHAIGH, G. Ó., 'Language, ideology and national identity', in CLEARY, J. & CONNOLLY, C. (eds), *The Cambridge Companion to Modern Irish Culture*, Cambridge: Cambridge University Press, 2005.

TWOMEY, D. V., *The End of Irish Catholicism?*, Dublin, Veritas, 2003.

UNITED STATES CONFERENCE OF CATHOLIC BISHOPS, *The Basic Plan for the Ongoing Formation of Priests* [Online]. Available: http://www.usccb. org/beliefs-and-teachings/vocations/priesthood/priestly-life-and-ministry/national-plan-for-the-ongoing-formation-of-priests.cfm [Accessed 12 March 2013], 2001.

VATICAN, Code of Canon Law. Available: http://www.vatican.va/archive/ENG1104/_PY.HTM [Accessed 5 February 2013], 1983.

VATICAN, *Statistical Yearbook of the Church 2007*, Vatican, Liberia Editrice Vaticana, 2009.

VATICAN, Vatican report on the Apostolic Visitation in Ireland. Vatican: Rome Reports TV News Agency, 2013.

VERDIECK, M.J., SHIELDS, J.J. & HOGE, D.R., 'Role Commitment Processes Revisited: American Catholic Priests 1970 and 1985', *Journal for the Scientific Study of Religion*, 27, 524–35, 1988.

VIRGINIA, S.G., 'Burnout and Depression Among Roman Catholic Secular, Religious and Monastic Clergy', *Pastoral Psychology*, 47, 49–67, 1988.

WALKER, G., 'Eunuchs for the Kingdom of Heaven: Constructing the Celibate Priest', *Studies in Gender and Sexuality*, 5, 233–57, 2008.

WALSH, W., 'Priest and Bishop', *The Furrow*, 53, 523–9, 2002.

WARD, C., 'Christians and Social Change', *Christus Rex*, xix, 247–56, 1965.

WARD, C.K., 'Socio-Religious Research in Ireland', *Social Compass*, xi, 25–9, 1964.

WEAFER, J.A., 'Change and Continuity in Irish Religion 1974–1985', *Doctrine and Life*, 36, 507–17, 1986.

WEAFER, J.A., 'Vocations – A Review of National and International Trends', *The Furrow*, 39, 501–11, 1988.

WEAFER, J.A., 'The Difficulties of Preaching in a Changing Ireland', *Priests & People*, 4, 2–14, 1990.

WEAFER, J.A., 'A Church in Recession', *The Furrow*, 44, 219–25, 1993.

WEAFER, J.A., 'Irish Attitudes Towards Religious: A Survey', *Religious Life Review*, 39, 201–10, 2000.

WEAFER, J.A., Irish Religious Monitor (unpublished), Leixlip: Weafer Research Associates/MRBI, 2007.

WEAFER, J.A. & BRESLIN, A., Irish Catholic Clergy and Religious. Maynooth: Council for Research & Development, Irish Bishops' Conference, 1983.

WEIGEL, G., *Witness to Hope*, New York, Cliff Street Books, 1999.

WEIGERT, A.J. & BLASI, A.J., 'Vocation', in GIORDAN, G. (ed.), *Vocation and Social Context*, Boston: Brill, 2007.

WHELAN, C.T. (ed.), *Values and Social Change in Ireland*, Dublin: Gill and Macmillan, 1994.

WHITE, J., 'Introduction', in: BAKALAR, N. & BALKIN, R. (eds), *The Wisdom of John Paul II: The Pope on Life's Most Vital Questions*, London: Routledge, 2002.

WHITESIDE, B., 'No Longer Servants', *The Furrow*, 39, 347–56, 1988.

WHYTE, J.H., *Church & State in Modern Ireland 1923–1979*, Dublin, Gill and Macmillan, 1980.

WIN-GALLUP INTERNATIONAL, Global Index of Religion and Atheism. Win-Gallup International/Red C Research, 2012.

WOOD, S., 'Priesthood: Forty years after Vatican II', in DIETRICH, D. (ed.), *Priests for the 21st Century*, New York: The Crossroad Publishing Company, 2006.

WOODMAN, K., *Media Control in Ireland 1923–1983*, Galway: Galway University Press, 1985.

WORLD HEALTH ORGANISATION, Defining sexual health. Report of a technical consultation on sexual health. Geneva: World Health Organisation, 2006.

YAMANE, D., 'Introduction to Goodbye father', in YAMANE, D. (ed.), *Goodbye Father: The Celibate Priesthood and the Future of the Catholic Church*, New York: Oxford University Press, 2002.

Notes

Chapter One

1   Unless otherwise stated, all references to Church in this study are to the Catholic Church.

2   This issue was not specifically included in the original research design. However, its significance emerged spontaneously in the interviews.

3   The servant-leader model of priesthood, which emerged following Vatican II, emphasised pastoral leadership, flexible Church structures, optional celibacy and toleration of theological differences. Conversely, a neo-orthodox model emerged during the papacy of Pope John Paul II, where priests are perceived to be attracted to traditional forms of piety, worship, clerical dress, and neo-scholastic theology (See chapter three).

4   The Second Vatican Council (1962–5) addressed the relationship between the Catholic Church and the modern world. It is regarded as one of the most significant events in the Church during the twentieth century (See chapter two).

5   In 1966, sociologist Fr Jeremiah Newman identified a number of factors that had a negative affect on vocations including, increasing affluence and materialism, the new emphasis on lay spirituality and particularly the spirituality of the married state, and the uninspiring, stereotyped image of religious vocations (Newman, 1966). Twenty-one years later, some of these factors were echoed in a study of vocation decline in the US: 'a pervasive materialism, a new ecclesiology which is still not clearly defined, uncertainty regarding the precise roles of priests, religious and laity in the Church' (Pro Mundi Vita, 1987).

6   A diocesan priest is typically ordained in a ceremony performed by the bishop of his diocese, which usually follows seven years of philosophical and theological studies in a seminary.

7   All diocesan priests in the Catholic Church are male and in 1994 Pope John Paul II declared in his letter *Ordinatio Sacerdotalis* that 'the Church has no authority whatsoever to confer priestly ordination on women and that this judgement is to be definitively held by all the Church's faithful' (Reference 4) (http://www.vatican.va/holy_father/john_paul_ii/apost_letters/documen ts/hf_jp-ii_apl_22051994_ordinatio-sacerdotalis _en.html). However, in spite of the threat of automatic excommunication for the bishops and

women involved, a relatively small number of women have been ordained by groups 'within' the Catholic Church, such as the international Roman Catholic Women Priests (http://www.romancatholicwomenpriests.org/index.php) and it is alleged that women priests are celebrating Mass in Ireland http://www.rte.ie/news/2012/0420/group-claims-women-priests-are-celebrating-mass.html.

8   Celibacy is an obligatory discipline of the Catholic Church, which, at its most basic, means that priests cannot marry or engage in sexually intimate behaviour (Canon 277, Code of Canon Law).

9   The code of canon law is an extensive body of laws and regulations used by Church authorities to administer the Church, http://www.vatican.va/archive/ENG1104/_INDEX.HTM.

10 Only the pope can create or change law within the Church. The College of Bishops exercises power over the universal Church but only when approved by the pope and in an ecumenical council. Official declarations of infallibility by the pope are very rare in the Catholic Church and only two instances are accepted as infallible declarations – Pope Pius IX's 1854 definition of the dogma of the *Immaculate Conception* and Pope Pius XII's 1950 definition of the dogma of the *Assumption of Mary*. However, some commentators, such as former Irish president Mary McAleese believe that the Catholic Church is arriving at a situation of 'creeping infallibility about everything' where it is no longer acceptable to discuss controversial issues, such as women priests (McGarry, 2012, p. 9).

11 An individual bishop is entrusted with a given territory called a diocese. He acts as a vicar of Christ in his diocese and not as a vicar of the Pope. Consequently, he is not answerable to the Pope and he can exercise his power personally and directly for the benefit of the people entrusted to his care. A bishop can make 'particular law' for his subjects as long as this law is in harmony with the universal law of the Church and/or divine law (Can. 393.1). The bishop must appoint a vicar general to assist him in the governance of the whole diocese and to deputise in his absence. His authority is the same as that of the bishop although it must be exercised in the name of the bishop. Canon law requires the establishment of a Council of Priests to assist the bishop in the governance of the diocese by providing advice and information to him when requested to do so or when required by law.

12 Although canon law describes the parish priest as answerable to the bishop, he is not simply his delegate but enjoys ordinary authority within his parish.

13 Many parishes have Parish Pastoral Councils, which are faith-filled leadership groups through which priests and people work together for the sake of the parish. However, they have only a consultative vote, and their activities are regulated by the norms laid down by the diocesan bishop.

14 Although there is an Episcopal Conference that meets four times a year in Maynooth to 'consider matters relating to Ireland as a whole' the day-to-day running of each diocese is left to the discretion of individual bishops (Fuller, 2002, p. 140).

15 Some commentators argue that Pope Benedict XVI diminished the authority of bishops when he acted on his own initiative through a *Motu Proprio* he issued in 2007, which revived a number of Church traditions, including elevating the (Latin) Tridentine Mass to a more prominent position (Hoban, 2009).

16 Research by the author in 1999 found that the majority of Irish adults were sufficiently familiar with diocesan priests to give an opinion of them – 52% of Irish adults had favourable impressions of diocesan priests, 29% had mixed feelings, 8% had unfavourable impressions, and 11% had no opinion. Furthermore, one fifth (20%) of Irish adults had attended a school run by diocesan priests and approximately one eight (12%) had a relative or friend who is a diocesan priest (Weafer, 2000).

17 More than four in ten (44%) respondents in a survey of adult Catholics in the Archdiocese of Cashel and Emly in 1998 said that one of the parish clergy had called to their home within the past six months, and just over half (53%) said this had occurred at least once in the past year (Irish Marketing Surveys, 1998, p. 14).

18 In May 1999, for example, *The Irish Times* ran a story of a county council in the south of the country that passed a motion to call on the Catholic Church to change its laws on celibacy and women priests in order to address the problem of falling vocations. In November 2009, *The Irish Times* ran a story of a priest who decided to leave the priesthood to be with a woman, while in July 2012, *The Irish Times* had a photograph of a young man being ordained in Cork. More recently, a priest who left to marry his partner was photographed on the front page of a national tabloid newspaper in August 2012.

19 Opportunities for any form of meaningful contact between priests and people are declining due to their ageing profile and a shortage of priests. It is increasingly likely, according to Fr Tony Draper, that 'more people will never have talked to a priest' in a 'human, person-to-person fashion' (Draper, 2001, p. 349).

20 The reason given for the statistical focus on Church personnel in Ireland was 'to provide an accurate and comprehensive statistical picture of the Priests, Brothers and Sisters in Ireland' in order to 'provide information and guidance for those whose task it is to direct and coordinate the affairs of the Church in the country' and 'to lay the foundation for future research' (Lennon et al., 1971, p. i).

21 Some dioceses have commissioned private studies of their priests and laity but the findings are not publically available.

22 www.associationofcatholicpriests.ie.

23 Denzin and Lincoln (2000, p. 3), for example, define qualitative research as 'a situated activity that locates the observer in the world' and which 'consists of a set of interpretive, material practices that make the world visible' and meaningful.

24 Etherington (2004:31–2) defines reflexive research 'as the capacity of the researcher to acknowledge how their own experiences and contexts (which might be fluid and changing) inform the process and outcomes of inquiry.

25 I have been told stories of elderly and middle-aged men who continue to feel guilty for leaving the seminary many years ago, or who regret their decision to become a priest and now feel unable to leave because of guilt or a misguided sense of duty. My recollection is that seminarians who considered leaving the seminary ('cutting') or who were uncertain of their vocation were made to feel guilty in different ways, or so it seemed to me at the time. References to scripture, such as Luke's 'Once the hand is laid on the plough, no one who looks back is fit for the kingdom of God' (Lk 9:62) added to the sense of guilt. Consequentially, students who left the seminary often did so without telling anyone, sometimes not even their closest friends. Some students left the seminary within weeks or sometimes days of their entering but most stayed for years before leaving as 'spoilt priests' (a term that had virtually disappeared by the late 1970s). The vast majority of the hundred or so students who entered Maynooth with me in 1976 subsequently left the seminary before ordination.

26 In the context of management research, for example, Skinner et al. argue that there 'are circumstances in which qualitative research could offer a richness and depth of understanding unlikely to be achieved with quantitative approaches' (Skinner et al., 2000, p. 163). Inglis notes that while social surveys are 'very good at mapping changes in religious belief and behaviour', they are 'not very satisfactory for exploring the transitions in the meaning of being Catholic' and other issues that have taken place over time (Inglis, 2007, p. 209).

27 Positivist research typically entails the collection of large amounts of quantitative data that is subjected to multivariate analysis in order to identify statistically significant correlations between variables in order to explain social facts and predict future trends.

28 Narrative research is 'an umbrella term that covers a large and diverse range of approaches' (Mishler, 1999, p. xv). Since a core element of the present study entailed the use of 'a methodology based upon collecting, analysing, and re-presenting people's stories as told by them', it may be classified loosely as a narrative inquiry, without complying with the conditions of a fully narrative approach (Etherington, 2004, p. 75).

Chapter Two

29 Unless otherwise stated, the information in this chapter relates to the Republic of Ireland.

30 Some commentators believe that the media has replaced the Catholic Church as the 'social conscience and moral guardian of Irish society' (Donnelly and Inglis, 2010, p. 1).

31 John Whyte concluded his 1971 study of Church and State in Modern Ireland 1923–1970 with the words: 'The extent of the hierarchy's influence in Irish politics is by no means easy to define. The theocratic-state model on the one hand, and the Church-as-just-another-interest group model on the other hand, can both be ruled out as over-simplified, but it is by no means easy to present a satisfactory model intermediate between these two' (Whyte, 1980, p. 376).

32 http://www.europeanvaluesstudy.eu/evs/research/themes/religion.

33 The 'swinging sixties' is often used by writers to refer to the greater freedom that accompanied the social and cultural change that took place throughout many parts of the world (Tobin, 1984). Tim Pat Coogan refers to Ireland from the mid 1960s to the late 1980s as the 'disillusioned decades' (Coogan, 1987). The term 'Celtic Tiger' Ireland is a colloquial term used to refer to Ireland during the boom years of 1995 to 2007 (Murphy, 2000).

34 Brian Fallon disputes the credit given to the sixties for 'Ireland's supposed leap into modernity' and instead argues that 'what happened in the sixties was largely the culmination of a process which had begun well before that' (Fallon, 1998, p. 257). Others, such as political scientist Tom Girvin (2010) argue that while Ireland's modernisation project began during the 1950s, it was delayed by conservative interests until the 1990s.

35 The Troubles denotes a period of sustained conflict between Catholics and Protestants, and between the British army and paramilitary groups, that erupted in Northern Ireland following riots in Derry in 1969, and which continued until the 1990s, http://www.infoplease.com/spot/northireland 1.html.

36 Catholics went to Mass on the first Friday of each month to venerate the Sacred Heart of Jesus.

37 There are different kinds of indulgences that result in a lessening of punishment for a person's sins in return for undertaking some penance or prayer.

38 It is difficult to portray the sheer number and impact of rules in the Catholic Church before the Second Vatican Council. For example, prior to 1957, it was obligatory for Catholics to observe a Eucharistic fast from midnight. This requirement was replaced with a three-hour fast from solid foods and a one-hour fast from non-alcoholic liquids.

39 For example, while most people accepted that serious matters such as murder, divorce, the use of contraception, and missing Mass on Sundays were mortal sins, the status of other activities were less certain, e.g. eating meat on a Friday, not abiding by the rules of lent, arguing with a priest, or a woman going to Mass without appropriate head-gear.

40 The *Penny Catechism* contained a long list of questions and answers on matters of faith, hope, charity, and the sacraments, many of which were learnt word for word by school children. It guided the behaviour of Catholics for most of the twentieth century until the publication of the new *Catechism of the Catholic Church* in 1994. Ironically, perhaps, given the more liberal nature of contemporary Irish society, the *Catechism of the Catholic Church* has more than six hundred pages, compared with less than one hundred pages in the *Penny Catechism*.

41 Novelist John Banville (2004:26) described Ireland during the reign of Archbishop McQuaid as 'unique' and akin to 'a demilitarised totalitarian state in which the lives of the citizens were to be controlled not by a system of coercive force and secret policing, but by a kind of applied spiritual paralysis maintained by an unofficial federation between the Catholic clergy, the judiciary and the civil service'.

42 This example was given to me by one of the older priests in this study. Although he personally disagreed with the liberal direction of the Church since the Second Vatican Council, he was highly critical of the legalistic nature of Catholicism in pre-Vatican II Ireland. He also said that many young people circumvented the law by going to dances in adjacent dioceses where it was not a sin to dance after midnight.

43 In 1950, Minister for Health Noel Browne proposed introducing a healthcare programme, *The Mother and Child Scheme*, which would provide maternity care for all mothers and healthcare for children up to the age of sixteen. However, following strong opposition from some conservative bishops (who saw the scheme as opposed to Catholic social teaching) the medical profession (who feared a loss of income), and some members of the government (who disliked Browne), it was defeated and Browne was requested to submit his resignation. Historian John Whyte subsequently expressed surprise at the relatively moderate opposition of the Catholic Bishops to proposed constitutional changes in the 'special position' of the Catholic Church, or to changes in the censorship law and education which were bound to reduce the Church's influence (Whyte, 1980, pp. 350–1).

44 Some organisations, such as the Knights of Columbanus, allegedly 'controlled official and unofficial censorship systems', acted as 'para-clerics for the bishops', and 'reportedly scratched each other's backs in business' (Garvin, 2005, p. 255).

45 English sociologist Michael Hornsby-Smith summarised some of the main features of the pre-Vatican Church as 'stressing the virtues of loyalty, the certainty of answers, strict discipline and unquestioning obedience' (Hornsby-Smith, 1992, p. 270).

46 The first document to come out of the Council was the *Constitution on the Sacred Liturgy* in December 1963, which came into effect in 1964. This particular constitution was to have 'a profound effect on the Mass in Ireland: introducing the vernacular, new translations of texts, and the re-ordering of sanctuaries to facilitate the celebration of the Mass facing the people' (Lane, 2004, p. 70).

47 Numerous articles published in Church journals during the 1960s focused on changes to the design and architecture of churches to facilitate the liturgical developments.

48 Writing some years after Vatican II, Fr Donal Flanagan made the point that the 'Roman Catholic Church in Ireland has shown and continues to show what seems to be an inherent anti-collegial tendency', which is 'evident in the mass of laity who do not want to be bothered or involved; in the many priests who would prefer the simple, straightforward decision handed down from above rather than to be asked to take counsel together and to help formulate decisions' and 'in those bishops who seem instinctively and collectively to want to isolate themselves as far as possible from the people and from the mass media when they are coming to a decision' (Flanagan, 1969, p. 106). However, whilst acknowledging the tensions that accompanied the drive towards more collegiality in the Church, both Flanagan and Houtart saw signs for optimism in the Vatican II Church.

49 This decision created considerable controversy 'at both pastoral and theological levels, not least because the encyclical went against the majority opinion of the expert Commission set up to advise Pope Paul VI on this most contentious question' (Lane, 2004, p. 72).

50 Church historian John O'Malley writes that three issues were 'so sensitive or potentially explosive that Pope Paul withheld them from the council's agenda – clerical celibacy, birth control, and the reform of the Roman Curia (the central offices of the Vatican) (O'Malley, 2008, p. 6).

51 Unpublished research conducted by Fachtna Lewis in 1961–2, suggested to Ward that there were different types of Catholics hidden under the cloak of uniform practice: 'Limited research already completed suggests that very many ordinary Irish Catholics are articulate, educated and intellectually committed to a mature apostolic faith.' However, the evidence also suggests that 'there are those who are ill-informed, those who are disinterested, and those who are alienated' (Ward, 1964, p. 28).

52 Political scientist, Tom Garvin, points out that Biever's 1962 study of

Catholics in Dublin highlighted a dilemma for Irish priests, who had to balance the needs of an emerging educated Catholic middle class, with the more conservative needs of the majority of Catholics who were 'hostile to change of any kind' (Garvin, 2005, p. 260).

[53] Most of the research on religious attitudes and practice was undertaken in the Republic of Ireland. Northern Ireland studies tended to focus on the political dimension of religious life, although some studies contained information on religious practice (Rose, 1971). A few studies adopted a cross-border approach (McAllister, 1983).

[54] The proliferation of survey research was a trend that was also found in other Western countries and one which was to continue in Ireland for some decades.

[55] Other characteristics of Catholics noted in the R&D 1985 report included attendance at novenas (21%), private reading of the Gospels (18%), practicing penance, such as not eating meat on Fridays or not doing something for lent (48%), wearing religious medals (44%), making the Stations of the Cross (52%), and going on pilgrimage (41%).

[56] Some of the conflicting data noted by Ryan included the observations that 'though nearly all believe in God, nearly a quarter are not sure about what sort of a God this might be; some 35% either reject or are not sure of a life after death; nearly half do not believe in hell or the devil; only 53% with third-level education fully accept papal infallibility; while only 35% of the same group agree that divorce should not be allowed; over a third of those surveyed have difficulty with some aspect of Church teaching' (Ryan, 1983, p. 5).

[57] Nic Ghiolla Phadráig suggested that eight different types of Catholics could be identified that help to understand lapsing Catholics. *Committed* (accepts religion fully); *Sinner* (attends Church, accepts beliefs, compartmentalisation of religion from everyday life); *Cultural* Catholic (attends Church but minimal faith commitment); *Conformist* (practices religion but does not believe or endorse Christian values); *Individualist* (accepts basic beliefs and values but does not practice); *Seeker-Rebel* (reacts against parents' religious practice); *Political-Radical* (rejects religious practice and belief but is deeply committed to certain Christian values that are pursued in a political arena); and *Alienated* (does not practice or believe).

[58] Pobal Dé have organised annual conferences on diverse aspects of the laity within the Catholic Church since 1986 (http://www.pobalde.ie/index.html).

[59] Conversely, article 44, which acknowledged the 'special position' of the Catholic Church, was removed from the Irish constitution in 1972, albeit with no public objection from the Catholic Church.

[60] The Health (Family Planning) Act 1979 provided that contraceptives could be dispensed by a pharmacist on presentation of a valid prescription for

'bone fide family planning or adequate medical reasons'. The Health (Family Planning) (Amendment) Act 1985 subsequently liberalised the law on contraception by allowing condoms to be sold to people over eighteen without a prescription.

61 In 1984 fifteen-year-old Ann Lovett died after giving birth in a grotto outside Longford. In another case the 'Kerry Babies' tribunal was established the same year to investigate how Joanne Hayes and her family confessed to the killing of a newborn baby found stabbed to death on a beach in Kerry. The tribunal concluded that Joanne Hayes was not the mother of the baby but that she was the mother of another newborn baby whose body was found on the Hayes family farm.

62 Following decades of opposition by the Catholic Church, the divorce referendum was passed in November 1995, albeit by a relatively small majority, while abortion is only allowed in exceptional circumstances. According to the X case in 1992, abortion is allowable under the constitution when the life of the mother is in danger. However, it took more than twenty years before relevant legislation was enacted in 2013. The Protection of Life During Pregnancy Act 2013 allows for abortion if the woman's life is at risk, including the risk of suicide.

63 In the second edition of his book, John Whyte states that Fr Liam Ryan's argument has 'force' and that 'although individual bishops, like Dr Newman, may appear to be using a different set of assumptions, the hierarchy as a whole, in its collective statements since 1973, seems to have stuck closely to the 'conscience-of-society' model (Whyte, 1980, p. 417).

64 In August 1982, for example, the Holy Faith nuns in New Ross sacked a teacher, Eileen Flynn, who had become pregnant by a married man with whom she was living and whose marriage had earlier broken down.

65 One memorable feature of the 1980s was the 'moving statues' phenomenon, where statues of the Virgin Mary were reported to move spontaneously. The first sighting was in Ballinspittle, Cork during the summer or 1985. Peader Kirby saw 'the phenomenon of Ireland's moving statues' as 'a cry by ordinary people for spirituality, an attempt to cling to some secure landmark in a fast changing society' and that it 'shows up the spiritual vacuum or crisis that exists' in the Irish Church (Kirby, 1986, p. 240). While this may be true of some people, I am sure others, like me, simply went out of curiosity.

66 In 1992, a three-part referendum on abortion was held. The proposal to amend Article 40 of the Constitution so that it would be unlawful to terminate the life of an unborn unless such termination was necessary to save the life, as distinct from the health, of the mother was rejected. Conversely, the right to travel and the right to information were passed. In 2002, the proposal to remove the threat of suicide as grounds for legal

abortion in Ireland and to introduce tough new penalties for those performing or assisting abortions was defeated. This was subsequently passed with the enactment of The Protection of Life Act 2013.

[67] The second divorce referendum was passed in 1995.

[68] The Criminal Law (Sexual Offences) Act 1993 repealed legislation prohibiting all homosexual acts between males and introduced seventeen as the age of consent for homosexual activities.

[69] A subsequent report by the UN Human Rights Committee released on 5 February 2014 reported similar findings.

[70] The initial disclosures of abuse followed the broadcasting of the three-part documentary series *States of Fear* on RTÉ during April and May of 1999, related to the abuse of children in Ireland's industrial schools. This 'provoked an unprecedented response in the country', culminating in the collapse of a government in 1994 as a result of controversy over the failure to extradite Fr Brendan Smyth to Northern Ireland on charges of child sexual abuse, the issuing of an historic apology by the Taoiseach on behalf of the State to the victims of child abuse within the system and the establishment of a Commission to hear testimony from those who had suffered as children (Raftery and O'Sullivan, 1999, p. 9). While these disclosures related to abuse by religious rather than diocesan clergy, the focus soon shifted to the abuse perpetrated by diocesan priests, with several high profile cases in the media concerning Fr Seán Fortune, Fr Ivan Payne and Fr Paul McGennis.

[71] The investigation was established in the wake of the broadcast of a BBC television documentary, *Suing the Pope*, which highlighted the case of Fr Seán Fortune.

[72] Unwanted, that is, from the Church's perspective.

[73] http://www.safeguarding.ie/3rd-tranche-nbsccci-reviews-april-2013.

[74] A significant issue for the Catholic Church related to the 'slowness of the Irish hierarchy to acknowledge the problem and the clear pattern that existed of moving abusing priests from area to area', which served 'to seriously undermine the credibility of the Catholic Church in this country' (Raftery and O'Sullivan, 1999, p. 255).

[75] It transpired that the Vatican's Congregation for the Clergy had written a letter to the Irish Bishops in 1997 directing them not to enforce the child protection policies they had published the previous year, calling for mandatory reporting of priests who molested children. The existence of the letter was broadcast on RTÉ in the course of a programme, *Unspeakable Crimes*, on 17 January 2011. Part of the explanation for the letter is that the Church has an obligation to protect the canonical rights of accused priests. The Vatican subsequently refused to cooperate with two inquiries on abuse in the dioceses of Dublin and Cloyne set up by the Irish state. These

revelations have undoubtedly seriously damaged the position of the Catholic Church in Ireland, and the pastoral letter from the pope to the Catholics of Ireland has done little to halt the public criticism. Seen in this light, the closure of the Irish embassy to the Vatican, although surprising, is understandable and according to journalist Patsy McGarry (2012) 'appropriate and proportionate'. It was subsequently reopened in 2014.

76 A national survey commissioned by the Iona Institute in October 2011 found that one in five Irish adults considered the government to be excessively hostile towards the Catholic Church, with the remainder split between those who did not believe the government was excessively hostile (40%) and those who could neither agree nor disagree (34%). An earlier survey commissioned by the Irish Bishops in 1997 found that 25% of adult Catholics did not think the media's treatment of the abuse scandals was unfair (Council for Research & Development, 1997).

77 Some international studies include longitudinal data on religion, e.g. the European Social Survey (www.europeansocialsurvey.org) and the European Values Study (www.europeanvaluesstudy.eu).

78 US theologian Richard McBrien believes that before the Second Vatican Council, most people 'inside and outside the Catholic Church had no apparent difficulty locating the line that separated Catholics from other Christians', even if their views were somewhat superficial, e.g. abstaining from meat on Friday, regarding birth control as a mortal sin, or recognising the authority of the pope as the successor to Peter (McBrien, 2004, p. 455).

79 It subsequently transpired that the Vatican decided to end discussions aimed at reintegrating the Society of St Pius X into the Church after a twenty-one-year schism over its implacable opposition to the reforms of the Second Vatican Council, because of their refusal to accept the reforms of the council (*The Irish Times*, 6 October 2012).

80 Various organisations have been established to promote the voice of the laity, the renewal of the Catholic faith in Ireland, and to support the spirit of Vatican II, including Pobal Dé (www.pobalde.ie), the Association of Catholic Priests (www.associationof catholicpriests.ie), and the Association of Catholics in Ireland (www.acireland.ie).

81 Noel Coghlan believes that active discipleship will renew the Church, a discipleship that is embedded in a 'consensual community'. It will also require changes in leadership style and organisational structures, together with an option for the poor and an 'inner transformation' (Coghlan, 2010, p. 404). Gerry O'Hanlon SJ believes that the 'way forward is abundantly clear – we need to insist on appropriate structures and institutions' which 'involve all the faithful, for more inclusive decision making and input into doctrinal formation and development.

82 Dobbelaere distinguishes different levels of secularisation, including individual secularisation, which is manifested in 'a decline in involvement in churches and denominations' leading to a more 'à la carte' individualistic religious commitment (Dobbelaere, 2005, p. 18).

83 A poll commissioned by *The Sunday Times* in March 2013 reported that 14% of 18–34 year olds attend Mass at least once a week compared with 34% of all adults. This research did not distinguish between Catholics and those of other faiths or none (*The Sunday Times* and Behaviour & Attitudes, 2013).

84 A similar situation also exists in other Catholic countries, such as Italy, where religious practice among young people is collapsing (http://chiesa. espresso. repubblica.it/articolo/1344389?eng=y).

85 http://www.ionainstitute.ie.

86 http://www.associationofcatholicpriests.ie.

87 A survey commissioned by *The Sunday Tribune* (2005) found that the majority of Irish adults believe the Catholic Church should (a) relax its views on using artificial contraception (83%), (b) relax its views on homosexuality (61%), support IVF treatment for couples (75%), relax its views on sex before marriage (73%), and relax its views on divorce (75%). This survey does not distinguish between the responses of Catholics and all adults.

88 http://www.indcatholicnews.com/news.php?viewStory=22514.

Chapter Three

89 The notion of a vocational journey is used widely in the Church within the context of vocational discernment, including the Irish Bishops' Conference *Programme for the Formation of Priests in Irish Seminarians* (2006). The Archdiocese of Los Angeles, for example, has identified four phases in this journey to the priesthood, http://www. lavocations.org/4-phase-vocational -journey.php.

90 Laicisation is the process whereby a priest loses the rights to exercise the functions of an ordained minister. However, even when laicised, a priest retains the character of a priest, as sung at his ordination: 'You are a priest forever, like Melchizedek of old.' In some cases, a priest may be dismissed by the Church as a penalty for certain grave offences, such as child sexual abuse. However, voluntary requests for laicisation are most common in the Catholic Church, when a priest wishes to be dismissed from the clerical state for personal reasons. A separate dispensation is required if priests wish to marry.

91 It is further highlighted in the first document published by the Second Vatican Council in 1964 – *Lumen Gentium* ('Dogmatic Constitution on the Church') – and in the document *Pastores Dabo Vobis* (1992), the Post-Synodal

Apostolic Exhortation of John Paul II, 'On the Formation of Priests in the Circumstances of the Present Day.'

92 For example, the impact of both personal and social factors on the vocational conflict and resolution of John Henry Newman are described by theologian Donald Capps in his study of vocational identity.

93 One former priest highlighted the difficulty of mandatory celibacy when he wrote that he was convinced he had a vocation to the Catholic priesthood but that he was 'equally convinced' that he had a vocation to marriage (Castle, 2009, p. 146).

94 www.pewresearch.org.

95 Journalist Fintan O'Toole reflects on what might have been if he had decided to pursue his original desire to become a priest. He was eight when the possibility first struck him, but that was not unusual for boys in the 1950s and 1960s.

96 The status of priests in rural Ireland was evident in colloquial sayings, such as a farmer being well off when he had 'a bull in the yard and a son in Maynooth' or 'a priest in the parish and a bull in the yard' (O'Morain, 2010, p. 14).

97 Professor Conor Ward observed that when a priest comes to a parish to do a particular job, 'He knows what he is expected to do, and how he is expected to act, and everyone else knows what they expect him to do and how they expect him to act' (Ward, 1965, p. 249).

98 Research by Hepworth et al. in the UK found that priests equated scrupulous behaviour with a 'religious manifestation of OCD' (obsessive compulsive disorder) (Hepworth et al., 2010, p. 1).

99 While some dioceses allowed their priests to attend horse racing, or the theatre, others forbade these practices.

100 Rubrics are detailed rules laid down for the recitation of the Divine Office, the celebration of Mass, and the administration of the sacraments. They governed, for example, how a priest held and moved his arms during Mass, how he changed the missal, and how he performed triple blessings and genuflections. Anecdotal evidence suggests that some scrupulous priests took great pains to ensure they did not violate any of the rubrics. One priest friend told me that his uncle believed that he risked potentially hundreds of mortal sins every time he said Mass.

101 See chapter five for a more detailed account of Church discipline.

102 A similar situation existed in seminaries run by religious orders. Redemptorist Fr Tony Flannery, for example, noted that 'uniformity was a way of life', where training was 'geared towards suppressing the individuality of its members, and developing people with similar ways of thinking and behaving' (Flannery, 1997, p. 21).

103 One elderly priest told me that he believed that a student from Kerry had been sent home because no one could understand his accent in Clonliffe college. However, due to the secrecy surrounding the expulsion of students, it is difficult to know if this was the reason or just an urban myth imagined by students.

104 Seniority in the seminary was determined by alphabetical order and students were identified by a number.

105 Articles in *The Furrow* suggest that priests were already considering their position in the world. Volume 9 of *The Furrow* in 1958 was dedicated to 'The Priest in the World'.

106 Anecdotal evidence suggests that some older priests resisted the changes and left the diocesan priesthood for the relative stability of monasteries and religious orders. I contacted two of these men during the recruitment phase of the research but, unfortunately, they did not wish to take part in the research.

107 Fr O'Carroll observed that while the Vatican II document, the 'Constitution on the Church', had chapters on religious and the laity, it had none on priests.

108 Fermanagh priest Fr McVeigh, for example, describes a typical day for himself in 1970s Ireland, as follows: 'Each day was very structured and everybody knew what he was supposed to be doing. One of the three priests was always on duty. There was Mass to be said either in the church or in the Convent of Mercy every day and a number of Masses to be said on Sunday. There were confessions at set times every week, home visitation, the Legion of Mary meetings, etc.' (McVeigh, 2008, p. 95).

109 The research was based on a sample of five hundred priests, religious and diocesan, randomly selected from the Irish Catholic Directory.

110 Some, like Bishop Laurence Ryan, argued that the development of lay participation in the Church should not depend on any shortage of priests, and that priestly and lay ministries 'need each other and complement each other' (Ryan, 1988, p. 26).

111 Informal inquiries by the National Conference of Priests during the 1980s found that while many priests experienced an 'overall sense of satisfaction', every priest contacted felt that their priesthood was 'an increasingly complex and difficult vocation' (Brady, 1989, p. 9).

112 Research by the Council for Research & Development in 1997 found that less than one third (29%) of Irish adults felt that their confidence in the priests in their parish had been adversely affected by the clerical sex abuse scandals. Six years later, a survey commissioned by RTÉ's *Prime Time* reported that 79% of Irish adults felt that the services provided by priests to the community in general were very or fairly important.

113 Doherty gives three definitions of clericalism. The first, from Scott Appleby, professor of history at the University of Notre Dame: 'a constellation of ideas and practices rooted in the conviction that ordination to the priesthood confers a special and privileged status that places the priest above the non-ordained priest'. The second is from Fr Hoban: 'cherishing a mentality that believes that clergy knows best; it is the idea of an exclusive club to do with status and privilege'. The third is from Doherty: 'a lack of respect for the role of lay people, or a feeling that their role is less important than that of ordained clergy; reducing them to passive by-standers when they should be active participants' (Doherty, 2013, p. 12).

114 The crisis of ministry is often linked to a decline in vocations to the priesthood, which is perceived by some commentators to have been caused by an 'all pervasive spirit of materialism' in modern society, leading to a loss of the 'elevated status' traditionally enjoyed by the priesthood (Dalton, 1990, pp. 92–3).

115 When asked what action should be taken regarding Sunday Masses if vocations continue to decline, half (50%) of all priests that responded to a national survey in 2004 felt there should be less Sunday Masses, while one third (32%) said that parishes should be amalgamated (*The Irish Catholic*, 2004). In 2012, six in ten Irish adults (60%) said that clustering of parishes should be introduced to overcome shortages (Association of Catholic Priests/Amárach Research, 2012).

116 In spite of the decline in vocations, only some of the men who apply to a diocese are accepted. In 2005, only 50% of applicants to the diocesan priesthood were accepted as candidates to the priesthood (O'Mahony, 2006). While the reasons for their refusal are not known, it may well be as a result of a psychological diagnostic test, which are increasingly used to test the suitability of candidates for the priesthood.

117 A reduction in the number of Masses is a feature of some parishes, and undoubtedly it is an issue that will become more serious in the next decade as more priests retire and die. Some dioceses are preparing for this eventuality by clustering parishes and seeking ways in which their combined resources can be most effective. However, this process is at an early stage and not yet universally accepted by priests or people.

118 The number of priests accused of abuse may be relatively few but it is still quite high. Archbishop Diarmuid Martin noted in October 2013 that the Diocesan Child Safeguarding and Protection Service (CSPS), and the civil authorities, had allegations of abuse recorded against ninety-eight priests. This represents approximately one in every fourteen priests who have served in the archdiocese over the past seventy years. He further noted that the CSPS estimates that over five hundred children may have been abused by priests in Dublin.

119 As previously stated in chapter two, Ireland is significantly more secularised in 2012 than in 1962, with less people participating in the sacraments or engaging with the Church at any level.

120 The Irish Bishops' Conference *Programme for the Formation of Priests in Irish Seminaries* emphasises the difference between priests and lay people by its use of the following wording: 'Nevertheless, as the Second Vatican Council states, while the ministerial priesthood and the priesthood of all believers come from the one priesthood of Jesus Christ, 'they differ essentially and not only in degree' (Irish Bishops' Conference, 2006, p. 9).

Chapter Four

121 As previously stated in chapter one, I did not explicitly request information on priests' sexual behaviour or orientation during the interview. Rather, I initially sought to create a space through a narrative-style interviewing process, which enabled the research participants to disclose whatever information they deemed relevant to their lives as priests. Some priests chose to give detailed accounts of their sexual history, while others were content to speak quite generally about the impact of celibacy on their lives.

122 Theological and philosophical aspects of celibacy are outside the scope of the present study.

123 The *Catechism of the Catholic Church* states that 'all of the baptised are called to chastity' (1994, p. 502) and accordingly, offences against chastity, such as lust, masturbation, fornication, pornography, prostitution, rape and homosexuality are sinful (Libreria Editrice Vaticana, 1994, No. 2348–2359, pp. 502–5).

124 While the call to celibacy is absolute, some married Anglican priests have been accepted as Catholic priests when they converted to Catholicism following the introduction of women priests and openly gay clergy into the Anglican Church. However, by creating a *Personal Ordinariate*, the Vatican disposed of a rule that is obligatory for the majority of priests. Celibacy is obligatory for all bishops in the Eastern rite and for any priest who was ordained while unmarried or if he is widowed. Conversely, priests of the Eastern Catholic Churches who are in full communion with Rome can be married if they are married before their ordination.

125 Two types of deacons exist in the Catholic Church, the transitional and the permanent. The transitional diaconate comprises men who intend to become priests, while the order of permanent deacons, which was introduced by Vatican II, comprises men who will not be ordained and who might be married and permitted to have conjugal relations with their wives. Ireland ordained its first permanent deacons in 2012, fifty years following the opening of the Second Vatican Council.

126 In a nationwide survey of US priests in 1971, Fr Andrew Greeley reported that 'about two thirds of the priests in the country expect a change in the laws of celibacy, and three quarters expect it to take place within the next ten years' (Greeley, 1973, p. 77).

127 US therapist and spiritual director Fr Paul Holmes believes that some priests are unable to express their true feelings to anyone, while others engage in multiple anonymous sexual encounters.

128 In his study of nearly six thousand priests in the USA, Fr Greeley (1972) found that most priests in the US would not marry if they were free to do so. Fr Rossetti (2005), in his study of more than one thousand priests surveyed from fifteen US dioceses in 2003/2005 reported that 67% of priests said, 'Celibacy has been a positive experience for me' and 53% endorsed the statement, 'I support the requirement that priests live a celibate life.'

129 Irish theologian Fr Dorr believes that celibacy is such 'a specialized and personal call that it is not wise' and in his opinion, 'not just for the Catholic Church authorities to insist that everybody who wishes to become a priest in the Western Church must take on celibacy' (Dorr, 2004, p. 143).

130 There is 'no scriptural evidence that Jesus practiced celibacy' (Sipe, 2007, p. 549), or conversely, that 'he had an intimate sexual-genital relationship with anybody' (Dorr, 2011, p. 431). It was an ideal of the emerging Church that would take hundreds of years to become a tradition and a discipline of priesthood (Pope Paul VI, 1967).

131 There is 'indisputable evidence' that 'many priests and bishops in good standing were married' in the third century (O'Malley, 2002, p. 9) and that married clergy lived alongside celibate priests up to the second millennium. De Rosa (1988) makes the point that 'priesthood itself was practically hereditary' around the middle of the first century (p. 402), and Sipe (1990) identified six popes who were sons of either bishops or priests during the second half of the first century. Conversely, while accepting that there is historical evidence for parish priests who lived in sin 'with a concubine and several children, or the lecherous friar molesting his female penitents in the confessional' (Laven, 2001, p. 866), Laven also notes that the interactions between male and female celibates in sixteenth-century Venice were frequently monogamous, long-term, and intense, although rarely overtly sexual.

132 The Council of Trent (1545–63) reaffirmed the discipline of celibacy following challenges to celibacy by Luther during the Reformation in the sixteenth century.

133 Code 132 of the *Code of Canon Law* of 1918 states: 'Clerics in major orders may not marry and they are bound by the obligation of chastity to the extent that sinning against it constitutes a sacrilege.' Canon 277 of the revised canon law published in 1983, reaffirms the obligatory nature of celibacy for priests.

[134] Celibacy was one of three topics, including birth control and the reform of the Roman Curia, that were considered 'so sensitive or potentially explosive' that Pope Paul withheld them from the agenda of the Second Vatican Council (O'Malley, 2008, p. 6).

[135] Senior Church figures supported the notion of optional celibacy following the Second Vatican Council. In his memoirs, Cardinal Daly recounts that Cardinal Suenens, 'one of the great figures of the Second Vatican Council' (Daly, 1998, p. 132) called for an end to mandatory celibacy at an international gathering of European Bishops in 1969.

[136] This encyclical countered the objections against priestly celibacy, including the fact that the gospels present celibacy as a gift from God, the exclusion of priests who have a vocation to the priesthood but not celibacy resulting in a shortage of priests, and the view that celibacy is detrimental to the development of a mature and well-balanced human personality.

[137] For Paul, sexual abstinence is 'a suggestion, not a rule' (1 Cor. 7:7). For those with the charism or gift of celibacy, it is judged as the better option by St Paul in 1 Corinthians 7 because an unmarried man can 'devote himself to the Lord's affairs' while a married man is 'torn in two ways' (1 Cor. 7:33).

[138] Caution should be exercised in the interpretation of statistics from studies that are based on samples of priests who have received therapy for personal issues. However, while it may be argued that the statistics exaggerate the extent of the problem, the studies are consistent in highlighting the difficult nature of celibacy for many priests and the likelihood that many priests do not live up to the ideal of celibacy.

[139] US priest Fr Stephen Virginia discovered that secular clergy experienced significantly greater depression when compared to religious and monastic clergy. He concluded that the lack of social support and a sense of isolation were key elements associated with secular clergy's experience of both burnout and depression.

[140] US research has found that 'loneliness tends to be more common among retired diocesan priests' because they have less interactions with other priests (Gautier et al., 2012, p. 63).

[141] Prior to the Second Vatican Council, the *Penny Catechism* listed four instructions related to the sixth commandment ('Thou shalt not commit adultery'), which forbade Catholics to have any impure thoughts concerning another's wife or husband; to engage in any looks, words or actions that were contrary to holy purity; to look at immodest plays and dances; and immodest songs, books and pictures because they are 'most dangerous to the soul, and lead to mortal sin' (*Penny Catechism*, 1985, p. 36). The revised version of the catechism published in 1994 contains considerably more detail on offences against chastity, fecundity and marriage.

[142] A similar situation occurred in the training of religious priests. The abbot of Glenstal Abbey, Mark Patrick Hederman, for example, describes the 'training' he received as 'a lonely journey of self-sacrifice' where the 'important thing was to cut yourself off from all human affection and attachment, to kill off conscientiously any natural urges of the body so that the new kind of heavenly fuel, supernatural grace, might flow through the human infrastructure. You tried to be solitary, chaste, pure. You shunned all earthly goods and material wealth. Above all, you fought against your own good taste, impulses, inclinations and will' (Hederman, 2010, p. 62).

[143] The behaviour of seminarians was controlled by ensuring students had minimal contact with females, and presumably males, when attending university. For example, students in Clonliffe were forbidden to speak with students when attending UCD in the 1960s. There were no female students in Maynooth until the late 1960s. Visits from female family members were also monitored to minimise any contact with other students.

[144] All forms of sexual behaviour remain a prohibited activity for students and priests, resulting in any such activity being conducted in secret, regardless of sexual orientation.

[145] In his memoirs, *Putting Hand to the Plough*, former Maynooth Professor, Msgr O'Callaghan writes that contemporary Irish culture has resulted in a different reality for 'very many priests' who 'spin out quite lonely lives' (O'Callaghan, 2007, p. 196). In the past, priests had live-in housekeepers who cooked, cleaned, answered the door and 'kept a light in the house' (O'Callaghan, 2007, p. 196).

[146] For example, Richard Power's novel *The Hungry Grass*, Michael Harding's *Priest*, and Frank O'Connor's *The Collar* depict what were essentially the lives of isolated and lonely men.

[147] Fr Desmond Forristal in his commentary on the survey findings warns of the dangers of drawing 'too many conclusions from this single response'. He writes that while the response to the question shows that 'many of the clergy regard celibacy as a considerable source of stress' it 'does not tell us whether they wish to see celibacy retained or abolished' (Forristal, 1997, p. 23).

[148] Homosexuality was only decriminalised in Ireland in 1993 and it has been persistently linked with sexual deviancy in the Church. US canon lawyer Thomas Doyle refutes any link between homosexuality and celibacy with sexual abuse when he says that it is 'both naive and even preposterous to assume that the inability to turn to women for sexual release causes clerics to prey on children or adolescents' and that mandatory celibacy 'alone does not cause sexual dysfunction' (Doyle, 2006, p. 195).

[149] Fr Patrick O'Brien, for example, wrote of 'being present on several occasions when priests wept openly and with evident grief over the abuse cases and

the death of a brother priest in a homosexual club'. The 'reality of homo-sexual and lesbian vocations' is one of the wider questions he believes that need to be raised by these events (O'Brien, 1995, p. 14). The 'anonymous' article was written by two 'closeted' homosexual priests living in the New York area.

150 I am aware of a few instances where older students acted in a sexually predatory way towards younger students in the seminary. Each of the predators subsequently left the seminary or the priesthood, usually but not always voluntarily, and not before they had interfered with many younger men and possibly spoiled their vocations and lives.

151 As previously stated, the eight priests and two former priests that comprise this cohort of pre-Vatican II priests entered the seminary prior to the commencement of Vatican II, and all of them were ordained before the conclusion of the council.

152 The term 'natural celibate' is used colloquially to refer to priests who have little difficulty living a celibate life.

153 In order to protect the anonymity of the research participants, references to individual priests will usually only contain two pieces of information, their priestly status and the decade of their ordination. All names are anonymised.

154 The Vatican II research participants comprised eleven priests and three former priests, all of whom were ordained in the 1970s and 1980s. With two known exceptions, the research participants in this cohort presented themselves as heterosexual men.

155 One priest said that the writings of St Paul (1 Cor. 7), which are often used to advocate support for mandatory celibacy were 'written by a man who was expecting the imminent end of the world' and thus in a very different context to today's Church (Parish priest, 1970s).

156 All names have been anonymised to protect the privacy of the research participants.

157 The third and youngest cohort of research participants is comprised of five priests and four former diocesan priests, all of whom were ordained in the 1990s and 2000s. Two of them said they were homosexual.

158 Jesus emphasised the high expectations he had for discipleship in Luke 9:62, when he said that, 'Once the hand is laid on the plough no one who looks back is fit for the kingdom of God.' Some priests in the seminary used this quotation to motivate seminarians or to make them feel guilty if they considered leaving ('cutting').

159 During my five years in the seminary I was aware of some students who were in sexual relationships with girls. Most of them voluntarily left the seminary and subsequently married. Conversely, I was genuinely unaware

of any homosexual activity amongst students, other than possibly ill-informed suspicions concerning some students who were effeminate. I subsequently learnt the identities of some students who were gay and sexually active while in the seminary. I also became aware of a small number of priests and older students who were effectively sexual predators, most of whom, to the best of my knowledge, were never caught or sanctioned. During a chance encounter some years ago with a former classmate, for example, he boasted of the bisexual affairs he had had with other students in the seminary and since then as a priest with married men and women. He did not see any contradictions in his lifestyle and neither did he experience any difficulties living this life.

160 I can recall a similar explanation being given about another priest who was a 'known' paedophile who lived in close proximity to seminarians. The priest was subsequently convicted of abusing a large number of children and dismissed from the priesthood. Two of the research participants made similar comments in relation to another priest who was seen on numerous occasions walking the grounds of their seminary even though he had been convicted of sexually abusing young children in the courts.

161 The Civil Partnership Act was subsequently enacted on 1 January 2011.

162 While most housekeepers were female, some were male, including one former butler who acted as housekeeper for one of the participants in this study.

163 The relationship between parish priests and curates is discussed more fully in chapter five.

Chapter Five

164 The term 'ordinary' is used to denote bishops, vicars general, episcopal vicars, and major superiors of pontifical clerical religious institutes. In the case of diocesan priests, it refers to the diocesan bishop and to vicars acting in the name of the bishop.

165 Occasionally, individual priests are reported in the media for their criticisms of the Church hierarchy. For example, one priest recently criticised the hierarchy for excluding women from the priesthood (Riegel, 2011). Most often, however, critical comments are made by groups of priests. In a letter to *The Irish Times* on Tuesday, 19 February 2013, for example, a number of prominent Irish theologians indicated their support for a 'Declaration on Authority' in the Catholic Church that calls for change in some aspects of Church governance (www.churchauthority.org). The Association of Catholic Priests have also been quite critical of some aspects of Church leadership www.associationofcatholic priests.ie.

166 He was reputed to have been exiled to work in Kenya by Bishop Lucy. However, in a letter to *The Irish Times* on 30 July 2008, Fr Good wrote that the enduring myth of him being exiled to Turkana by Bishop Lucy was 'entirely untrue'.

167 www.independent.ie/national-news/bishops-gave-editor-sack-over-articles-on-sex-abuse-1764670.html.

168 The demise of the NCPI was inevitable according to Fr Hoban, who served on its executive for six years. It was an organisation that gave the impression of facilitating 'a distinctive priest-voice but not listening to what it had to say' (Hoban, 2009, p. 351).

169 The formation of the ACP was severely criticised by some interests within the Church. Journalist David Quinn, for example, branded the organisation as representing the interests of a sub-section of priests 'who want the Catholic Church to adopt the failed project of liberal Protestantism'. Some priests have also expressed their concern at the direction the ACP at national level seems to be taking as reported on the ACP website: (http://www.associationofcatholicpriests.ie/2013/02/clogher-group-unhappy-with-acp-leadership-and-content-of-website).

170 There is no evidence to suggest that the ACP is anything but loyal, albeit critical of some aspects of Church policies and practices. For example, in a letter to Cardinal Brady sent in June 2012, the Association of Catholic Priests was critical of the lack of 'real engagement' in the Irish Church. However, they stressed that the Association is not 'against' the Church. Rather, they say they are 'part of it' and that they 'care about it' and 'want it to survive' (www. associationofcatholicpriests.ie).

171 Six Irish religious priests that were silenced or censured by the Vatican are, Fr Seán Fagan (Marist), Fr Tony Flannery and Fr Gerard Moloney (Redemptorists), Fr Brian D'Arcy (Passionist), Fr Iggy O'Donovan (Augustinian), and Fr Owen O'Sullivan (Capuchin). The Vatican's treatment of these priests has been criticised by various Church groups, theologians and priests. One theologian, Augustinian priest Fr Gabriel Daly, for example, spoke out 'against the unjust and sometimes cruel tactics resorted to by the papacy and its curia against good men and women who are genuinely concerned with making Christ present to the world' (McGarry, 2012). The websites of the ACP and CORI have both published statements of support for Fr Flannery, while many individuals have expressed their outrage at the treatment of these priests.

172 Fr Reynolds was excommunicated for his public celebration of the Eucharist when he did not hold faculties to act publicly as a priest. Agnew believes that Reynold's views in favour of women's ordination and same-sex marriage were contributing factors towards his excommunication.

173 Unless otherwise stated, the institutional church is used in a broad sense to include persons and structures with formal authority over priests.

174 In the pre-Vatican II seminary, this task was relatively straightforward as the role of the priest was 'taken for granted' (Ryan, 1972, pp. 23–4) and seminaries were 'formally structured systems with rules and regulations' (Ryan, 1972, p. 24) that were widely regarded as places with 'text-book professors, walled-in virtue, and docile students answering bells' (Ryan, 1972, p. 10). Students were only allowed home during holidays and visits from family members were regulated. Strict discipline was enforced in areas dealing with personal friendships and the observation of strict silence, except at times when speaking was permitted (Dunn, 1994).

175 Although quite rare, the threat of dismissal is nonetheless real. For example, Pope John Paul II dismissed two Catholic priests convicted of sexually abusing children in the Ferns diocese from the clerical state in December 2004. This was the first time the Vatican had dismissed a priest in Ireland over sexual abuse. Since then, the practice of laicising priests found guilty of child sexual abuse has become more common, although still very infrequent, and not without difficulties.

176 Anecdotal evidence suggests that most dioceses had parishes to which priests were sent as a form of punishment. Some 'punishing parishes' were significantly poorer or more isolated than others, while other parishes had parish priests who were regarded as 'difficult'.

177 This practice has been replaced in most dioceses by a standard salary arrangement, which is more evenly distributed. The change has been made easier possibly due to the reduction in the number of curates in the Irish Church, with the result that most priests can expect to become parish priests much earlier than was previously the case.

178 For example, every priest is expected to live a celibate life, to wear clerical garb during official services, to work in designated priestly ministries, to be holy and to be loyal to the Church and its magisterium.

179 As previously stated in chapter one, the eight priests and two former priests that comprised this cohort of pre-Vatican II priests entered the seminary prior to the commencement of Vatican II, and all of them were ordained before the conclusion of the council.

180 Quotations from the research participants are identified by their clerical status (parish priest, curate, semi-retired, retired) and decade of ordination.

181 The research participants attended a number of seminaries, including Maynooth, Clonliffe, Thurles, Carlow, and Rome, with some priests attending more than one college.

182 A biretta is a square hat with three ridges or peaks, worn by clerics.

183 One priest recalled how he was refused permission to play in an All-Ireland

final, even though he had been part of the team that had won the Munster championship earlier in the summer, and how he, together with other students, had to crouch below the open window of a professor's room to listen to the match on the professor's radio. Others noted how sorry they felt for some of their classmates in Clonliffe who were refused permission to play in Croke Park although they could hear the match being played just outside the walls of the seminary. This was particularly galling for one priest who argued that the GAA and the Catholic Church were closely connected at parish level and that more tolerance should have been shown by the Church to allow their participation in important GAA activities.

[184] Students received various Orders as they progressed through their training, including reader, acolyte, diaconate and priesthood.

[185] When asked if their seminary training had prepared them for priesthood, most of these priests said their training was very poor, with outdated theology and few opportunities for personal development.

[186] Priests are appointed to their ministries by their bishops.

[187] The introduction of changes to the wording of the Mass generated quite an emotive response from many priests at the time. However, the controversy quietened down within a relatively short period of time.

[188] This is not his real name. This is the first of two stories recounted in this chapter of priests who were falsely accused of sexually abusing children but subsequently cleared of all charges. Both priests were deeply affected by their ordeals, yet both remain loyal to the Church and their sense of priesthood has, if anything, been strengthened rather than diminished.

[189] The Vatican II research participants comprised eleven priests and three former priests, all of whom were ordained in the 1970s and 1980s.

[190] I am aware of one priest who insisted on getting ordained against the advice of many people and allegedly, the reservations of his bishop, only to leave the priesthood some months later. He had allegedly become a priest to show he could beat the system.

[191] Not his real name.

[192] The third and youngest cohort of research participants is comprised of five priests and four former diocesan priests, all of whom were ordained in the 1990s and 2000s.

[193] I was fortunate to have been present in Maynooth college chapel on the day the pope visited Maynooth in 1979. The chapel was full to overflowing with seminarians from around the country.

[194] Bourdieu argued that the social world was divided into a number of different, relatively autonomous social fields, where people and institutions interact and compete with each other. One of these fields is the religious field, where the institutional Church is dominant.

Chapter Six

[195] As previously stated, the eight priests and two former priests that comprised this cohort of pre-Vatican II priests entered the seminary prior to the commencement of Vatican II, and all of them were ordained before the conclusion of the council.

[196] Life for students in a minor seminary or diocesan college resembled a seminary in many respects, including its Catholic ethos and a regimented, almost monastic regime. Mass attendance was compulsory and students were expected to go to confession and Holy Communion. Most of the staff were priests and most students were boarders. Most colleges also had spiritual reading in the refectory during meals.

[197] Anecdotal evidence suggests that Irish dioceses had first choice of candidates from the junior seminaries, which were populated by better-off students, leaving other students for foreign dioceses and religious orders. One priest recalled that diocesan priesthood attracted the 'cream' of the students wishing to be priests.

[198] Papesh defines clerical culture as 'the constellation of relationships and the universe of ideas and material reality in which diocesan priests and bishops exercise their ministry and spend their lives' (Papesh, 2004, p. 17).

[199] The magisterium is the teaching authority of the Church. Priests are expected to respect the Church magisterium and to obey the rules of the Church without question. In the pre-Vatican II Church, Irish society and the Catholic Church were strongly regulated and everyone was expected to conform to established rules and regulations. For example, as already discussed, rubrics determined the minutiae of how a priest should celebrate the Mass, while canon law controlled his general behaviour.

[200] This is not his real name. All names and details that might identify an individual have been removed or altered throughout the study.

[201] As previously stated in chapter one, the Vatican II research participants comprised eleven priests and three former priests, all of whom were ordained in the 1970s and 1980s.

[202] I understand that this phrase refers to a fugitive priest that stood by his people during penal times, saying Mass in secret locations.

[203] A number of priests across the different cohorts made a similar comment, suggesting that there is a culture of practice within priesthood that allows priests to be true to their personal beliefs and principles, whilst remaining within the Church.

[204] The interviews took place in 2010, two years before the new wording was introduced. I am not aware of any priest retiring from public ministry because of this initiative.

[205] Two priests spoke of having a mystical experience in prayer.

[206] An interior locution is a mystical concept that refers to a set of (usually auditory) ideas, thoughts, or imaginations from an outside spiritual source. These locutions are most often reported during prayer.

Appendix A

[207] The most comprehensive source of statistical information on the Catholic Church in Ireland is the Irish Bishops' Conference Council for Research & Development. Since its establishment in 1970, the Council for Research & Development has collected detailed information on various aspects of Church personnel including, total personnel numbers, vocations, ordinations, deaths and departures. The current data represents the most up-to-date information on Church personnel in Ireland at the time of writing.

[208] The number of ordinations increased in this period, due in part to the inclusion of ordinations for foreign dioceses since 1981. However, the number is relatively small and the downward trend in ordinations continued in the 1990s.